Praise for *Fathom*

'One of the most immensely read[...] memoirs of the year. His book is an engaging account of eccentricity, curiosity and a profound spiritual journey. I give it a screamingly camp, happy-clappy thumbs up'
Sunday Times, 'Books of the Year'

'Full of wit and humour about finding god, and Jimmy Somerville' *Independent on Sunday*, 'Books of the Year'

'Sex, drugs, death, religion, more sex, many more deaths – it has got it all. Like a sparkling old style chasuble worn by a Spanish priest, it is difficult to ignore' *Guardian*

'He writes with charm and erudition and his take on 1980s Britain is fascinating' *Sunday Express*

'Beautifully written, disarmingly frank and utterly charming'
Mail on Sunday

'Richard's devastating honesty makes his journey from gay pop-star to celibate parish priest comprehensible even to atheists' Linda Grant

'It is a tale of redemption and of a sinner come to transformation . . . The Church of England is all the better for having such a priest within its ranks' *Literary Review*

'Richard Coles has achieved a rare thing in writing an astonishingly honest autobiography, which, alongside the sex and drugs, presents Christian faith in a way that will surely be invitingly intriguing to an audience well beyond the church . . . immensely enjoyable' *Church Times*

The Reverend Richard Coles is the presenter of *Saturday Live* on BBC Radio 4. He is also the only vicar in Britain to have had a number 1 hit single – the Communards' 'Don't Leave Me This Way' topped the charts for four weeks and was the biggest-selling single of its year. He read Theology at King's College London, and after ordination worked as a curate in Lincolnshire and subsequently at St Paul's, Knightsbridge, in London. He is the author of *Lives of the Improbable Saints* and lives in the parish of Finedon, Northamptonshire.

@RevRichardColes

FATHOMLESS RICHES

RICHES
OR HOW I WENT FROM POP TO PULPIT

THE REVD RICHARD COLES

WEIDENFELD & NICOLSON

A W&N PAPERBACK

First published in Great Britain in 2014
by Weidenfeld & Nicolson
This paperback edition published in 2015
by Weidenfeld & Nicolson,
an imprint of Orion Books Ltd,
Carmelite House, 50 Victoria Embankment,
London EC4Y 0DZ

An Hachette UK company

1 3 5 7 9 10 8 6 4 2

A CIP catalogue record for this book
is available from the British Library.

ISBN 978-1-7802-2619-4

Printed and bound in Great Britain by
CPI Group (UK) Ltd, Croydon, CR0 4YY

The Orion Publishing Group's policy is to use papers that
are natural, renewable and recyclable products and
made from wood grown in sustainable forests. The logging
and manufacturing processes are expected to conform to
the environmental regulations of the country of origin.

www.orionbooks.co.uk

For David

Genesis 2:18

Contents

Acknowledgements

I would like to thank Alan Samson, my publisher, and everyone at Orion; Robert Caskie, my agent, and everyone at Peters Fraser & Dunlop.

Special thanks to my editor, Gillian Stern, who discerned from my tweets a story of more than 140 characters waiting to be told and then rescued it from my 160,000-word sprawl.

Thanks also to my parishioners: long-suffering, forgiving and kind.

PREFACE

In a plain little room out of the sun, religious zealots in robes and beards meet to study the teachings of the founder of their sect. In the hum of their discourse and the rhythm of their prayer summaries of his teachings emerge, are worked up, recorded and broadcast to the communities he founded, fractious and disobedient, in the cities and towns of that hot and volatile region.

The teacher we know as St Paul. He lived in the first century in Palestine, and those summaries we know as his epistles, or letters, to the communities he founded. Paul was born a Jew and became a brilliant scholar, so devout and so rigorous he was charged with putting down a weird little sect that had sprung up around an itinerant rabbi from the north, Jesus of Nazareth, whose teaching was so scandalous, so threatening, that he had been handed over to the Romans and executed.

And then something extraordinary happened. Paul, who had never seen Jesus or heard him teach, encountered him in a way that was so dazzling he was at first blinded by it. When he recovered his vision he saw something never seen before: the God who created the universe fully realised in a man, the expectation of the Jewish people not only fulfilled but surpassed, and the offer of salvation for all.

Paul exhausted his exceptional intelligence and gave his life to set out why this is so, and to pass on the good news – or gospel – to everyone else.

'Of this gospel I was made a minister according to the gift of God's grace, which was given to me by the working of his power. To me, though I am the very least of all the saints, this grace was given, to preach to the Gentiles the fathomless riches of Christ . . .'

Paul's followers sent this document out as a round robin to the churches that waxed and waned in the cities of the eastern Mediterranean, among them Ephesus. In time the document became known as St Paul's Epistle to the Ephesians, and in that form made the final edit of the New Testament. And so for many centuries it has captivated and mystified and transformed its readers, among them me, who came into this inheritance like a ne'er-do-well in a Victorian novel suddenly and undeservingly enriched by an unimaginable and unforeseen largesse.

I am a sinner. My best efforts to return Christ's generosity are inadequate, and even devalue the currency they're paid in. This matters, because my lack of generosity and meanness of spirit and self-absorption contribute, in their own small way, to building a hell in heaven's despite. But in spite of my inadequacies, and the inadequacies of all who struggle to live in the gap between Jesus' love and our best efforts, God continually restores to us that inheritance, no matter how thoroughly we fail to be what God would have us be, no matter how insistently we fritter ourselves away on the diversions that the world in all its splendour and awfulness can offer. I have frittered much in splendour and awfulness, and I have tried to be as candid as I can about that, in order that – if disgraced myself – I do not disgrace Paul's calling: to preach to the Gentiles the fathomless riches of Christ.

1. A Boy is Born

I know a priest who, after he had shut up shop on Christmas Day, would get into his pyjamas and take a bottle of vodka alone to bed, watch *The Sound of Music* and cry. An irony that a festival so commonly thought to be the one time of year when vicars come into their own should for him be a time of particular *tristesse*. Since the enchantment of childhood dimmed I, too, have had at least ambivalent feelings about the festive season.

One year, between falling out of pop music and getting ordained myself, Christmas for me began with a migraine, which lasted the whole day. I was with my brothers and my parents and after lunch and the Queen I went upstairs for a lie-down and tried to play *Sonic the Hedgehog*, the only computer game I have ever possessed. After a couple of goes, I decided I didn't need any more garishness and unreality than the day had already provided, so after a sleep I went downstairs and rejoined my family, dozing, reading, waiting for tea and Christmas cake. My mother, at least, was alert and suddenly into the silence she spoke: 'Darling,' she looked at me, 'I was driving to Northampton the other day and a record came on the radio which I thought I recognised and I was right, it was the CommuNARDS' (she always pronounces the name of my band with an odd emphasis on the last syllable). 'And, do you know, I thought it sounded really marvellous, so marvellous I was dancing around as I drove along. If anyone had seen me they would have thought I was crackers. Don't leave me this waaaay. It was really, really great.' I felt myself puff with pride. 'I don't care what anyone says,' she added.

Later on, like many gay men after a family Christmas, I decided to

seek the comfort of strangers, only where could I find a comforting
stranger on a freezing cold Christmas night in the middle of Northamptonshire? I pulled into a lay-by, hidden by woodland, expecting
it, on this most holy night, to be deserted, but it wasn't. A car was
parked in the darkness, the engine turning over but with no lights
on. I parked in front of it, a few yards ahead, and noticed in my rear-
view mirror something stir within. The headlights flashed. A signal.
I switched on my interior light and switched it off again. After a
moment the car's headlights came on and stayed on. A figure got
out and came and stood in front, illuminated by the headlamps. It
was a man, doing a dance, and he was completely naked apart from
a bow of tinsel, which he had tied round his balls. Merry Christmas,
I thought: Happy Feast of the Nativity.

My own nativity was on this wise. I was born in the Barratt, on 26
March 1962. As I appeared the midwife exclaimed, 'Ooh, Mrs Coles,
he's got clickers' hands.' This was a good omen. Clicking – cutting
out the shapes from a hide to make up a shoe – was the best-paid
job in a shoe factory. And it was shoe factories that had not only
funded the Barratt but had also funded my mother's stay and my
arrival there.

It was the first maternity unit in the county, given in 1936 by
William Barratt, one of the magnates of the Northamptonshire boot
and shoe industry. Private fortunes, thanks to nonconformist Christianity, were then often used to fund public projects and to this day
the manufacturing towns and cities of Britain are much the better
off for the largesse of the men in suits and hats and beards and watch
chains who stare confidently at us out of black and white photographs printed on thick board. I am the great-grandson of another,
John Wallace Coles, who, in 1908, started our family firm in Burton
Latimer, a small town about twenty miles from Northampton. He
was a Congregationalist, a Liberal in politics and man of energy and
purpose, renowned as a public speaker and the first mayor of the
town. He had worked for another firm as a salesman, but somehow managed to get the wherewithal to set up on his own. The

catastrophe of the First World War was, with bitter irony, very good for business – for armies, despite Napoleon's assertion, march on their feet not their stomachs – and those first shoe factories boomed. He prospered, the county prospered, the firm grew.

When John Wallace expired over an early morning cup of tea in the same year Barratt gave Northampton his maternity home, my grandfather, Eric Keith Coles, inherited. He was another man of great energy, although his was invested more widely, shall we say, than his father's. The firm continued to prosper, the Second World War, a boot-hungry conflict like the First, enriched it and him. My father, Nigel, grew up during those years, suffering few of the deprivations others did thanks to his father's wealth and complete disregard for the virtue of austerity. Eric Keith was a man of terrific appetites, for food and drink and luxury and company, and would illegally trade pairs of shoes for sirloin and whisky and cigars.

As my grandfather's firm – Coles Boot and Shoe Ltd – prospered, he acquired more factories, in Burton Latimer and in the neighbouring town where I am now vicar, Finedon. After visiting the Caribbean, which he adored, he even opened a factory in Jamaica, a tax-deductible excuse for going again, I suppose. A number of my parishioners today remember Eric Keith well. He was a peacock, in Prince of Wales check, and a waxed moustache, and drove a huge black Rolls-Royce, NNV 1, a 'prestige' number plate, *avant la lettre*. One told me my grandfather would leave the car at the factory for the workers to clean, but they liked doing this because they could sit in the back, help themselves to the cocktail cabinet and sprawl out on the leather seats imagining what it was like to be the boss. In photographs I have of him giving out the prizes at the town carnival, he is the picture of *noblesse oblige* – only the expressions on the faces of the rector and the lady at the big house suggest they were thinking something different. He was loud and emotional and dominating and rather adorable in a Mr Toad sort of way. Another parishioner told me that when he was sixteen, and had just started working at the factory, he took a morning off to get married and was late returning to work. Walking to the factory he saw my grandfather's Rolls-Royce lumbering down the street and as it arrived alongside him it stopped and the window was wound down. He thought he was going to be sacked but instead was handed a bottle of champagne with my grandfather's compliments.

I loved him. He was flamboyant and funny and constantly showing off, singing comic songs at the piano and giving tasters of whisky and puffs of cigarettes to my two brothers and me when we were only four or five years old. These things I, too, came to love, and my endless fascination with food is his, transmitted through my father, who would walk through fire for a decent fish soup. In this we are dogs, easily distracted from our mongrel purposes by a good dinner, and in our family history food rituals were significant. After Eric Keith died, my father took his place at the head of the table, and having carved the joint of beef on a Sunday my grandmother, Kathleen, would take a tablespoon of the meat juices down to him to slurp them as she held the spoon to his mouth.

Kathleen was the youngest of thirteen whose father died of the cure for drink when she was only six. Her mother, widowed at forty-seven, had to rely on her late husband's father for a living; another bearded, hatted, watch-chained paterfamilias, he was the inventor of the bacon slicer (at least according to him), which he neglected to patent. He also invented machinery for shoe factories and, most spectacularly, a car, the Robinson, one of which survives in Kettering's museum. It was made for a local doctor and has a fold-down operating table on which appendices could be removed. He was a Baptist, signed the pledge and ruled like an Old Testament patriarch, so maybe it was inevitable that his son and heir became a sot. Kathleen, his youngest granddaughter in a family of beauties, was the most beautiful of all, and caught Eric Keith's eye at Kettering Fair when she was five and he was seven, so the story goes. When she grew up she wanted to be a dancer but her grandfather forbade it and she became a secretary instead, only not for long. She married Eric Keith in the Toller Baptist church in the summer of 1923.

It was a marriage both life-long and life-giving, as the C of E service puts it, but she had to acquire extraordinary patience due to Eric

Keith's insatiable appetites and restless ways. After the war they took a liner to Istanbul at a time of tension between Britain and Turkey, because my grandfather had 'business interests' there. They were advised not to go ashore but my grandfather insisted and she had to climb down a ladder in a fur coat and get a tender to the quay. There they were picked up by a driver and taken to an address in the Old City. The driver warned them it was dangerous but my grandfather ignored him, told my grandmother he'd be twenty minutes and then disappeared for three hours, leaving her stuck in the back of the car, the focus of unfriendly interest.

In spite of these minor humiliations and some major humiliations, she loved him and when he died, suddenly, she went into shock. They were halfway through building a bungalow but work stalled because she found she couldn't make a decision, until one day the builder told her to snap out of it and her three decades of widowhood began.

The bungalow was on a plot of land next to their house in Barton Seagrave, an ancient village that had been swallowed up by Kettering. At the top of its hill, which claimed a great-uncle who died when he fell off his penny-farthing at its bottom, houses were built between the wars to accommodate those made prosperous by shoe-making. They had names like 'Fieldways' and 'Fourwinds', names I cannot write without thinking of doilies and rockeries and ticking clocks. They were the equivalent of the executive residences built today, with loggias and sunrooms and nurseries instead of en suite bathrooms and media rooms and triple garages. My grandparents lived in Poplars Farm Road, just round the corner from my uncle and aunt and their glamorous children in Ridgeway Road, where we lived, too, my parents and my two brothers, in a new house, 'Longmeadow', built for them when they'd got married in 1959. On Sundays we all went for high tea at my grandparents' house, a meal so defeatingly big and splendid it turned hospitality into a sort of challenge. There were sandwiches and cakes and sardines on toast and little stainless steel dishes of radishes and hard-boiled eggs and two kinds of tea: 'India or China?'

Not far away, on Pytchley Road in Kettering, lived my other grandparents, in a house just along the street from where my grandmother, Joan, had been brought up. Her father, the town's dentist, had raised his family in 'Grey Gables', a musical plural which conveyed both a sense of style and the suggestion of grandeur, but later, Joan – who married his junior partner – lived at 'number twenty-nine', which, as a child, I found a little disappointing. My grandfather, Leonard, not only married the daughter of his senior partner, but also inherited the business, measures of his own achievement, having been brought up the son of a dental technician in Devonshire. He was clever and caught the wave of opportunity that came after the First World War, studying dentistry at Guy's, while helping to keep the trams running during the General Strike. I wish I'd known Joan better but she died when I was fourteen. She seemed rather severe to me as a boy and was an uneven cook. Her marmalade tart makes me tearful even when I think of it now. Very unusually, she and her sister had studied maths at University College London, which must have opened up an unimaginably wide horizon, and I wonder what she made of her return to Kettering and marriage to her father's junior partner. She smoked like a chimney, loved cards, and said little, although even as a boy I sensed intelligence at work and judgements being formed. I think she found us tiresome and after my brothers and I stayed for a weekend she had a short conversation with my mother and we never stayed again.

I adored Leonard. He was creaky after a car accident and smoked a pipe and had a gin at six and was extraordinarily well read. He knew Shakespeare and Milton and Bunyan and Dickens practically by heart and liked my company because I was interested in things like that, too. My father's side of the family could not be described as cultured and it was this side that dominated, so, while Kathleen's intelligence, under wraps, intrigued me, my grandfather's, more readily expressed, engaged me, and we would talk about history and literature and religion. He was a low church Anglican, and a churchwarden in the village where they built their retirement bungalow, 'Paddockwray'. After my grandmother died, of lung cancer, he lived there alone, with his pipe and his Sunday Times Wine Club deliveries and his books and cricket and British Dental Association business.

My mother was the eldest of their three children, born in 1936 in Kettering. During the war she used to walk around town with a collection of animals from her Noah's Ark and push them through strangers' letterboxes until they opened the door and then she would say, 'Hello, my name is Elizabeth and I like sweets.' She liked to give people what for – she still does – and once brained the vicar's son, whom she found a bit pious, by poking a stick through the front of his bike as he was going along so he fell over the handlebars on to the road. She had great enthusiasm for things as a child but was only prepared to do them on her own terms. Playing the part of the green fairy in a junior school production of *A Midsummer Night's Dream*, she couldn't be bothered to attend Titania and flitted around the stage amusing herself instead until someone made her go and sit down. At St Leonard's – a fiercely dour boarding school in Scotland – she was as happy as she's ever been. She loved sport, cricket and hockey in particular, and my favourite photograph is of her in the Miss Jean Brodie uniform of the day cross-legged wearing pads in the school cricket team photograph. After school she went to Domestic Science College in Gloucester and once, reading the lesson at Evensong in the cathedral, had to say 'the pricks of the Corinthians', which I think must be the only time she has ever blushed.

By the time of her twenty-first birthday she was engaged to my father. I have a photograph of them dancing at their party, he in black tie, she in one of those wonderful fifties dresses that look like chintz sofas on the move. My father, after leaving the minor public school which my brothers and I would also attend, did his national service in Korea, just missing the war, but not its aftermath, for one of his men, stopping for a pee, stepped on a landmine and was blown into pieces next to him. I find it difficult to imagine my father, the gentlest and most gentlemanly of men, in armed conflict, but he was, serving as a second lieutenant in the Royal Tank Regiment, under a Captain Partridge and a Major Pidgeon. At Aldershot, where he trained, he nearly drove his tank into Field Marshal Montgomery's Humber and once after firing practice absent-mindedly rested his hands on the all but red-hot barrel of the tank's gun and had to be sent home. After the army he went to college in Leicester to learn the mysteries of the shoe trade and spent the weekends driving around Kettering in his MGA, going to dances, playing badminton and meeting my mother.

My parents were married in the summer of 1959 at St Andrew's Kettering, on a blazing hot day, so the beaks on the ice-cream ducks she'd requested wilted. In the wedding photographs, they all line up, my father's father, rich and glamorous, looking like it is all about him, next to my mother's mother looking pensive. She once forgot herself and spoke of her new in-laws as 'trade'. My father, smart and confident, and my mother, happy and triumphant, on the brink of a life they must have expected to be much like their parents' – steady, prosperous, in a world that would not change so much. Of course their world changed as much as mine has, as it had for their parents, too, but weddings make us salute the values of permanence and stability amid all the changing scenes of life.

I got lucky with my parents. I have never once doubted their love nor for a moment thought they might not endure. They never really argued, though once, spectacularly, when a plate and a poached egg launched by my father flew without warning across the kitchen and Mum burst into tears and ran off in her quilted dressing gown, I thought the end of the world had come. Now I know this sort of explosion happens when resentment is left unexpressed, arguments go unrehearsed. I still have a doomsday reflex that fires whenever people argue, but there are many worse things you can lay at your parents' feet, if you are lucky enough to still have them, than a dislike of quarrelling.

2. *Salus in Arduis*

I followed my older brother, Andy, to St Peter's School, 'An Independent Day School for Boys and Girls' in a house called 'Sunnylands' built by Kettering's only distinguished architect, Henry Gotch. It was run by a Miss Brown, who loved to crush you to her bosom, which was built for such things. I started in the kindergarten, which looked like a tuberculosis sanatorium at the bottom of the garden, and there it was discovered that I had a reading age of twelve when I was six. One morning the class was told about a boy who had done exceptional work and was going to be fast-tracked to the top stream and it was only when my teacher, Miss Buckby, took my chair and slid me across the floor to the top table that I realised it was me. I wasn't conscious of being clever, I was conscious of being competitive, and I discovered I could boost my performance by sticking stars on my own star chart like a tiny Jeffrey Archer. I also remember – is it a memory or something I imagine? – moments of insight. Running round the garden, in an aimless way, I stopped dead in my tracks when the thought occurred to me that things were not necessarily as they seemed, my first awareness of the gap between how things are and how they appear to be.

I was certainly creative, throwing myself wholeheartedly into Music and Movement, which Miss Brown led from a glowing radiogram. We had to prance around the Music Room interpreting her record choices with the body in motion and, less frequently, repose. I rather excelled at this both at school and at home. My mother had a group of friends who would meet in our sitting room for Knit and Natter. At one end French windows opened on to a sunroom, and these I would fling open to appear, dressed in a bedspread, performing an interpretative dance to 'My Bonny Lies Over the Ocean' played on my Dansette. I don't remember their reaction; perhaps they just looked into their coffee cups until I went away. But I wasn't really interested in their reaction; I was overwhelmed by the enchantment of my own choreography, its spell broken only by my mother snapping, 'Oh, Richard, stop showing off!'

I loved music from as early as I can remember, and could be reduced to tears by a bar of plangent French horn. I still can. Through music I accessed a world of richness and beauty and complexity that might not otherwise have troubled us particularly in Ridgeway Road, a place where I learned very early on what it is to be bored. I thought I was owed more than that, more than my circumstances allowed, and was haunted by the idea of people living glamorously beyond my provincial horizons. My grandparents, Leonard and Joan, with their literature and canasta and student days in London, and my father's stories of flying down to the South of France after the war, where his father had somehow moved the family to the Hôtel Belles Rives on the Cap d'Antibes and become friendly with Duke Ellington, intensified that feeling. My brothers, however, seemed content to dress up as cowboys and Indians, kick footballs around, admire cars. I read constantly, books that were beyond the reach or interest of most boys of my age, and when I was eight my father took me to hear a concert at the Albert Hall, Charles Mackerras conducting the Royal Philharmonic in a performance of Beethoven's Seventh Symphony. I was so affected by this, according to my father, that I kept trying to stand on my chair and conduct, too. I was fascinated by the big white acoustic-enhancing dishes suspended from the ceiling. On another trip to London, when I was nine or ten, I made my parents take me to Harrods and buy me a purple fedora, which I insisted on wearing to another concert at the Albert Hall. As I strutted around the Albert Memorial before the concert, oblivious to the remarks of passers-by, one of whom, according to my mother, said 'who's that peculiar little boy?', a gust of wind blew my fedora off my head and into the traffic of

Kensington Gore and my father had to rush into the street to retrieve it.

Trips to London were once-a-year treats, so I used to write off for things, casting a line into culture's rushing stream and hauling in, among many other things, a series of richly illustrated wallets containing ten-inch records of music by Haydn or Beethoven or Mozart. I played them so often that I cannot hear the pieces live without hearing in my mind's ear the faint vinyl pre-echo anticipating every entry. They fed my ambition to be a musician, but not *any* sort of musician, a great musician like them, and I struggled with a hard reality that I had not, by the age of eight, matched Mozart's short-trousered achievements. I wanted glory – I ached for it – and became very single-minded in my pursuit of it, striving always to add burnish to my own. I had started playing the piano when I was only four, in an effort to copy my grandfather who liked to sing 'Sam Sam Pick Oop Tha' Musket' while accompanying himself on his pretty little baby grand ('baby grand': very Barton Seagrave). My first teacher was Mrs Bowness, a lady with a glamorous gold tooth, who got the measure of me very quickly and persuaded me to take up violin, too. It was infuriatingly reluctant, however, to offer a decent sound as I sawed away, with no sustain pedal to depress till those swift passages are done, and so it was harder to fake competence. But one can try: we had a very nice gardener who, one afternoon, I noticed working in the back garden while I was playing the violin in my bedroom. Seeing an opportunity, I fastened a hanky round the part of the strings the bow is drawn over, put on my ten-inch of the Bach Chaconne in D Minor for violin, turned it up and stood by the open window pretending I was playing it. I don't think he even looked up.

From very early on I had an extraordinary propensity for lying. When I was young (and not so young), I found I not only enjoyed it but I was quite good at it, too. There were occasions when I over-reached myself. I stole my mother's jewellery when I was around four, buried it in the garden and triumphantly dug it up again when she discovered the theft, expecting to be praised but getting the short shrift of the whacking brush instead. The whacking brush also came out when I miraculously discovered a pin in a Brussels sprout about to be served to my Great-Aunt Polly at Sunday lunch. At school I became more elaborate, and constructed a fantasy in which I was the son of a duke and duchess who had died in an air crash in Switzerland and had been adopted by my parents who, for obvious but unexplained reasons, wished to keep my real identity secret. Friends who came to stay would be vouchsafed with my secret, shown a photograph of the doomed duke and duchess – really some friends of my parents sitting in the loggia of their house in Chesterfield – and led quietly to a map of Europe that I had on my bedroom wall, an area in the Alps of which I'd shaded black to show where the crash that made me an orphan had occurred.

When I was eight I went to prep school at Wellingborough, a red-brick institution propped up by pale-blue iron fire escapes on the edge of the sort of town you could imagine Philip Larkin finding dullish. It had a small and peculiar chapel and a large and peculiar cricket pavilion, the Thatched Pav, that had the doorstep that once stood in front of W. G. Grace's house, which gives an idea of the relative importance of religion and cricket. My older brother had gone before me, as indeed had my father, whose name I found in fading gold on an honours board inside. Like him, thirty years earlier, and my brother, twenty-eight years later, I was turned out in a uniform of maroon blazer and cap, grey shirt and V-necked sweater, a school tie which went through complicated permutations depending on rank and aptitude, and peculiar sage-green corduroy shorts, never encountered elsewhere.

In spite of dating back to the sixteenth century, Wellingborough was not a grand place, but a day and boarding school for the sons of shoe manufacturers, farmers, soldiers and sailors and middle-ranking diplomats. Perhaps conscious of being second rank, it held to its traditions with a certain strain and would rather wither when confronted at sport by the prestige of Uppingham or Oundle. Condescended to by them, we were actively hated by the local state schools whose toughs would nick our caps if they caught us day boys in the alley going down to and from school. Known locally as the Plum School because of the colour of our blazers and caps and our privileged status, when the toughs beset us they would shout 'Plummers are Bummers!' as they threw our caps over a wall, a scenario which both frightened and thrilled me – though more of the former than the latter – and I would dawdle at the entrance to the alley like a shy bride.

There were internal candidates too for my affection. Our school's principal adornment was a boy so glamorous I still melt a little at the thought of him. He was good-looking and self-possessed and outstandingly good at sport, all things I was not, and everyone fell under his spell. I fell more spectacularly than most and for a whole wretched term tried hard at football because I thought, if we both made it to the First XI, whenever he scored I could hug him for as long as I liked. But I was always, always, last to be picked for football and can still hear a voice from my childhood going 'Oh no, not COLES!' as I stepped from the lonely sideline to join whoever got unlucky that day. The god-like boy left our school – parental financial embarrassment or something – and the last I heard, at the age of thirteen, had impregnated a teacher.

Coles Major and Minor were joined by Coles Minimus, my younger brother, Will, who arrived at the prep school in 1972. You might think that three brothers together in the same school would form a tight gang but it was not so. Age difference counted for more than kin, so we did not see much of each other at school apart from in choir, where we all sat in surplices and ruffs, warbling the hymnody of Ancient and Modern. My mother has a photograph of the three of us in choir kit looking angelic, but there was nothing angelic about our behaviour to each other. For a while I got on badly with Andy, who was fighting the fights of the first-born and saw me, I think, as an irritant, a show-off, and perhaps someone getting more attention than he deserved. There was a period when he would punch me as a matter of course if we passed each other going about our daily affairs and for a while I would, by reflex, turn my shoulder towards him if I saw him coming to reduce my surface area. On one occasion he did really hurt me, not physically, but by an act of wilful destruction that will live long in the annals of infamy. I made from clay a head which I called Mr Schtumpf, my first successful work in the plastic arts, and kept it on my bookshelves alongside my plaster busts of Beethoven and Bach. When I came home one day Andy stopped me in the drive and pointed to a mess of brown sludge at the edge of a puddle. 'Do you know what that is?' he asked. 'It's Mr Schtumpf.' I was devastated.

Will was, also for a while, someone for me to inflict suffering on and I remember when he came out of hospital aged four from having his tonsils out, making him eat a teaspoon of dried ginger in an experiment to see if the wounds in his throat were still raw. They were. Andy and I sometimes ganged up on him, too, a method of deflecting hostile attention by redirecting it to another and forming an alliance with your aggressor. We once tortured him with Cossack hairspray until he wailed his surrender and we discovered, too, a way of driving him mad by singing over and over again the word 'treyka' while waggling our fingers in his face.

That was home, but I was much more absorbed by school and my relationship with other boys. Boarding schools are notoriously, or famously, places for what we now call same-sex fun but back then was referred to as unmentionable vice. Of course before puberty such things were only faintly sensed and the ardour of boys' friendships was unselfconsciously expressed and acknowledged, or so it seemed to me. Puberty changed that and the thickening hormonal soup of teenagehood produced simultaneously a desperate desire for sex and a desperate fear of being thought 'queer', the greatest taboo in our churning world. There were, of course, moments when sex happened, boisterous wanking competitions that were not thought to provide any mutual satisfaction, so were OK. There were also sleepover romps, wrestling that got a bit intense. For me they were mostly seemly, for pyjama moments came infrequently. I longed to be a boarder, partly because it better befitted my noble though secret birth and partly because I was excluded from the boarders' Jennings-and-Darbishire sodality. I yearned to have midnight feasts, and torment the weak by making their entire lives a misery rather than just in school hours, and to be current in the ups and downs of boarding life and escapades of the dormitory. Perhaps this was in part to do with awakening sexuality, but it was also to do with not wanting to miss out on anything, that feeling of helpless frustration at delights being enjoyed just over my horizon, just out of reach. I think this comes from strict bedtimes enforced by my mother and the awfulness of lying awake on a sunny evening hearing the sounds of play outside. This discipline turned me into an insomniac party-goer, a vocation I only really abandoned in my forties.

In spite of being day boys, we had school on Saturdays, the afternoons filled with the misery of sport, and on Sundays, in chapel, for my brothers and I (we had been joined by Coles Minimus, my brother Will) were choristers. It was in the choir stalls that I acquired my love of the Anglican choral tradition and a sense, long dormant, that I was more at home in it than anywhere else. We had chapel every morning, congregational practice on Fridays, which comes rushing back to me whenever I preach at public schools on Sunday evenings and hear the more roistering hymns of Ancient and Modern sung unselfconsciously and very loudly by teenaged boys (and now girls, though there was none of that back then). I had quite a good voice and with my competitive nature clawed my way to become Head Chorister, singing the solo of 'Once in Royal David's City' at the candlelit carol service at the end of the autumn term, a rather shrill if confident performance, wobbling a little when I saw wax from a candle dripping on a lady in the congregation's hat and forming a little flourish of what looked like icing on its crown. We sang our way through *Carols for Choirs*, the green book in Advent and for Christmas, and *Oxford Easy Anthems* through the year, a book we had to place in our folders, for the Director of Music, Mr Ostler, did not want the 'Easy' to be displayed. We sang also the Evening Canticles, printed on yellowing and tatty paper, T. Tertius Noble in A Minor, Stanford in B Flat, Dyson in F, names which are as redolent of childhood for me as Spangles, Aztec and Trebor Sherbert Fountains.

My best friend in the choir, in the whole school, was Matthew Gammage, still my best friend more than forty years later, though it sounds preposterous for a middle-aged man to say that of another middle-aged man. Matthew was the most handsome boy in the school and another into whose orbit we ineluctably fell, though he was charmingly unaware of this. He and I sat at the back and with another friend, Mark Berry, whose glamorous dad was a jazz musician in Bermuda, whiling away the sermon playing poker dice. I cared nothing for the mysteries of Christian doctrine and as soon as I was capable of thinking about it dismissed it as utter nonsense. In fact, I started an atheists' club and enjoyed asking the Chaplain impossible questions. I did a project in Divinity ('Div.', as we called it in the school lexicon) that set out the scheme of salvation and redemption as a board game, a sort of celestial snakes and ladders, which so annoyed him I had to do it again. And I remember a clergyman coming to give a lecture about William of Ockham. I was irked by this poor man and made him declare, by leading questions, that he had based his entire life on something as insubstantial as fairy dust. I thought that was a triumph at the time, although maybe for a moment the weirdness of basing your life on fairy dust opened a chink through which a new and unaccustomed light blipped for a second.

But I did love the music, working hard and competitively with other good singers, and learned a lot in choir practice. I learned that loudest is not necessarily best, I learned to lead a musical line, I learned the rudiments of four-part harmony, I learned the rudiments of word setting. I learned without realising I was learning.

It was not simply the music that shifted something inside me, it was the atmosphere of the chapel. As I grew more proficient on the piano I started to play the organ, which gave me an excuse to be in chapel whenever I was free. I felt then, as I feel now in an empty church, a release from anxiety, a sense of peace, a refuge from trials, a feeling I wish I had paid more attention to back then. But I was full of resistance to the blandishments and iniquities of religion and left it unexamined. Where Christianity was more explicit I was at first puzzled and then indignant. There was a stained-glass window at the west end of the chapel and whenever we left we left beneath it. It showed a scene from the gospel of Luke, Christ among the Doctors, when the boy Jesus was found by his parents astounding the men of learning at the Temple with his teaching. Perhaps it was meant to present to us an improving, if impossible, model of pedagogic excellence but the text written underneath, from the old Author-ised Version of the Bible was 'wist ye not that I should be about my Father's business?', or as a modern translation puts, 'did you not know that I must be in my Father's house?'. As a boy I completely misunderstood it, and day after day left chapel thinking it said '*Wish* ye not that I should be about my Father's business' and thought, dimly, that it was a divine injunction against pursuing a career in the shoe industry. Good advice, as it turned out.

The British shoe-manufacturing industry died in the 1970s and took with it our family fortune and prestige. Cheap imports were our undoing, from Portugal and Spain at first, and I remember my father inspecting a pair of gents' shoes that were cheaper and better than anything we made and looking suddenly very worried. Over the next year or two he got greyer and more silent. Production shifted from men's fashion in high volume to smaller runs of specialised footwear, motorcycle boots and work boots with steel toe caps, but it was not enough, and one evening he sat at the dining table in the sun room signing a thick pile of letters notifying customers and suppliers that the company was to be sold to a competitor. It was a devastating time for him, with people's livelihoods at stake, friends, and mem-bers of the family, not to mention the thousands who worked in the factories of the little shoe towns on the A6. We sold our house and stayed with my grandfather, Leonard, at his bungalow before moving to a smaller newly built house ('Springfield') in a pretty and tiny village that still had a post office and a pub where, round the back, a blacksmith would shoe horses and cut your hair. Will was taken out of prep school and sent to a comprehensive and my father got a job working in sales for a firm in London, which obliged him to get up at five and get in at eight, up and down the M1 five days a week. To my shame I was only really concerned with the damage to my own prestige and I doubt I had the grace or the wit to contain my feeling of resentment. It was not my father's fault that the industry collapsed, and shoe firms withered like supermarket herbs in those years, disappearing so quickly and devastatingly that towns that once roared with shoe machinery and stank of leather and glue were quiet and odourless before the seventies were out.

Around this time a hardness entered my soul which, combined with my ambitious nature, must have laid the foundations for the success story, partial narrative though it is, which was to come.

3. The Dark Field

When does becoming gay happen? Some would say puberty and the arrival of sexual desire and performance; others might say earlier, nurture playing its part as well as nature. Can we say that someone as young as ten or nine or eight is gay? I think you can have a good guess. A friend of mine, who thought that her eight-year-old son might be gay, asked me if I would meet him and have a chat to see if I could divine from our conversation the direction of his future sexual orientation. We met and I asked him what sort of things he was interested in. 'I particularly like Victorian neo-Gothic church architecture . . .' was his reply.

When I was his age I, too, gave off indications. I loathed football and asked to do knitting with the girls when I was at kindergarten (and was allowed to). I was very sensitive and wept bitterly when a boy knocked over my snowman at junior school. I met him years later at a concert in London and felt a tiny spasm of grief for the casualty of his childish malice. By the age of thirteen, however, something else was stirring. I knew what sex was from about the age of eight, an activity so rude I felt a mixture of prudish recoil and obscure fascination, but I didn't begin to understand the dynamics till I was into my teens, and my voice, vehicle of my success, failed. As Head Chorister it fell to me to sing a solo in a lovely little eighteenth-century anthem at a special service in chapel attended by parents and dignitaries. There's a pretty sustained note, during which I liked to put on my most angelic face, but on the great day my voice cracked and I fell off the note, like an angel crashing into the earth. It was the end of my glorious treble career and the beginning of a downy blur appearing on my top lip, the outward visible sign of an inward invisible change. I hated it, dreading my imminent demotion and the loss of cachet that would follow, so, childishly, pretended it wasn't happening, and developed an irrational fear not only of singing anything that went above an E, but also of the paraphernalia of shaving. One day my father, gently, gave me an electric razor and showed me how to use it. That first touch of its buzzing rotors on my skin, the first harvest of its down, the loss of my treble voice, the handing back of the thick red ribbon from which to hang my Head Chorister's medal, marked the passing of my childhood.

Sexual maturity arrived in the long hot summer of 1976. I was fourteen, and it was a summer of water shortages and standpipes and pictures on the news of the evaporated Pitsford Reservoir a few miles away. It was also the time of grandmother Joan's death. In the late spring she had developed a cough and by midsummer had died of lung cancer. My grandfather came to stay and Andy and I were sent to sleep in a tent in the garden, the mystery of adult mourning compounded with excitement at this adventurous change to the routine. The adventure grew even more exciting when, alone in that tent and wearing a much-loved pair of pale pink corduroy jeans, I discovered that great pleasure of the adolescent male quite by accident. At first I thought it was some sort of funny turn, highly enjoyable, but in need of research, and by a series of oblique questions to older boys discovered that it was, in fact, all the rage. I heard from some that there was a risk it might have a deleterious effect on your eyesight but my own eyesight was so bad anyway I felt it a risk worth taking. In fact I enjoyed it so much I would have continued even if it threatened immediate blindness.

But what was the object of my desire? I can remember getting extraordinarily persistent and social disabling hard-ons, once so rigidly I wanted to fill the sink in my bedroom with cold water so I could immerse my throbbing and unbiddable organ in its quenching shallows just for some relief. Was the urgency of those desires intensified by a particular person or persons? I am not really sure, but among the contenders were two sisters who lived at the end of Ridgeway

Road, both blonde and beautiful in that seventies Pirelli girl way, and I fell a bit in love with the younger.

This was a bit awkward because in childhood I had betrothed myself to my cousin Judy, also blonde and beautiful, who lived at the other end of Ridgeway Road ('The Red House') and, in spite of once encouraging her older sister to shoot me in the hand with a steel-tipped arrow, she offered no reason why, in due course, we should not lawfully be joined in holy matrimony. Fickle Judy, not long after this betrothal, put dog shit in my wellingtons, discovered only when I put them on, so my love for her faltered. As Judy waned, the younger of the two sisters up the road waxed. We did a lot of sitting around innocently in trees that summer, among Red Admirals fluttering around the buddleia to the rather jarring music of the ice-cream vans. I think all I did in acknowledgement of my growing regard was buy her a Mivvi, but I told a friend that I had snogged her. It got back to her, of course, and one blisteringly hot afternoon she confronted me in front of my friends. In the middle of this humiliating dressing down she said that she quite liked me, too, and had been working up to a snog but certainly wouldn't now.

There were other objects of my desire. One was a boy, mad, bad and dangerous to know, who I became friends with, sort of, the nerd and the ne'er-do-well (what a recurring theme that has been in my life). I discovered in him a disregard for authority that I admired, envied and deplored; and he was also a creature of impulse and during what people now call sleepovers there was some horseplay in pyjamas in his bedroom that I was too young to understand, although I certainly enjoyed it. He, being older, perhaps did understand. He spoke one night of 'Edward and Ebenezer' and when I asked who they were, I discovered, with a throat-catching thrill, that Edward was his dick and Ebenezer his bum. One night, perhaps a year or two later, when I did understand things a little better, he came on a sleepover at mine and we went to see a friend, who lived near the Field, the place of our unsupervised adventures. The hour of curfew arrived and it was time to go home. As we got on our bikes he said, 'Fancy a fuck?' I was so taken aback I could only respond with 'What did you

say?' There was a pause. Then he got on his bike and turned left for
my house rather than right for the Field, which now lay shrouded in
darkness and transgression, perilous with danger. Later, in our pyjamas in our twin beds, I asked him in a sing-song voice, 'What did
you meeean earlier?' He said nothing and eventually went to sleep
while I lay awake, nursing a regret that has lasted me all my life.

There were other boys who came for sleepovers and with one or
two I would engage in vigorous wanking competitions. There were
near misses too: one day down the field I was taking a piss and
flashed my dick at my friend as a 'joke'. He said nothing, but as we
walked on further into shrubby privacy said, 'This is just the place
for a homosexual encounter.' My mouth went dry, and I knew that
further along the path there was an old roofless barn and when we
got there we lay in it looking up at the sky, side by side, and I said,
'Yes, just the place for a homosexual encounter' but neither of us
actually moved. Suddenly I was overwhelmed by hay fever, sneezing
uncontrollably, my eyes streaming. And then we heard the voices of
boys coming down the path to where we were lying and I thought
if we had started to fool around they might have caught us and that
would have been a fate worse than death. My friend, like me, longed
to escape, and, like me, succeeded. Years later I came across him in a
gorgeous hotel where he had become rich and successful and famous
and heterosexual.

I never did become heterosexual, though I wished I would for
a while, because to be labelled a pouf then was about the same as
being labelled a paedo now. In spite of the dread of exposure, my
most cherished near-miss was with an older boy at school. Although
he was senior to me we got to know each other through smoking,
a prohibited activity, which took place democratically in the gents'
toilets on the north side of the senior school quadrangle. Perhaps we
grew to understand each other via rudimentary gaydar, too, because
one sunny Saturday afternoon I was in the Music School playing the
twiddly cadenza of the first movement of the Mozart piano concerto
in B flat and I was so absorbed in it I didn't notice that he had come
in until I stopped and turned to find him standing right next to me.

He had just finished games, hearty creature that he was, and was wearing nothing but a pair of plimsolls and some dark blue washed-out shorts, so short and so well worn they were barely able to do the fundamental job of an item of clothing. And, of course, I was seated, so when I turned I practically got a faceful of his middle section, golden from the sun and with droplets of sweat running down his abdomen and darkening the turned-down top of his shorts. 'Do you want to come to mine for a fag?' he said huskily – I think it was huskily – and that was the end of Mozart for the day. We walked up the path to his House and up the stairs into his study bedroom and I thought, 'This is it, I am going to have sex with him.' He shut the door, said, 'We can have some privacy here', which made my heart leap, and then stuffed a towel along the bottom of the door lest cigarette smoke betray us in the stairwell and beyond. He sat in an armchair, legs apart, and I sat opposite him and we smoked fags and I remember telling a stupid joke about blow jobs and he sort of played idly with himself when suddenly there was a knock on the door and he opened it to a master so junior he cannot have been more than a year or two older than the prefect and – again – the moment passed. Did I want it to pass? We vaguely arranged for him to come for a sleepover, but it never happened, not because I wasn't stupid with frustrated desire but perhaps because, in a way, I liked the insanity of frustrated desire.

But also, and this grew as I got older, I believed that I was so undesirable no one would want to transgress with me on a sleepover, nor consider snogging me up a tree. Puberty made me gawky and spotty and for the first time physically self-conscious. This was not helped by my teeth, which in my teenaged years looked like a First World War trench. When I was ten I had gone round to a friend's house to play trampolines on the twin beds in his room. In those pre-duvet days they were covered with bedspreads and these were pulled over the bed posts so when, in a spectacular display of athleticism, I dived on to my front, my open mouth connected with the hidden bedpost with such violence it broke one and chipped the other of my front teeth, one of which actually stuck in the wood.

With the arrival of puberty this display was made even more Gothic by the narrowing and lengthening of my jaw, which pushed my broken teeth into crooked formations. This left me with a smile like a calving glacier, so a dental brace was made for them. I couldn't bear to wear it to school where I thought it would be interpreted as a sign of physical incompetence so in the end I threw it away. From then on, or at least until pop music made me rich, I just kept my mouth shut and never smiled and began to look serious rather than carefree.

And I wore specs, too. I had put this down to a bold and daring move – looking at the sun through my grandfather's bird-watching binoculars aged eleven – but later discovered, less romantically, that my myopia was down to a bout of German measles. Losing your eyesight to a disease with a colloquial name sounds rather Victorian, but this was 1973 and it contributed to a growing and disappointing sense that, far from the hero I wanted to be, I was really, in Larkin's deadly phrase, 'the guy who's yellow and keeps the store'; or worse, not a Siegfried but a Mime.

I had allergies and hay fever, my eyes itched and ran and I sneezed and sneezed in the summer months when the grass pollen blew. I went to the doctor to have an allergy test, for which puncture marks were made down my forearms with some sort of stylus and a letter in biro marked against each one. They all instantly went red and swelled. Pollen, food colouring, base metal, I even found the sound of the Hoover unbearable, so sensitive to everything I made Marcel Proust look like Ian Botham.

An excruciating moment stands out for me. At the Caledonian Ball in Kettering, Burns Night I suppose, we were made to do dancing by a ceilidh band. I enjoyed dancing, I still do, and there was a complicated one in which women danced round in an outer circle in one direction, men forming an inner circle going in the opposite direction. When the music stopped you had to peck the cheek of the girl opposite you. There must have been a time, in some under-populated Western Isle, when this was how you found your spouse, but Kettering offered a wider range of opportunities for the young and ardent to engage with one another in the 1970s. Perhaps that is why, when the music stopped and I bent forward to kiss the girl who had arrived opposite me, she physically recoiled and said 'eeurgh!' At the time the humiliation was so intense it was as if more than the music had stopped. Even down the years I can still be stopped in my tracks remembering.

4. Scorn and Noise

Aged sixteen, I began to look to the horizon, I saw the future rise before me, and to meet it my Dad got me a fizzer, a Yamaha FS1E moped, 50cc of purple freedom. Mopeds were *de rigueur* for a sixteen-year-old boy in rural Northamptonshire – Yamahas, Suzukis, Kawasakis – and the smell of a hot Japanese two-stroke makes me feel giddy with teenagehood even now. Social life, such as it was, was connected by the high-pitched whine of little cylinders, racing pathetically at thirty along the A6, fifty down Crow Hill.

And then girls arrived at Wellingborough in the sixth form, Candy Willmot among them, a driver with a dazzlingly smart TR7, and my horizons expanded even further. She and Matthew and I became a trio, first at school and then outside it. Ruthlessly protective of my relationship with Matthew, at first I felt threatened by a girl coming into the field of my 'secret' desire. But Candy seemed completely immune to Matthew's handsomeness, and before long we were spending hours and hours sitting in her attic bedroom in the tall red-brick house next to her father's photographic studio in Rushden. Her mother was German and had met her older husband in what was left of Dortmund after the war. He had been a soldier in the British Army; she'd been a nurse and the daughter of an official in the city government. She had a rather innocent way about her and reminisced about her childhood, the Third Reich and the destruction of Europe, in a sing-song voice, when she appeared in the attic room, bringing trays of sandwiches and coffee in cups and saucers, her tone never faltering even when she recalled the area bombing of Dortmund and seeing her father's secretary caught in a firestorm's updraught, dragged along a street, shedding papers, into the roaring blaze.

Candy and Matthew and I would sit for hours listening to Rod Stewart's *Atlantic Crossing*, Pink Floyd's *Dark Side of the Moon*, and Santana, discussing the utter futility of life. Rather, Matthew and I discussed the utter futility of life. Candy was more interested in the arrival of punk and its impact on the local music scene, and substituted the mullet-haired rockers with scratchy little records from bands in Milton Keynes. She took us to see Jilted John, the Four be Twos, bands I wanted to like but didn't, and Matthew's older sisters and older brother enriched the cultural diet with the rock and folk heroes of the sixties and seventies. We even went to see Bob Dylan at Blackbushe aerodrome, hiring a minibus which abandoned us, so we were up all night and had to make our way home on foot and then on a milk train to London, then across London and finally on to a Northampton train from Euston. As it pulled out an older woman sitting opposite us with a little girl grimaced and pitched forward with a fatal heart attack. I don't remember anything of Bob Dylan, apart from pretending to like him and affecting a look of rapt fascination while he played a quarter of a mile away. And Joan Armatrading's tiny arm, black against the golden belly of her guitar, going up and down out of sync with what we were hearing.

The futility of life, inescapable; the fruitlessness of impossible desire; the boredom of a teenagehood in Kettering and its environs – over the course of some months it became evident to my parents, my teachers, myself, that my career at Wellingborough School was in doubt. By now I had become so Bolshevik, as I liked to think of it, or simply so disturbed, that fresh fields and pastures new needed urgently to be sourced. And while I loathed the music of Candy's punk fixation and was both embarrassed and frightened by the stagey outrages of its heroes and heroines, I loved its antinomianism and contempt for everything.

My revolutionary spirit, while profound and powerfully felt, was outwardly expressed weedily, limited to making a sort of brooch from safety pins, bolts, nails and screws, a tiny scrapyard which I wore like a badge in the lapel of my charcoal-grey school jacket. I did so with guarded pride, for it infringed the uniform rules and I had to hide it if a master with an eye for such things came by. One day I was in chapel playing the organ when the headmaster, a rather stiff individual we nicknamed the Plank, came in with some prospective parents and, while executing with my right hand a rather brilliant passage from a piece in the series *Early English Organ Music for Manuals*, attempted to disassemble the punk brooch with my left. Unfortunately it fell apart and as I watched, aghast, the screws and nails and bolts cascaded on to the pedal board and into the gaps between the pedals where they may still be today.

My O-levels were a grave disappointment. My most sustained act of resistance in these terrible years of puberty was to refuse to do any work and when the envelope arrived I discovered that I had done even worse than I expected, securing four undistinguished passes and an unclassified result in GCE Mathematics. My father, hard up and under pressure, must have wondered if the sacrifices he had made to keep paying the school fees after the company was sold were worth it, but my mother, rather brilliantly, saved the day when she discovered a pioneering course offered by the South Warwickshire College of Further Education in Stratford-upon-Avon. It had a Department of Drama and Liberal Arts, which had been founded by Gordon Vallins, a pioneer of theatre in education and one of the designers of the Theatre Studies A level, which the college offered along with the usual syllabus. It had a drama studio with a lighting rig and a Green Room and connections to the Royal Shakespeare Company. I loved the theatre and had excelled at drama at school – no surprise there – so the thought of studying drama at Stratford with the added freedoms of being at college rather than at school were exciting, but it also, magnificently, gave me my ticket out of Kansas. It was a different and more generous world then and I was offered a local authority grant sufficient to pay my fees and my maintenance at the age of only sixteen.

Goodbye school. I felt a little disappointed walking around on my last day, expecting some sort of emotional charge or sense of significance at moving on, but there was none. My mother had given me a bottle of sherry to give to my housemaster, the long-suffering Stephen Ostler, but I dropped it on the way to see him and the only detail I remember of the day is the sourish odour of Croft Original ('one instinctively knows when something is right') that rose from the shards of dark green glass at my feet and then was gone.

At home the kit list arrived from the drama department, or DLA as it was known by everyone. Black footless tights, 'loose comfortable clothes', plimsolls, a jock strap or 'dance belt' as I think it was called. There was a reading list, too, and on it were Stanislavski's *An Actor Prepares*, which I don't think I ever read, and Peter Brook's *The Empty Space*, which was to be our bible.

DLA began, in Tiddington Road, Stratford-upon-Avon, where, on the Sunday evening before term began, I unpacked my bag with my new room-mate, Adam Sindall, son of the sculptor Bernard Sindall, who had sat, scarily silent, his eyebrows bristling, downstairs as my parents tried to make small talk with him and his much less frightening wife. I found out later that the unpacking had rather alarmed Adam, because among my possessions was the double album *Saturday Night Fever*, which I thought then, and still think now, a work of rare brilliance. Adam unpacked Siouxsie Sioux, Punishment of Luxury, Kevin Coyne and Pere Ubu, which occupied a very different space in the cultural spectrum, but we nevertheless became friends. Also living in the same house were Joss and Sarah, chalk and cheese, Joss the daughter of the technical director of the National Theatre and a former ballerina, and Sarah, who was called Babe. Joss was intense and a little shy, a bit like Saffy in *Ab Fab*, and Babe was anything but. She had the most enormous bust, '36 double D' she announced, which for a girl of sixteen was quite something. We were, I suppose, typical of the kind of people who got to DLA, a mixture of middle-class delinquents, gay boys (some gayer than others), the children of bohemians and one or two who it was harder to place. The college was a mixture, too, with DLA students running around in pixie boots and granddad shirts, and catering students, who we hated and thought beneath consideration, and school dropouts

who were drinking in the last chance saloon of A levels. Apart from
Theatre Studies I also did English, which was not so different – we
did a staged version of Eliot's *Waste Land* in which I played 'Tiresias,
old man with wrinkled dugs', a line which always got a laugh and set
a precedent in my performance praxis of always being funniest when
I was trying to be my most serious. I also did art, which I was no
good at, and French, which I rather enjoyed, though we were horrible to the lecturer. The 'we' was me and the preposterously named
Tarquin Murray-Holgate, like me a public school dropout, was, I
think, the handsomest boy I had ever seen. He was a sportsman and
had a body that anticipated Abercrombie & Fitch by thirty years,
not that I ever saw much of it. He was also a biker, in jeans and leath-
ers, and so was I in an underpowered moped sort of way, but he had
a 125cc Suzuki trail bike, and when my Yamaha fizzer broke down
and was off the road for some time, he would pick me up on his way
into college and I would very, very happily ride pillion, longing to
hold him round the waist but this was not done and I had to hold
on to the 'sissy bar' behind me preserving a proper distance. Once
at a junction a car pulled out in front of us, he slammed the brakes
on, and I shot forwards and upwards in a thrusting motion, which
was as near to an act of congress as I ever got with Tarquin. He had
a complicated but firmly heterosexual love life and a pretty biker
girlfriend with whom he would fight constantly and who hated me.

Tarquin was, in more senses than one, not in my department, and
I began to form more lasting relationships with my fellow drama
students, some of them still friends today. I was closest to Fergus
Durrant, a local boy from Kenilworth, also a biker (Honda CB500),
and his girlfriend, Romy Dixon, the only person he had ever dated
and they are still together now. I am ashamed to admit that my affection for them at that time was unequal, but I was by then locked
into a pattern of having undeclared and futile crushes on boys whose
quite forgivable lack of sexual interest in me I found not only unforgivable but possibly wrong-headed, and felt that with a bit of hard
work on my part their latent homosexuality would not only awaken
but also ontological fulfilment would follow in discovering that I

was the no longer obscure object of their desire. This formed an ob-
bligato to most of my close relationships with men for longer than
I care to admit. Graceless, thoughtless, ungenerous, damaged boy
that I was, in my frustration and furious sense of exclusion failing
to see that a real reciprocity was formed in these relationships, my
mystifying (mostly) anger must have been hurtful. If noticed at all.
Of course, these asymmetrical relationships were for me a mighty
Sturm und Drang of passion, undeclared, unmet and unchecked by
the resistance of reality – of course they had to be unrequited or it
wouldn't have worked – and I am not entirely sure that those on the
receiving end necessarily noticed this at all. So I brought to relationships with my male peers an indistinct mixture of things visible and
invisible.

Drama school was a fertile environment for drama queens and
I greatly enjoyed the wider latitude for acting out that it provided.
Gordon Vallins was of the generation of theatre practitioners who
used papier-mâché as a revolutionary tool and there was much mask
making and puppetry attempting to show the ineluctable forces of
history going about their business. He was not slavishly ideological,
though, and we had a full diet of Greek theatre, *commedia dell'arte*,
Noh and Kabuki and the classics of English drama from Shakespeare
via Sheridan to Shaw. Nevertheless, the end of year show always
seemed to fill the stage with girls in mob caps and aprons singing in
stagey cockney, arms akimbo, while the menfolk deposed tyrants or
went on strike.

Tantrums and tears were not unusual and adolescent passions
were intensified in the half *Kids from Fame*, half Shakespearean atmosphere of the place. We were very fortunate, at the Shakespearean
end of things, to have been there at the end of the seventies when the
Royal Shakespeare Company was probably at its strongest. The first
play I had ever seen was the RSC's production of *Macbeth*, directed
by Trevor Nunn, with Judi Dench and Ian McKellen, a production
of international significance and career-building brilliance. I still remember thinking 'so that is what evil is' as the drama played out
without scenery in a plain circle of black beer crates. Peter Brook,

the author of *The Empty Space*, arrived in Stratford at the same time
as I did and my class was invited to a rehearsal of *Antony and Cleo-
patra* at the Royal Shakespeare Theatre. It was our first week and
we sat in the stalls watching Alan Howard and Glenda Jackson love
each other to death. At the end Brook, this legendary man, came to
talk to us and asked if we had any questions. No one said anything,
so, like a trouper, I thought of something and put my hand up.
I had noticed that there were cushions of different colours in the
feast scene, thrown hither and thither by Patrick Stewart, playing
Enobarbus, while everybody sang a drinking song. I asked what was
the significance of the colours of these cushions. He replied: 'None.
They haven't all been covered yet.' And we all went home.

Digs with a landlord and landlady, for whom I would do tarot
readings, was not home for long, as I discovered a place for rent
nearby. A terraced house with a bay window, freezing cold, and a
terrible dank lean-to kitchen with a lavatory at the end, it was surely
illegal even then, looking like something from a documentary about
slum housing. But it was unsupervised; ours, and we could live as
we wanted if we could make the seven quid a week rent. We did
this by asking a mixture of first- and second-year to share, which
broadened my social horizons considerably. Stratford, and Leamington Spa down the road, were bohemian places, at least by the
standards of Kettering, so there was a generation or two above us
who all looked like Eleanor Bron and Anthony Sher, caftan-wearing,
red-wine drinking, who had children who grew up and had to work
their own rebellion. The rebellion was drugs. There was a white/
black crossover ska scene in Coventry so there were people around
smoking weed, but I remember more clearly – clearly? – exotics who
passed through town on the hippy trails from India to Amsterdam to
London, Greeks and Catalonians wearing berets and keffiyahs who'd
come and crash on the floor and sit up late at night telling us they
believed they were put on earth for a reason. The reason seemed to
be to sell us marijuana, which came in great sticky blocks of black
resin, marbled with opium, or so we thought, and we saved up to
buy it in quarter-ounce blocks wrapped in foil. It was precious stuff

and when news of Moroccan or ganja in town reached us there was sometimes a scramble to get into the queue. We smoked it, mostly in spliffs, which we made in ceremonial ways, like geishas at a tea ceremony, but for more hard-core attempts at stupefaction we used bongs or chillums and, the deadliest of all, hot knives. You placed the blades of two dinner knives on the gas ring until they glowed red-hot and then got a friend to drop a lump of resin on one and cover it with the other so it instantly vaporised. You sucked it up, as hard as you could, through a rolled-up newspaper and did your best not to cough. It turbocharged the hit. The first time I did it all seemed to be fine; the next thing I was standing in the street, a sunny afternoon, sort of aware of people looking at me; then I was in Key Markets in the shopping precinct surrounded by boxes of Weetabix with someone shouting at me.

These stories sound like bravado, teenage high jinks, but I never really liked being stoned. I liked full awareness; I liked to be alert to what was going on in the world, not dulled to it, so the great drug discovery for me was speed. Amphetamines, in the form of torpedo-shaped tablets or snorted as a white powder, were also available, through a slightly different network, and I loved them. I loved staying up all night talking and really didn't need a stimulant to achieve this, but taking speed kept others up all night, too, which meant hours of fun. Others liked drawing or writing or making stuff, but for me it was talking and I talked and I talked and I talked.

Talk, language, speech, song was very rich in Stratford in that period. Cicely Berry was the voice coach at the Royal Shakespeare Company and had worked up a house style which is very of the period and may sound a bit mannered to our ears now, accustomed to different ways of speaking and acting. But she knew her Shakespeare and she knew how to get people to speak his texts with a clarity which I do not hear so much today. We would get visits from actors at the college, master classes and Cicely Berry herself came once, but I don't remember anything about it apart from the excitement that she was coming.

While the RSC set a high standard, our own productions were

uneven. We did lots, from a Medieval Mystery play to mystified shoppers in the precinct at Coventry, to a Japanese drama in which I played the ghost of the warrior Atsumori and came on slow-motion shadow fighting in a dressing gown, masked and with a stick, which, again, brought the house down. We did Sean O'Casey and Pirandello and Shaw, then as fundamental to the syllabus as Shakespeare and Chaucer, and a lot of Brecht. Gordon Vallins was this unlikeable man's greatest admirer, I think, and our own house style in the DLA drama studio was relentlessly Brechtian; but Gordon was also a great admirer of Noël Coward, who seemed to me then not even remotely Brechtian (I am not so sure now), and he encouraged me to make my own piece for an exam in which I performed a medley of his songs at the piano, dressed in the dressing gown I wore for Atsumori but clenching between my teeth a fag in a cigarette holder to give an authentic twenties note. I had the live recording of Noël Coward from the Desert Inn at Vegas and tried to sound like him, effortless, unflappable, but it came out like Kenneth Williams. Again, when I tried to be funny there was silence; when I tried to be solemn there was laughter. There was some fundamental error here, a failure to understand how I went over, a failure to actualise what I wanted to convey.

Another advantage of the liberal and bohemian atmosphere of college was the opportunity it gave me to come out as gay. In the late seventies we were just beginning to see a public face of homosexuality that wasn't entirely blurred with disgrace. Gay Liberation had arrived from the United States and by 1979 had got as far as Leamington Spa where there was a club that had a gay night on Rogation Days, or something like that. I never went, but it was there and there were gay men and women around about, some of them, if not quite out, not quite in either. I was too scared of exposure, sex, rejection, acceptance, and so on, to go to the club myself – and how would I get there? Who would I go with? – but I did know that there was *Gay News*, a national weekly publication with contact details for local groups, and I thought it might be my portal to this world of undiscovered acceptance and fulfilment. I could not bring myself even to look on a newsagent's shelf where it might be stocked, along with the jizz mags and the fortnightlies for peculiar hobbyists, so I didn't quite know how to go about getting a copy. My brother Andy, then at university in Swansea, invited me down for a weekend and on the way back, at a newsagent's near the bus station, I saw a clutch of *Gay News* held together with a bulldog clip. The shop was empty, I was alone and far from home, so I reached up and pulled out a copy, but unfortunately all the others came with it and they fell apart fluttering to the floor like big gay butterflies all round me as the door opened and a rugby team walked in. Someone kindly, but excruciatingly, tried to help me gather them up and put them back together, but I was so embarrassed I fled.

In the end I got *Gay News* through the post, in a manila envelope that gave nothing away. It was thrilling, not only because it did open a door into a world I wanted to be part of but did not know how to access, but also because it had an edge, a radicalism, a politics that made being gay a bit respectable. Like black people, like women, we were unjustly oppressed – hooray! – and found in that an identity that rescued us from the hateful caricatures only too readily encountered. There was a scandal at the time, I remember, a prosecution for blasphemy brought by Mary Whitehouse against the *Gay News* publisher, Denis Lemon, for printing a poem about the centurion at the Crucifixion having what we could call 'inappropriate' thoughts about Jesus. *Gay News* started a fighting fund and was represented in court by famous human rights lawyers. A *cause célèbre* was born and, although Mary Whitehouse won, she and the like-minded were surprised, I think, by the strength of the resistance to the prosecution – even Monty Python contributed to the fund – and there arose a growing sense of pushing back against the unthinking antipathy that was so common then.

It also gave me a way of outing myself that would be less embarrassing than just declaring my love, as I would have called it, for the unfortunate succession of straight boys who were close enough and attractive enough to have had it flung at them. So I did one day. I very much enjoyed telling people the news, and lined up appointments over a week or two with everyone I knew to make sure no one was left out and actually felt, halfway through this marathon of disclosure, a little disappointed that my revelation did not get more attention. This was not because I felt I deserved a more scandalous reputation but because I realised a truth once expressed by the mother of a friend of mine: 'No one's thinking about you.' She's from Yorkshire.

I suppose my parents thought about me from time to time, and so I told my mother one afternoon at home in Great Addington. I played her Tom Robinson's ('Sing If You're) Glad To Be Gay' two or three times before she said, 'Darling, are you trying to tell me something?' I said 'Yes'. She said, 'Do you think you might be gay?' And I said, defiantly, 'I KNOW I am.' This must have been difficult for her to acknowledge and she said, as an aside, 'Let me tell your father', which she did, but he made no comment about it, at least not to me. In fact, no more was said about it explicitly until I had moved to London and appeared in a television programme about young gay people and the law, a programme which was broadcast without any warning from me in advance and did the job of outing me explicitly to any members of the family or friends of my parents who had not yet either heard about it or worked it out for themselves.

Coming out, while an immense relief and the right thing to do, had two unexpected consequences. The first was to make my dark, secret love no longer secret, which altered the angles of my relationships to the men I was asymmetrically attached to. The second was to send me quite mad for a while. I think it was the release of a huge accumulation of tension, the acknowledgement that I was not as other men and that my life would be different from the mainstream lives of others. For some today, friends of mine, the discovery that a child or a friend is gay would be something to celebrate, but my own chorus of ('Sing If You're) Glad To Be Gay', like the original, was ambivalent. I wasn't particularly glad to be gay. I was very happy to be different and special, I liked all the cultural benefits that came with membership, but at a profound level I felt I was out of tune with nature, with the essential forces of the world, and would for ever be excluded from full participation in the business of being human. Some find this bracing; I found it agonising, but it was difficult to admit this because there was a fight to fight, a polemic to engage in, an existence, in fact, to defend and there was no place in that for ambivalence.

One evening, in a rented farmhouse in North Wales where a group of us had gone on holiday, I was talking to Fergus, the kindest of friends, and this feeling of alienation suddenly splurged out of me in huge hammering sobs. It was quite different from the self-dramatising versions of the story I had rehearsed with others – authentic feeling I suppose – and it suggested something of the damage which I had sustained as I was growing up.

I sank into depression, which was not helped by the amount of psycho-active drugs I was taking, so desperately I used to go from chemist to chemist buying bottles of kaolin and morphine, leaving them to settle and drawing off the clear liquid, which I presumed had the morphine, with a straw. I went to the doctor and got prescribed antidepressants but instead of taking them I stockpiled them and also got hold of some Mogadon, the rather well-named soporific of the time.

Means was one thing, but I was held back by the fear of the bourne from which no traveller returns, and by the thought of the consequences my death would have for my parents and those who loved me. But one day I came to the realisation that non-existence simply won the argument over existence. It was an epiphany. There would be no guilt, no regret, and no pain, if I did not exist.

And so it was while we were in the bar at the Arden Hotel in Stratford, from which we would sometimes steal toilet paper, and Donald Sinden was sitting in a corner, his voice filling the room as it would a theatre, that I suddenly felt it was time to go. I always kept my stash of stockpiled drugs on me, so left and walked back towards home diverting down an old railway track where I sat on a verge, in some bushes. I took out my stash and considered my options. I thought I would be quite alone tucked away there, but two men walked by in conversation and stopped when they saw me sitting there in the bushes. I looked at them, they looked at me, without acknowledgement, they went on their way and I decided this was not the moment and went home.

But I hadn't changed my mind and when we broke up for the summer holidays I took this cocktail of drugs and vodka one night while my parents were away. I left a note by my bedside and I fell into unconsciousness.

The next thing I remember was being half awake lying in a bed by a window, my brothers standing in front of it, in order of height, looking at me. A psychiatrist came to see me, an unsympathetic nurse, and after a day or two I was discharged and my mother drove me home through Kettering's indifferent streets and told me that a place awaited me at a private psychiatric hospital, St Andrew's, Northampton. I was lucky. In spite of my father's tribulations with work his health insurance covered the cost. St Andrew's had been built in the days of a different kind of enlightenment, as the General Lunatic Asylum, and looked like a stately home, set in a park on the edge of the town centre. It had been home to John Clare, the Northamptonshire 'peasant poet', whose completely unexpected verse, guileless poems about nature, had been feted by literary London and then passed out of fashion, leaving him stranded between an early life to which he could not return and an exalted one to which he could not hang on. He suffered severe depression, was confined in an asylum in Essex but then walked back to Northamptonshire and was eventually committed to the General Lunatic Asylum 'after years of poetical prosing', according to the admission papers. It was a humane regime, fortunately, and he was encouraged to write and eventually to come and go as he pleased. He liked to sit in the portico of All Saints Church, the town's principal church, and watch the passing scene. He composed his most famous poem in Northampton, 'I Am', heartbreakingly sad, and for me, lost in depression, almost a hymn.

I am: yet what I am none cares or knows,
My friends forsake me like a memory lost;

I am the self-consumer of my woes,
They rise and vanish in oblivious host,
Like shades in love and death's oblivion lost;
And yet I am! and live with shadows tost

Into the nothingness of scorn and noise,
Into the living sea of waking dreams,
Where there is neither sense of life nor joys,
But the vast shipwreck of my life's esteems;
And e'en the dearest – that I loved the best –
Are strange – nay, rather stranger than the rest.

I long for scenes where man has never trod;
A place where woman never smil'd or wept;
There to abide with my creator, God,
And sleep as I in childhood sweetly slept:
Untroubling and untroubled where I lie;
The grass below – above the vaulted sky.

I love his nature poetry now, preferring extrospection to introspection in his work, but at the time I felt an extraordinarily strong sense of identification with him. This was a little forced, because when I was admitted – not committed, as he had been – my overriding feeling was one of relief, relief at not having to cope with the necessities of living and lying any more, and beyond that a peculiarly pleasant sense of being not quite present in the events of my own life.

But I was present, in a psychiatric hospital, not in the classical main block, where John Clare had lived, by then reserved for patients with more difficult illnesses than my 'clinical depression'. I was booked in – checked in, really – to the Isham Centre, a modern block in the grounds, which looked more like a spa than a psychiatric unit. We had our own rooms, with en suite bathrooms; chefs rather than caterers, and on arrival entered a world that fascinated me. I was assessed by the psychiatrists on the staff, a rather frightening woman with a foreign name, who checked my reflexes by tapping my knee with a little rubber hammer, and a genial man who turned out to have a column in a glossy magazine. They decided group therapy was for me and so I found myself in a room sitting in one of the comradely circles group therapy produces, the youngest and oddest-looking of twelve.

I discovered, thrillingly, that among the twelve were the alcoholic wife of a politician; the heroin-addicted son of a foreign tycoon who had been flown in on a private jet; and a peer of the realm who was, for much of the time, as drunk as a lord. In the wider community there was a singer-songwriter who used to entertain us at the piano when he could bear to; a Jewish princess from St John's Wood; one of the country's leading growers of fuchsias (a plant I still can't abide); and the surviving partner of an aristocratic landowner, confirmed bachelors, who lived as companions in a magnificent house, but when the landowner died found himself no longer part of the family's plans for the future. There were also the much more obviously damaged – wives of bullying husbands whose grief and anger were so locked down they had become like ghosts; a young woman, in her twenties, who stopped coming one day and we found out that she had killed herself; another who would be found lying in the corridors in despair so frequently people would step over her without interrupting their conversations.

There was lots to do. We painted and modelled things and swam and played tiny rounds of golf on the hospital's tiny course. I discovered the only sport for which I have a natural aptitude: trampolining. A handsome former army instructor in a track suit took us to the gym and had me soaring and tumbling almost immediately, an activity which was at least as therapeutic as medication. There were characters who worked there, too, a lugubrious lady who ran the tuck shop with rather a graphic way of answering enquiries. I asked one day for some razors but she said, 'Oh, we don't sell razors . . . you know', and drew her finger across her throat. Matthew would call in to see me. He was working that summer driving an ice-cream van round Northampton, so when he did call a queue of the mentally fragile would form at the van and he kindly, but perhaps unwisely, gave free 99s to everyone until someone told him to stop. The confirmed bachelor friend of the late landowner had a certain asperity about him, which I enjoyed, too. When one of our number returned from a course of electro-convulsive therapy at the main block he said, 'How did you find being plugged into the pylon this morning?'

There was the therapy. We spent hours in that intense circle, talking things through, exploring our evasions and illusions and self-deluding and self-promoting strategies, sometimes with striking results. In one session a woman suddenly experiencing her own grief, wept for the first time in years, her tear ducts opening like rusty taps. One morning the drunken lord, normally the most amiable of men, declined my offer to accompany him on a walk. Later that day one of the nurses on the team made us do an exercise in which we had to touch our toes. He immediately overbalanced, was challenged, and taken to his room, which was found to be full of empty vodka bottles. Tables were turned when one of my fellow patients caught the husband of that nurse, also a nurse, having it away with another member of staff in a storeroom. He brought this up in therapy, like a scene from Whitehall farce dropped into an exercise in method acting, and she ran, crying, from the room. *Quis custodet ipsos custodes?* I thought, and still do when I see or get drawn into therapeutic circles.

And so I spent that summer as an in-patient at St Andrew's. I remember thinking 'well at least life will never be this bad again', and I have been right, so far, though there are times that have been tougher. At seventeen I did not have the experience or the resources to imagine something beyond the frontier of my misery so floated through it rather than engaged with it. But one afternoon, in group therapy, I think I did. The stern doctor with the foreign name was leading our session and asked me a question, which led to a long answer. She seemed particularly interested in what I was saying, 'Go on,' she repeated, so I did. Then, in a pause, she said, 'I think what you're saying is tremendously significant', and at that very moment I not only lost my thread but also any memory of what I had said. Not long after that I woke up one morning and knew I was better.

5. Small-Town Boy

London 1980

I went back to Stratford, completed my second year, and returned home, jobless and directionless. In desperation, my mother made me take the civil service entrance exam, and bought me a horrible pin-striped suit from Burton's in Kettering. I was put on the train to London and found myself in a large hall full of desks and chairs with an invigilator and a printed sheet face down in front of me. I sat down, looked around, and knew at that very moment that I was not going to be a civil servant. So I got up, walked out and spent the day wandering around town, watching Joseph Losey's film version of *Don Giovanni* and then going to London's first unroman-tically named gay shop, Zipper. I bought a porn mag that featured a young skinhead in some very dubious play on the secret love we bear those who want to beat us up, and then got a train home. When my mother asked, I said it had gone fine and hoped she would forget about it rather than notice the non-arrival of the mandarins' marks.

She did notice and I was in trouble, but a friend I'd met in St Andrew's then invited me to rent the spare room in her flat in West Hampstead. Without hesitation, I moved to London. It seems un-usually adventurous to me now to have done so without a job, without money, but I was so desperate to escape that I would have slept on the sofa if she'd let me. And also in those days, with the Thatcher government only just elected, the welfare state was generous, easy to access and routinely exploited by people like me. Rent was paid on the nod, dole was paid without demur, and in the culture, or at least the culture I lived in, welfare was seen as a sort of Arts Council grant, sufficient to cover the necessities of life. It was a golden age for the middle-class wastrel although this was not a view universally shared. My landlady took a different view and made me apply for jobs which she found in the *Standard*. In fact, there was only one, as an assistant at a motor factor in Cricklewood. I failed the interview before I even opened my mouth – what could I say that wouldn't have ruled me out? – and I can still see the look of disdain on the owner's face as my paltry CV and utter lack of interest in retail or motoring or work was made plain. It was just as well. I knew as surely as he that I was never going to be a motor factor. I was much more interested in the sights and sounds of a big city, where I was anonymous and so was everyone else. Following a skinhead, dressed in boots and a Crombie and those marble denim jeans that seemed like a good idea at the time, down West End Lane, I was a step closer to the sexual fulfilment promised by the porn mag I'd bought at Zipper. Actually, this was as near as I got to sexual fulfilment, although the city was full of opportunities if I'd had the nerve to exploit them.

Although I enjoyed living in West Hampstead, when Fergus and Romy called to tell me they were moving to London so that Fergus could start at Middlesex Poly on the Performing Arts BA course, I jumped at the chance to rent a house with them in Finchley. I journeyed north to a tall, narrow, done-up house overlooking some allotments let to us by a trusting man who had gone to work abroad. I had the top floor, an attic conversion, with a Velux window and an aluminium ladder so noisy and cumbersome that I took to peeing out of the window rather than using the bathroom on the basement floor. The house came with two cats, renamed Anthrax and Thyroxin, and there I dwelled for a year or so. Fergus and I spent most of the time lying on opposite sofas in the sitting room. He had fixed up a remote-control model car with a device for holding a joint and this little machine would whine to and fro between us for what seemed like an entire summer. This must have driven Romy mad, but we were too wrapped up in ourselves to do anything about it.

I did take the initiative one day to call FAGS, the Finchley Area

Gay Society, an organisation rather at odds with the spirit of the neighbourhood, represented in Parliament by Margaret Thatcher, whose policies were taking hold. FAGS was a more genteel form of protest, men too settled or too shy for pubs and clubs, meeting fortnightly in a member's house. It was a big deal for me to show up one night, the first deed to match the words, but I'm happy to say my first visit ended in my first proper sex with a shy boy who offered me a lift home. In the car I think I said, 'Fancy a tumble?', an excruciating attempt at nonchalant ribaldry, and he did, to my surprise, although it was obvious we were as desperate for sex as stranded whales for the sea. We did not repeat the exercise.

Not long after this I saw an ad in *Gay Times* for people interested in joining a gay theatre company. I got in touch and was invited to an audition, come get-to-know-you which was held in a room in a community centre in King's Cross. The company was called Consenting Adults In Public and like its better-known precursor, Gay Sweatshop, was interested in theatre by and for gay people seeking to radically and creatively engage with a patriarchal homophobic – although then we didn't say homophobic – world. It seems so quaint now, in an era when being gay is far less noteworthy, and when cynicism about politics is so widespread, that a radical gay theatre company could be taken seriously, but we did take ourselves seriously, and saw an opportunity to take control of our own identity in a world which forced upon us an identity of hopeless victimhood at best, one of toxic evil at worst. Theatre gave that impulse shape and voice and body, and we sang the Body Electric.

This conviction was unevenly shared by those who turned up that night. One, a man in his sixties, rather let himself down during a trust game in which we allowed ourselves to be passed unresistingly round a circle, but in spite of that I was recalled and a week or two later a group reassembled in that community centre around our leader, although he would have hated being called a leader. Eric Presland was the kind of long-haired dropout the *Daily Express* so loved to hate, a Cambridge graduate who lived in a squat, cared little for the standards of middle-class behaviour, cared nothing for the values of a consumer society and was radical by reflex. He had a circle of like-minded friends, some of them even more radical than he was. One of them, a nervy and sometimes unpredictable young man, was so upset by patriarchy that when we had a meeting with a radical lesbian feminist group about a proposed joint project he lay on the floor as a way of rejecting the privilege of domination his male body imposed on their female bodies, a well-meant gesture which unfortunately was lost on the lesbians who I don't think would have seen him as a threat in anything other than the most theoretical sense.

Those of us who arrived as a result of the ad in *Gay Times* were more mixed. I especially liked Lorna, a woman whose badges-and-braces appearance belied a gentler, less confrontational, nature. She was a lawyer, but had abandoned her Articles to work for a publisher in Mayfair where she seemed to spend most of the time proofreading ornithologists' notes to aid in the identification of birds. One species had a distinctive call, 'a harsh chack-chack', and as we discussed how it might be spelled, a friendship began that has been one of the richest and most durable of my life. Lorna lived in West Hampstead, just up the road from where I had made my London landfall, in the bottom floor of a house divided into two flats, with a small front garden in which she took great pride. The first time I visited I asked if I could see the garden, imagining something fancy round the back, but she replied, a little hurt, that I was standing in it.

Consenting Adults in Public made its debut in its reinvigorated form with a play called *Latecomer*, by Eric Presland. Four gay men on holiday in a country cottage go over their entanglements, a romantic comedy but with fewer X chromosomes than usual. The director, somewhat peculiarly, decided to set it on a tennis court rather than in a low-ceilinged cottage. The curtain came up with me banging my head on an imaginary beam, but it must have looked like I'd just been hit on the head with a tennis ball, for we stood on a stage cloth painted green with white lines and Lorna, stage manager, dressed as an umpire in blue blazer and white pleated skirt, sitting in a chair at the side of the tennis court calling 'fault!' from time to time. My character had to take all his clothes off and get into a sleeping bag with a man much more handsome but much less naked than me, which drew an audible sigh of disappointment from the audience.

We played in the upstairs room of a pub in Islington, sometimes to fewer people than were on stage (four plus umpire) and after the performance we were obliged to discuss issues raised by the play with the audience. The only person I remember doing this was the man who had let himself down playing the trust game at the audition, who appeared to have had more than his consciousness raised by the final scene.

Another member of Consenting Adults was Toby Kettle, a red-haired punk teenage troubadour with a guitar and practised incivility, a boy dancer from the Arts Educational School who appeared as one of Tadzio's friends on the Lido in *Death in Venice*, dodging von Aschenbach's offstage as well as onstage attentions. He wrote sour, rather brilliant songs about transgressive desire and the futility of everything, Barnes's answer to Jacques Brel. We became friends and could have been more perhaps but I found I was just as terrified of my desire for someone who might have reciprocated it as I was for someone who wouldn't. One night on the tube, the smoking carriage on the Piccadilly line westbound, he asked me back to his place – a bedroom in his middle-class parents' Thames-side flat – but I declined, pretending I had to go on to see my boyfriend, and spent the next couple of years longing for him hopelessly.

In my last year at Stratford I had been knocked off my bike one morning on the way into college and a cheque arrived in compensation. Two thousand pounds, a fortune, which I spent on getting my ears pierced, buying some dreadful clothes and a soprano saxophone, which I taught myself to play very badly. I loved Sidney Bechet, great soprano player of the golden age of jazz, who I discovered through Philip Larkin's poem in homage, but I could only make a dreadful blary, leaky sound with mine. It went quite well with Toby's songs and we performed a couple on a travelling cabaret show that Consenting Adults toured once to Newcastle-under-Lyme, where we appeared in the town hall to an audience who seemed so unexpected and unlikely that Toby put down his guitar and said he had to go to the toilet, leaving me alone on stage. We were put up in people's houses, where there was groping and bed-swapping in the name of the radical repudiation of heterosexist norms, and we travelled in a minibus so decrepit it broke down on the M1 near Leicester on our way back to London. I called my parents and my father and my younger brother drove out thirty miles to ferry us from the hard shoulder to our house, where my mother, daughter of the WRVS, made up beds, cooked us something and asked no questions that might have led to embarrassing answers.

Back in London, Toby and I were asked if we wanted to move into a flat in King's Cross that had been found by a friend of an exemplary gay radical who had re-spelled his Christian name because it was a 'Christian' name and also because he wished to divest it of the male power such gendered things endow. We accepted Greyum's offer, and so I left Fergus and Romy, in a fug of hash smoke, and moved into a flat above a television repair shop on the Caledonian Road at the red-light end of King's Cross. There was an alleyway behind our flat that was often used by women and their punters. We ached to express solidarity with them, but they were more interested in earning whatever living they could and resented our efforts to reach out to them with our best consciousness-raising intentions.

Life got very gay. I was living with two other young gay men, working in a gay theatre company and hanging out with other gay men and some male-friendly lesbians to leaven the lump. It seemed like a good idea at the time to construct for ourselves an exclusive identity, individually and together, that gave us room to be fully human, not reduced to caricature, although we quite liked aspects of that caricature, too. Along with the sense of solidarity the best thing about being so gay then – and now – was the humour. Julian and Sandy, from the BBC's radio comedy of the fifties and sixties *Round the Horne*, were rediscovered, their double entendre and campery not a cleaving to the hatred of others but a reappropriation of it, or so we liked to think when it suited us. Some gay men, like Julian and Sandy, still spoke Polari, the gay slang of the theatres and fairs. 'Bona to vada your dolly old eek' – nice to see you – would have been familiar to audiences of *Round the Horne* but 'living out the national handbag' for being on the dole must have been a more recent coinage. It was a language of resistance and that was to be applauded, but sometimes it also carried the taint of misogyny and sometimes cruelty that was not so lovable. Enjoying it, therefore, produced a sort of anxiety and we would sit, when we could be bothered, in earnest discussion attempting to purge our consciousnesses.

Greyum could be especially strict in this. He wore a leather jacket decorated on the back with a large pink triangle surrounded by concentration camp barbed wire and the slogan 'Never Again!'. For Greyum, for all of us in our coterie, that sense of homosexuality as a sharply defined political identity was unarguable, the victimisation of gay people by the Nazis was a fact, identified by pink triangles rather than yellow stars in the concentration camps. Our sense of common cause with all the oppressed, black people, women, the working class, was so keen that to waver from this orthodoxy was seen as a cowardly capitulation to the oppressor. It was neat and tidy, it suited the temper of the times and I think it did a lot to heal my generation of the pain we had suffered growing up. It was also, like all enterprises of this kind, a bit ridiculous, but I dislike it when people sneer at it or dismiss it as nothing but ridiculous. It was richer, freer than this far more cynical era, and I feel an intense nostalgia for that time of *City Limits*, and badges and calling each other comrade.

Not far from our flat – renamed Wee Nooke – was Gay's the Word, London's first and only gay bookshop, in the middle of Marchmont Street at the council end of Bloomsbury. It stocked everything that you now find in mainstream bookshops on the shelves marked 'gay and lesbian interest', from scholarly works on Magnus Hirschfeld to histories of the Hollywood musical. At the back there was a coffee shop, really just a table surrounded by chairs, and it was there I first met Jimmy Somerville. Well, where I first met Jimmy Somerville by name and in daylight.

He was very short, very striking, very unintelligible. We exchanged a few words but I couldn't understand many of them because his

Glaswegian accent was so strong. For the first six months of our friendship I got only a fraction of what he said but nodded politely, or so I thought, until one day he challenged me about it. 'Wise up,' he said, 'Wise up!' I tried to wise up. We were all a bit overpowered by Jimmy, who had extraordinary charisma and self-possession, although he was only a year older than me and so tiny, a little over five feet tall, that he must have been used to being literally overlooked. If Jimmy ever thought his size a deficiency you would not readily know, for he had turned it into a strength, by becoming not boyish – there was nothing boyish about Jimmy at all – but as if a Glaswegian had been miniaturised by a brilliant designer. He was compact, physically strong, he was a wonderful dancer, he was always well turned out, and he had an extraordinary style about him, a look that expressed both vulnerability and strength and a degree of charge, like electricity, which would switch off street lights as he walked by (a useful superpower for a man who relished so much the cover of darkness).

As my ear became tuned to his accent, I got to learn more about him. He was a Glaswegian from Maryhill who had run away to London after a life of extraordinary toughness and fight. By the time he hit puberty people mistook him for a girl. He was, he said, the only boy in his year to bunk off school to watch the Bay City Rollers open a carpet shop, which did little to secure him an easy place in the macho culture of his family and peers. Jimmy, tough and resourceful and resilient, turned it to his advantage, and discovered first, that if it doesn't kill you it makes you strong, and second, that looking like a girl was enough for beer-filled horny Glaswegian men turning out of the pubs on a Friday night looking for 'hole'. Jimmy, liberal with his affections, made the most of these opportunities. In fact I can say with confidence that I have never met anyone more liberal in his affections than Jimmy. His sexual appetite was immeasurable, his bedpost, had he notched it, would have whittled away to a lace bobbin in a fortnight, and he could switch on at will a kind of tractor beam which, once it had locked on, drew its target unresistingly in.

He dazzled me, with his toughness, his sexual confidence, his stylishness and his interest in me, which I don't think I have ever really understood. Perhaps it was the attraction of opposites? Me, physically shy, intellectually precocious, awkward, geeky and posh? Being gay in the way that we were being gay at the beginning of the eighties levelled social differences, class and regional and national differences, a bit like the French Foreign Legion, I guess. I both enjoyed and valued finding common purpose with people in whom you struggled to recognise yourself. Jimmy was really not like me in so many ways and one of the greatest lessons I learned from knowing him is to try not to make assumptions about people whose lives are unimaginably different from your own. And tougher than your own.

Jimmy lived with his flatmate, Constantine Giannaris, in a squatted Peabody flat without a bathroom round the corner from the British Museum. Connie was Greek, spoke unaccented English, was politically fluent, well-read, had something of Sally Bowles about him, and was a foil to Jimmy at his most egregious. Jimmy could explode without warning, into rage or tears or random shrieking that used to throw me, but Connie could make it better, make a joke, calm him down, put him to bed. Gay's the Word was equidistant between our two flats so we got into the habit of meeting there and soon we started seeing each other in our flats. Flats were more than where you lived then. Because we were all on the dole, our lives happened in our flats; what we said there, thought there, how we did them up with zero budgets, became our work. Our work was forming what sociologists were to call the 'alternative gay scene', launched on the first wave of gay liberation but formed in the aesthetics of punk and the politics of the hard left. We were not like our immediate gay predecessors, with their moustaches and leather caps and hanky codes, at the Colherne and Copacabana in Earls Court; we rejected the look, the culture, the woefully inadequate politics.

I don't know how it emerged or where it emerged or upon whom it emerged, but our look was different. We had flattops at the barber's, razored back and sides and a level cut on top, we wore Levi 501 jeans, button-flied, we wore white socks, which seems unforgivable now but made sense then, and Doctor Marten boots. Check shirts, white t-shirts under, and a bomber jacket, were standard issue, but there was a sort of rockabilly flourish to this, which distinguished it from the skinhead look. Caps were worn, like Fidel Castro's, and sometimes black Chinese slippers in a gesture to Mao. We had no money so it was a look put together second-hand, from places like Flip in Covent Garden and then the charity shops of north and south London, where fifties clothing, even demob suits, still smelling faintly of austerity and Sir Stafford Cripps, could be cannibalised or adapted. I was hopeless at getting this right. Jimmy, Connie and Toby had effortless style and could put on anything and look good. I had no idea, unable then and now to see what goes with what and what doesn't, and so poor at seeing a job through I would buy a jacket that was too big, and wear it tucked in like a tramp rather than look further for something that actually fitted. I had terrible specs and terrible teeth and a terrible dislike of my reflection in the mirror, so looked unconfident and unsure of myself. And I was caught between two identities, never an easy place to be; scruffy hippy who rejected societal norms, and sharp-dressed foot soldier in a new and exciting urban subculture. In retrospect, even when my countercultural kudos was at its strongest, there was always a vicar struggling to get out.

Our social circle widened when Jimmy and Connie introduced us to a club night, which took place on a Wednesday evening in the upstairs of a pub in Islington. 'Movements' was the midweek night out for this 'alternative gay scene'. It felt slightly like a meeting of a north London Socialist Workers Party but had a bar and a DJ who played music like Visage, and Kraftwerk, electronic pop made by boys in make-up, and some who went there were to become famous in bands themselves. It was also where I met a close friend of Jimmy's who was to become a major influence on my life and the life of many, Mark Ashton.

Mark was in his early twenties, from Northern Ireland, had come up through the Marxist left, was General Secretary of the Young Communist League and could hold his own in a conversation about bourgeois formalism and address people as 'Comrade' without embarrassment. I could not. He was also outrageously fun and flamboyantly cheerful and sexually bold. He, like Jimmy, who looked like cousins if not brothers, was a brilliant dancer and they would, when drunk, which was a lot of the time, go rockabilly jiving across dance floors with such exuberance people would be knocked off their feet if they got in the way. Mark had also worked for a while as a barman at the Conservative Club in King's Cross, or, rather, as a barmaid, in drag, with a blonde beehive wig. I was never sure if the patrons worked out that he was really a man or if he had perhaps oversold the story, but like Jimmy he had a degree of self-possession and authenticity which impressed us all. They were very close but had quite a difficult relationship, both capable of wickedness, both unafraid of a fight, although Jimmy was always undefeated because we knew that if backed into a corner there was nothing he would not do. There was either peace or nuclear war. Mark was tough, too, but more circumspect, and would look for ways to take the heat out of an argument or sometimes just back down.

Mark was also a keeper of conscience. Jimmy was impulsive and emotional and, while he was good at keeping the fires of commitment and action stoked, he avoided the cooling rill of theory. Mark was good at theory, had an instinctive grasp of it, and more tellingly a feel for putting it into practice. Occasionally it misfired. I remember a dreary evening in support of a benighted South American nation. Top of the bill was a protest singer from that country, but she stopped halfway through what felt like the thirtieth verse of a song to ask us, the audience, if we would mind being quiet and pay attention to her song and the plight of her people. We did not, too absorbed in ourselves to pay much attention to her howling and twanging, and she left the stage crestfallen. As a punishment Mark made me come on stage and read an incomprehensible poem, as the volume of chatter rose, to soak up some of the ignominy. He was usually much more successful in getting people's interest because he was at home with an emerging popular culture, the 'alternative' of the 'alternative gay scene', and that made all the difference because the message was mediated in forms and by people that audiences were excited by. There were venues in London such the Oval House and the Albany Empire, which were run by people sympathetic to this and where Toby and I, and Consenting Adults, and Gay Sweatshop, were able to perform.

At the Oval House, Eric Presland from Consenting Adults and I performed a cabaret show he had written, a sort of parody of ourselves, with me as a Liberace-like figure singing camp songs on the piano wearing a powder-blue suit and a pair of rhinestone-encrusted glasses, Eric as an earnest activist. He had the best song, though, a version of 'These Foolish Things' which he had adapted to suit a different lifestyle from those of the twenties and thirties: *'The cleats and chains when you got into SM; the vicar in leather you brought round to bless 'em: my arm is still in slings, these foolish things . . .'* One night, during a performance, we were interrupted by a heckle from the audience that I hear again now: 'I am finding this very offensive!' I faltered and answered, pathetically, that I hadn't written it, and a debate opened up between Eric and the heckler, a person notorious for her exacting propriety, which rather killed the rest of the evening. There was a lot of that in those days, interruptions of righteous indignation, a feature of the tensions which both informed the show and underlay the relationship between Eric and me. One day, dispirited, I made the mistake of putting my frustrations on paper and sending them, with my resignation, to him. Eric called round to pick up costume and props a few days later, by which time I was already ashamed. I still am.

At the Albany Empire I appeared at a benefit with Tom Robinson, the singer whose song I had used to persuade my mother that I was not as other sons. Toby and I did a couple of numbers before Tom and his band headlined. I watched him at the sound check, taking his time giving very detailed instructions to the sound engineer. It paid off. His performance of his song 'War Baby' – Tom on guitar and vocals and a great sax player, Mark Ramsden, on soprano – and it was one of those occasions when words and music and performance captured something distinctively of the moment and yet also sounded like they would endure beyond it. Fortunately they were distant enough on the bill from Toby and me, also on guitar and soprano, for their performance not to sound too like a judgement on our own.

That evening was recorded and made into an LP, my first recorded performance, of historic interest only, and I lost the album years ago; but it was also filmed and a bit of me appears swanning around backstage holding a soprano saxophone. Then I address the camera in an irritating mock-camp voice: 'This is for all those lonely gay teenagers out there . . . IN STRAIGHTSVILLE!'

6. Revenge of the Teenage Perverts

It was the generation before ours on London's gay scene that were the real pioneers, the founders of Gay Sweatshop and *Gay News*, and one of the most able of the pioneers was Andy Lipman. He was a blond nice Jewish boy from Leeds, grammar school alumnus, clever and driven, who had gone to Oxford to read Law, dated an aristocratic girl, very sketchily, and then came out as gay. He went home to tell his mum. 'Thank God,' she said, 'I thought you'd married a shiksa.' Andy worked at a Law Centre by day and on creative projects in his spare time. He and his friend, an actor called Philip Timmins, were very involved in the theatre groups that came and went at the Albany Empire and other radical venues, but were also connected to people with real jobs in the media.

One of them, Alan Fountain, was working as a commissioning editor for the soon-to-arrive Channel Four and he had a budget and the new Umatic video system, low-cost and easy to use. He was looking for something new in documentary form, so offered people budget and kit and told them to make something interesting.

Andy and Philip took him up on this offer and the Lesbian and Gay Youth Video Project was founded. They felt past the cut-off age themselves, veterans in their late twenties, so needed to assemble a group of young gay men and lesbians to actually make it. Word went out and a group of us met one night at Philip's flat in a red-brick council block off Argyll Square in King's Cross.

From this group much followed. Toby and I and Jimmy and Connie were among the dozen or so who were involved daily, although some blew in and out, in the months we took to make it.

First the kit arrived, and we set up shop in an office in Effra Road in Brixton. We were profligate with tape, shooting everything because we did not know what we were doing, but if only for that reason we captured something that had not been seen before – the texture of our lives, the look and feel of the young gay people in London in that gap between liberalisation of the legislation concerning sexual offences and the arrival of HIV. I saw it again recently and was surprised by its rawness – at the time we thought we were wonderfully sophisticated – by its gang feel as we ran around London, and by our youth. Some of it seems ahead of its time: it begins with Isaac Julien, world-famous filmmaker today, shooting a close-up of himself in a mirror saying, 'You should show everything'. Everyone is filming or photographing everything all the time. It cuts quickly and raids other images as comment on what interviewees say or don't say. Nothing is still, it judders and shakes, and wobbles, but there is a truthfulness about it especially when Rose Collis, interviewer out of shot, confronts people in a market in Hackney with her lesbian self and elicits an extraordinary range of reactions from them.

We were all sleeping together, even me, though nervously, in the spirit of Walt Whitman's 'army of lovers', and the intensity of those relationships tell on the screen. To sleep with someone was not only to form an attachment, however fleeting (some very fleeting indeed): it was an expression of autonomy, of freedom – the personal really was political – and while today we might think the bedroom door a good place to check our ideological baggage we brought it right in with us then. The whole experience was charged and exciting, and unlike Consenting Adults, which felt underpowered and behind the times, the Video Project was in the forefront, and doing something new. As the badly shot, grainy images slowly came together we put on a soundtrack, the Eurythmics and Soft Cell, genderish electro pop just coming up – I still can't hear the opening bars of 'Love Is A Stranger' without thinking bliss was it in that dawn to be alive . . . – but we also wanted to create something of our own. We were young and didn't know what we were doing, so we took risks without knowing they were risks, and tried things we wouldn't try now.

And that is how my musical partnership with Jimmy Somerville began. One day we were talking about a sequence of images and decided to try to make something up to go with them, something more screamed than sung, with howling saxophone and a beat and a vocal. But whose vocal? Jimmy, whose deep and gruff Glaswegian voice bore no token of what was to come, volunteered, opened his mouth and sang.

It was an extraordinary moment. What came out was so at odds with what we saw. Jimmy, who looked like a street urchin, produced a voice like an angel. The room fell quiet, partly at the extraordinary quality and power of what we were hearing but also because it seemed to come right out of the heart of who we were. The noise he was making was what we sounded like. Someone programmed a tiny beat box and I got my saxophone and because we had only a stereo tape recorder and no effects we actually made up a song, vocal, drum track and soprano saxophone, and recorded it in an underground gents near King's Cross; tiled, acoustically live, sexually notorious; how perfect. It was called 'Screaming', a scrap of a song, not really a song at all, but a star was born.

Toby and I sort of fell out during the making of the video. There was a competitiveness about our involvement in the project and sometimes this spilled over, his into aggression, mine into passive aggression. As the end approached there was a bit of jockeying to get credit – and indeed to get in at the edit – and I moved to the side or was moved to the side. When I saw the rough edit I was disappointed not to see more of myself and to see rather more of Toby. But then he had the edge because he wasn't constrained by having to pretend that he didn't care about it. I did pretend, some self-denying ethical circuit firing whenever my ambition flared, which was a lot of the time. It was a sign of suitability for ordination, I see now, the Christian tradition of the last being first and the first last, making for some awkward postures of humility with the more careerist clergy.

At home this resentment rather coloured things between Toby and me. He got more vocal about it. I got more silent about it. And as his clamour and my resentment grew I arranged to move out of Wee Nooke and back into Lorna's flat in West Hampstead. When the moment came to tell him, he had fallen ill with hepatitis, and looked on me yellow-eyed as I told him of my plans. I left him there, in King's Cross, with a boil-in-the-bag cod in parsley sauce, and headed north-west.

The video, when it was finally finished, was called *Framed Youth: The Revenge of the Teenage Perverts*. It was raw and uneven, but when I saw the final version I sensed we had made something good. We sent it to Channel Four and when they finally broadcast it we watched it at Philip's flat, where it all began. Much to our surprise, *Framed Youth* was chosen to receive the Grierson Award by the British Film Institute, for documentary of the year. There was a big do at the Festival Hall to which we all turned up looking like Fagin's kids gate-crashing the Biennale. After a rather grudging speech from the chair of judges, who expressed some reservations about the decision of his peers, Philip went up to collect the award. He made a speech, we ate the buffet, drank the wine and stole a wheel of Stilton as we left.

Framed Youth had a powerful effect on all of us who participated in it. For me, in spite of having waxed and waned during its production, two things in particular stand out. First, that we could make something of our lives that looked original and distinctive and that had an edge; and, second, I realised that I needed to do something with my life that would get me off the dole. I was not really cut out for a gutter life, although I quite enjoyed hanging around other people who were. I could never quite shake off the fear of penury and failure that ran deep in my family background, small-town people in hats and moustaches, who never quite got to believe their luck. I remember telling my mother about *Framed Youth* and laying on thickly Channel Four and the BFI and her thinking about it for a moment and then asking me if it was 'under the gay umbrella?' Under the gay umbrella, could I find a place where I would be not only protected from the storms of contumely but also could stride out into the world? I began to pick up little bits of work, through contacts in fringe theatres, and wrote a score for an earnest show about the Spanish Civil War at a little theatre in north London. I also looked at the ads in the back of *Melody Maker* and there saw one for a band signed to Polydor called Two People. They wanted a third person, someone to play keyboards, and I went to meet them and played and they must have liked me a bit because I did a couple of rehearsals with them. I can't remember how it happened, but someone put me in touch with Pauline Black, singer with the brilliant Coventry ska band the Selecter (on my radio, on my radio). She was doing a benefit in London and needed to put a band together so I joined to play the piano and met in that line-up the drummer June Miles-Kingston, who had been in the Modettes and played with the Specials. We all got on and took numbers, and I suppose things were coming together.

Much more exciting things were happening for Jimmy. After *Framed Youth* revealed the beauty of his voice, he was approached by two friends living on the same council estate in Camberwell as him. Larry and Steve were keyboard players and they had some ideas for songs. A band was formed, brilliantly named Bronski Beat, a reference to the little boy in *The Tin Drum*, the 1979 Volker Schlöndorff film version of Günter Grass's novel, whose high-pitched scream could shatter windows. Thanks to Ken Livingstone – who we all adored – Bronski Beat made their debut at a gay arts festival funded by the GLC. They also got a slot supporting Tina Turner, just reinventing herself, at the Venue in Victoria, and another at St James's Church in Piccadilly, where Jimmy worked for a while in the coffee shop. What I remember of those first appearances is Jimmy's total assurance on stage. That he looked to the manner born was remarkable considering he had never done any public performing before. His stagecraft experience amounted to dressing up as a child in his auntie's clothes when she was out and hoovering her flat singing along to Motown records she'd brought back from the United States; and yet there he was in front of us, on full power, totally assured, transformed, transfigured even, in bright light and the object of fascinated attention.

His voice was just extraordinary, and seeing others hearing him sing for the first time was intensely exciting. A&R men from record companies began to appear in that widening circle, scouting for talent, and as word got out about Jimmy and the band they began to close in. Among them was Tracey Bennett, A&R man at London Records, a label that behaved like an independent but was actually part of the Polygram group, a major, with a major's resources. Bronski Beat signed to London in 1983 after only a handful of gigs, and the next I heard Jimmy was recording a single.

I was both gratified and envious. Gratified that success was coming their way, and not only for the band but for what the band stood for; and envious that it was happening to them and not to me. I was still living on next to nothing with Lorna. Winter arrived and one day the bathroom ceiling fell in. We called the landlord, a mysterious man who used to send florid letters from his home in Wales, and he sent round the experts who discovered that it was so damp we might as well have been living in a swamp. When the builders started doing calculations in pencil on the kitchen table top, I had a feeling things weren't going to go well. They arrived the following week, took our windows and window frames and then disappeared, leaving us freezing cold, damp and unsafe. I came down with glandular fever and during the wretched weeks of recovery that feeling I had to get my life in order grew stronger.

Jimmy appeared on the front of the *NME*. It stopped me dead, seeing, for the first time, something significant out there in the world acknowledging his potential. A few weeks later Bronski Beat released their debut single, 'Smalltown Boy'. It was about running away from Glasgow, from Kettering, from anywhere, running from awful teenage years of misery and shame and violence to London and its opportunities and temptations. Opportunities and temptations were sometimes the same thing and the record is full of pain and pleasure, desire and resistance, fulfilment and frustration. Jimmy's voice, simultaneously fragile and strong, rises from bluesy velvet in the verses to howling power in the choruses. He had an extra dimension of power and fury, and the track, spare and electronic and in that most unsettling of keys, F minor, gave him room to soar. 'You leave in the morning with everything you own in a little black case . . .': we heard it and we immediately recognised it as our own experience, a vindication of what we stood for and an endorsement, like the Grierson Award, of who we were.

It would have been good if it had just been that, a soundtrack to our lives, but it was more. As soon as it got airplay others responded and within a week or so of its release Bronski Beat was booked on to *Top of the Pops*, then the most influential music show in Europe. Peter Powell introduced the band saying, 'You're not going to believe what these guys are all about', and there was Jimmy, singing a live vocal faultlessly, while on podiums men in mullets and women in legwarmers interpreted the song in wildly unsuitable dance.

The record, like the vocal, soared, and got to number three in the charts, alongside Frankie Goes to Hollywood and George Michael. How gay is that?

7. The Workers United Will Never Be Defeated

Bronski Beat's rise coincided with the miners' fall, the two most significant influences on my life at the time, the sound of gender-bending electropop for ever conflated with people shouting 'the workers united will never be defeated' at exactly the moment they were being beaten into submission. The two could not have seemed more different, but were not unrelated, both attempts to define and defend identities and communities under threat. While Margaret Thatcher – icon of all the awfulness of the time to us – overlooked the entrepreneurialism and dynamism of the alternative gay scene (imagine!) she did not ignore the miners. Nor did the miners' leaders ignore her and for a while it was like living through a civil war.

I had started going to Socialist Workers Party meetings, a Trotskyist group on the hard left, immensely active but also notorious for the ruthlessness and relentlessness of its politics and for fielding about ten students for every proper worker on its demos. I once took Lorna along to a meeting in West Hampstead but she was denounced for offering to pay for some literature by cheque, an act of collusion with the military–industrial complex that dismayed the comrades. Other friends of mine were involved with the International Marxist Group, who ran jolly camping weekenders when everyone fell out; the Spartacists, whose slogans were almost as long as manifestos; the Workers Revolutionary Party, which seemed to appeal particularly strongly to artists; and then the Revolutionary Communist Party, which I seem to remember split, with the frequency of boy bands, into the Revolutionary Communist Group and the Revolutionary

Communist Tendency. It had an annual conference which one year, with commendable ambition, was called 'Preparing for Power'. It seems a very distant world now, not least the passionate conviction of both left and right, and the bloodthirstiness of the revolutionary impulse. The violence was a bit theoretical for me until, on an SWP outing to the picket lines at Eddie Shah's newspaper printing press at Warrington, where the NGA, another powerful union, was taking on a rising press baron, I discovered that I was not cut out for the front line. I chanted beautifully and pushed to the front, but when I was confronted by police officers with batons I changed my mind and got caught trying to retreat in the push forwards, whacked a few times and then caught under a crush of falling comrades. Unable to breathe I panicked and screamed, letting the side down, and was chastised for this in the minibus on the way home by a solemn and righteous young woman.

Armchair socialism was more my thing, until I met Mike Jackson, who had been a gardener in Regent's Park, living in a grace and favour cottage plotting the downfall of the Establishment while planting fuchsias for the Crown. Mike, along with Mark Ashton and others, saw the need for an organisation to get involved with the striking communities and so in 1984 Lesbians and Gays Support the Miners was founded. It sounds like the beginning of a joke about loony lefties, but it was a profoundly affecting experience for all. LGSM 'adopted' a mining village in South Wales, Dulais, as traditional a working-class community as ever went down a pit, and with traditional working-class values, like self-reliance, and toughness, and what we would have thought of as an unreconstructed view of the respective roles of the sexes. I have no idea what they thought of LGSM before they met us, but with all the earners out on strike, and deep uncertainty about the future of the industry and the communities it supported, the offer of help and solidarity was welcomed. So Mike went down to Dulais with an advance party and if there were anxieties on both sides they seemed to just vanish as two communities found they had more in common than anyone might have thought. We offered practical help, too, as we shook buckets on street corners up and down the country, raising thousands of pounds – enough to buy Dulais a minibus which I would love to think was still ferrying pensioners to lunch clubs in the livery of the NUM and LGSM. But the real change came about when LGSM members went to visit miners' families in Dulais and Neath. These encounters were so rich in comedy and pathos that they have been made into a film, *Pride*, written by Stephen Beresford and directed by Matthew Warchus. Stephen came to see me to talk about that episode in 1980s social history, and left me with the tantalising thought of people I know being recreated on screen by Bill Nighy and Imelda Staunton and Dominic West.

Why did these unlikely friendships flourish? Perhaps, in spite of the geographical and cultural distance between us, there was a growing sense of common experience due to shared status as pariahs. One of the great achievements of Thatcherism, I think, was to unite the communities it despised, from what was left of industrial Britain to the newly forming subcultures of the cities. LGSM was an early example of this. The friendships made, we discovered, were more durable than the industry they formed round, and while the miners were roundly defeated in only a year, the relationships forged in the strike brought benefits. Miners joined the Gay Pride March in 1985 and supported gay rights in the TUC and the Labour Party, which played a part in the dramatic shift in attitudes to gay people in the thirty years since. Some of those from the mining communities found a voice they didn't know they had, particularly women, and went on to add theirs resonantly to the Labour movement in Wales and beyond in the years to come.

I suppose I had rather a good miners' strike. One of the achievements of LGSM was organising a red-hot Bronski Beat benefit concert at the Electric Ballroom in Camden. Jimmy, who I had run into at a club, asked me if I wanted to play saxophone and I somehow managed to find time in my crowded schedule to oblige. I borrowed my best friend Matthew's tenor sax and spent days and days practising to tracks from *The Age of Consent*, the band's first album. I practised so much I nearly bit through my bottom lip and stuffed the bell with socks and played under a duvet lest I drive the upstairs neighbours mad. Another gig followed, at Hackney Town Hall, and to my surprise, and the surprise of anyone who knew any-thing about saxophone playing, the band asked if I would like to join them for live gigs as a regular thing. It took me a while to work out why Bronski Beat, which had been managing very nicely without me, were doing me such a favour. Their manager could quite easily have hired someone who could have done a much better job. But I soon began to think, as I was one of Jimmy's friends, it was a way of trying to keep him happy. Jimmy was never at ease with the fame and success that had come his way so quickly and so abundantly; not quite to the point of striding purposefully away from it, but there was a volatility about him that could be very concerning for those who depended on him for it to work. Stars tend to be like that; the qualities that make them fascinating also make them difficult, and a lot of work and teeth-gritting compromise goes into keeping them happy and functional. I was soon to discover just how wearing this could be but back then, in the ante-room of success, Jimmy's unpre-dictability was not really my problem.

These tensions grew, though nobody said anything about it. I went and bought a rather sober grey suit from a charity shop, fifties-style. I needed a new look. Things were happening.

I wore it on my first trip abroad with the band to the Montreux Pop Festival. Geneva airport looked like Madame Tussaud's. There were famous people everywhere, pop stars arriving from all over the world for the half-gang show, half-trade fair, televised throughout Europe to an irresistibly enormous audience. There is an unwritten pop star etiquette and one of the fundamental rules is that when two pop stars meet, the overture, if there is one, must come from the more famous. That's easy if you're an *X Factor* finalist meeting Paul McCartney, but when all the pop stars you can think of are in one small Swiss town those judgements can get frighteningly fine. Rod Stewart or Sting? Ray Davies, royalty but venerable, or Vanilla Ice, suddenly, bewilderingly, everywhere? At the airport, unacknow-ledged by anyone, I stood at the baggage carousel, my grubby hold-all crushed between the immaculate bags and aluminium flight cases of my betters. The best among them would never pick up their bag at all and had people to do it for them, unsmiling men in mullets who had their own pecking order, mirroring that of their masters and mistresses, like servants in an Edwardian country house. But pop stars still have to get off a plane, clear customs, get their passports stamped, even if it is through the VIP channels, so there were un-likely clumps of the famous awaiting their entourages, checking each other out to see who should make the first move. Jimmy was new and red-hot and got a lot of attention. Larry and Steve and I moved without resistance through the airport, on to a minibus, and into town, through the occasional sputter of flash guns.

Hotels afford some protection from journalists and fans, and the bigger the star the longer they end up living their lives in them. At Montreux, however, there were so many stars in town there was not enough accommodation of sufficient splendour to go round the number of people who thought they deserved it. Dreadful protocol issues followed. You spend so much of your time as a pop star in a cocoon of acquiescence, everyone stroking you and making a fuss; but before long this is mistaken for a state of nature rather than the peculiar lottery of success. However, when there are more stars than suites, the terrible reality of the pecking order, or the strength of the team in your corner, is revealed. The cocoons burst, but not in a good way, and there are scenes.

Something of these tensions was foreshadowed on this trip. We brought Marc Almond with us. He had joined Jimmy on vocals in the Bronski Beat cover of 'I Feel Love', one of the great disco anthems of the seventies. Marc had become very famous with Soft Cell, pulling off a leather-wearing synth-playing pop-punk thing, which was very distinctive. Jimmy was a great fan, their looks and their sounds were complementary, and we felt it was rather a coup to get Marc on board. The trouble was that his star was slightly waning while Jimmy's was vividly waxing, so there was an uncertainty about who took precedence, nothing obvious, nothing stated, but there.

We were all staying in a giant wedding cake of a hotel on the shores of Lake Geneva, dazzlingly luxurious to me, full of deferential waiters dressed like dukes and rude pop stars dressed like Fagin's gang. Marc, as soon as he checked in, took off to his room – or was it a suite? – and stayed in it, coming out only to rehearse and for the performance. There he ran up a quite spectacular room-service bill and entertained his entourage, but he did not seem to want to come out and play. Jimmy, growing apart from Larry and Steve, and not really at home in the millionaires' spa atmosphere of the town, did not want to go out to play with them either, so he and I stuck together while Marc Almond drank champagne with his entourage and Larry and Steve had meetings. I quite enjoyed being around my suddenly famous friend, getting a bit of sun in his reflected glory, although Jimmy's nonchalant attitude to the schedule could be a little alarming. On the day of our performance we saw an old-fashioned steamboat about to leave on what we assumed was a pleasure cruise of Lake Geneva. We got on it only to discover it was in fact going to France and would not get back in time. Fortunately they let us off.

So we played that night in the Casino at Montreux, 'I Feel Love' with Jimmy in a blue Paul Smith top and chinos, looking like Tintin, and Marc in a sort of spangly top and jeans, his hair, blond coiffed, slicked back. I watched it on YouTube just now and saw myself in an Oxfam suit and tie looking thin and beaky and playing the saxophone so badly I wondered why it was put up in the mix at all. I suppose there had to be a reason for me to appear in shot.

The next day we flew back to London and got the train from Gatwick to Victoria. There, in a moment of sheer nastiness and in an acknowledgement that times were a'changing, we took the car booked for Steve and Larry rather than wait for our own.

I don't suppose I was worried too much by the distance that was growing ever wider between Jimmy and Larry and Steve. Jimmy and I had already talked a little about doing something together as an aside, an album of standards with piano, so if he were to decide to look for something new to do I hoped he would look no further.

Then, quite dramatically, Jimmy's circumstances changed. He was still living in a council flat in a tower block, not always a comfortable place to live even when he had been anonymous. There was heroin on the estate, and the crime that went with it, a threat of violence in the air, and Jimmy was not someone you could describe as gifted with silky diplomatic skills and the violence often became real. When Bronski Beat signed a deal with Elton John's company Rocket Music, Elton invited them to join him at a concert at Wembley. He sent a car to pick them up and when the buzzer rang they went downstairs and in front of the whole block found a huge black limousine, the door opened by a uniformed chauffeur. I don't know if this was the last straw, but shortly after this Jimmy's flat was raided by thugs who kicked the door down and roughed him up. When they'd gone he called me at Lorna's and he came round and moved in, a move that made it even easier for us to imagine a future working together.

My grandfather's baby grand, secured for me by my mother, stood in my room in Lorna's flat, occupying more space than the bed, and there Jimmy and I worked together on the first song we really wrote together. 'You Are My World' was a hymn to love in C major, with a lot of fiddly piano work, scales and arpeggios, and a section in B flat, which sounded a bit Tony Hatch, and built to a howling chorus back in C major. I listen to it now and feel sorry for anyone confronted by such shrieking affection, but it wasn't bad and the record company told us to go and work it up into something. We went to a studio in Camden Town and there laid our first proper tracks.

There I was, in a studio, like a proper musician, with a pool table and someone who made me coffee, listening to anecdotes about a star so awful the tape op left a shit in his flight case.

8. Communards

My future was in the balance. Would Jimmy leave Bronski Beat behind and start something new with me? I was consumed with anxiety and uncertainty about what would happen next.

Bronski Beat had been enormously successful but Jimmy was conflicted, uncomfortable with the effects of pop stardom, the pressures intense, the evacuation-speed departure from his life-before, wrenching. His night-time rambles, risky enough when he was anonymous, had become much riskier and he was arrested for importuning at one of his favourite spots near Hyde Park Corner. It was really a case of entrapment: handsome plain-clothes policemen were used as bait at that time, and one of them nabbed Jimmy. He was taken to the police station but there did not suffer the humiliation that he expected; instead the policeman fetched his copy of *The Age of Consent* and asked Jimmy if he would mind signing it. He did sign it – a different kind of a humiliation. The press got hold of it and Jimmy brazened it out in court, but he was not unaffected by it.

I think also he found the tension of the rewards and burdens of success quite complicated. He disliked being pointed at in the street, he cared nothing for the luxuries money could buy (apart, oddly, from Le Creuset cast-iron cookware), but it wasn't only good-bye yellow brick road. That sense of vindication mainstream success brought to a minority sensibility was powerful and with it Jimmy's allure intensified to the point when it became almost supernatural. He was no slouch when it came to romance in his pre-famous days but post-fame there was an endless succession of men, some in and out, others sticking around, others so fleeting they barely registered. I remember once Jimmy standing in a street off Oxford Street hailing a black cab. It stopped, but as Jimmy got in the door on the other side opened, and a businessman in a suit got in, mistakenly thinking the cab had stopped for him, I assumed. But, no, he was actually a conquest, whom Jimmy had managed to seduce from the other side of the road, wordlessly, in the time it took for the cab to stop. Around this time Jimmy met Steve Maclean, a dizzyingly handsome man with dark Irish looks and deep blue eyes, Armada Irish, and Steve was a sticker. Caught up on the slipstream of Jimmy's success he sort of moved in to Lorna's flat, too, which created a little pressure between us new men in Jimmy's life, and, although he was romantic and I was professional, there was a tinge of competition about it. More than a tinge sometimes. I came in one day and found a photograph of me cut into tiny pieces strewn on my bed.

Bronski Beat's album *The Age of Consent* was a huge hit and the US, with its infinitely bigger market, beckoned, most insistently when an invitation arrived to support Madonna on a world tour. Jimmy turned it down. I don't know why he arrived at his decision but as you can imagine Larry and Steve were incredulous and then furious, and who would blame them? And in this weird, heightened period Jimmy decided to leave Bronski Beat and form a band with me, something that would be truer to his instincts and conviction; something, also, his actions implied, that would be less successful. I could see how well that went down with the record company. They could see how well that went down with me.

Jimmy eventually announced his departure from Bronski Beat and there was a little flurry of comment about it in the press and an interview with Larry and Steve in which they seemed unenthralled at the news. Just after this came out I ran into Larry in West End Lane and, with fake indignation, had a go at him for saying ungenerous things about Jimmy. We shouted at each other, ridiculously, outside Barclays Bank, and I slunk off feeling ashamed of myself and I suppose a bit guilty.

Jimmy and I needed a manager and found one under our noses,

Lorna, who was by now working as the assistant to the boss of perhaps the last vaudeville agency in London, looking after Danny La Rue and Tessie O'Shea. She agreed, turned her back on Tin Pan Alley, and off we went to London Records, which, for all its heavy corporate structure, was still run as an indie by the managing director, Roger Ames, a laid-back white Jamaican who sounded like Michael Manley but swore more. We were taken to lunch at a Japanese place in Mayfair, where we were served something new to Britain, sushi, already mocked as the food of yuppies, little parcels of cold rice and raw fish which I found singularly unappetising. Far more appetising was the deal London Records offered, a three-album contract with all the trimmings, and for me an advance of £60,000, a dazzling sum that was more than I could possibly imagine. After a nanosecond's worth of what we in the Church call 'prayerful consideration', I agreed, and was asked what I would like as a present from the record company, the golden hello which was the custom when someone signed a major deal. Most pop stars asked for a car or a motorbike. I asked for a washer-drier, a durable device that outlasted my pop career by fifteen years.

London Records also gave us money to make some demos. The songs were arriving regularly, Jimmy and I in the fruitful honeymoon of our collaboration, written in my unheated bedroom at West Hampstead, Jimmy in a jumper, me on the baby grand. Most of the songs on our first album were written thus, just piano and voice. I would come up with a piano figure and Jimmy the words and melody, and we quite quickly wrote about a dozen. Made this way they were quite different from Bronski Beat, which was much more about synthesisers, partly because we were trying to be a bit jazz, partly because we consciously didn't want to sound like Bronski Beat, although Jimmy was always closer to where he'd been than to where we thought we were going. When a larger cheque arrived I was able to buy some kit, a Yamaha DX7 keyboard, the first synthesiser that did professional-sounding things at amateur prices, and a Linn Drum, a box with buttons that produced sampled percussion sounds that you could program. All these went into a four-track recorder, which meant we could produce songs that sounded not entirely distant from a finished product.

Some people, like Larry in Bronski Beat, a boffin, could do amazing things with these spare bedroom resources, but we were not so competent. Everything we did was a bit ragged, and not only technically. I think we lacked the focus of Bronski Beat's sound and songs, their comfortable, unselfconscious groove. I was trying to be clever all the time, and our songs lacked the integrity and honesty that theirs achieved.

The contract signed, song writing under way, it was necessary for London Records' head of press to handle the announcement of the birth of whatever our new band was going to be called. I came up with two names, Gloria Mundi, which sounded too much like a drag queen, and The Crockery Club, which was too close to Culture Club. It is difficult to launch a band without a name and by the time our first gig arrived we still hadn't thought of one. Our first gig was to be in Paris, a city Jimmy loved and a city that loved him, too, in so very many ways. Bronski Beat had sold a lot of records in France and Jimmy, short red-headed Glaswegian – that Tintin thing perhaps – appealed to Gallic sensibilities. Frenchmen appealed to him, too. He had become close friends with Didier Lestrade, a journalist and publisher who ran *Magazine*, a French gay version of *The Face*, with a cover that seemed invariably to show a shaven-headed paratrooper looking ambiguous with his shirt off. Such things were like catnip to Jimmy and he threw himself into Paris's gay whirl, often staying with Didier (or 'DJ' as he called him) in his apartment in rue Blomet in the 15th. Didier had an instinctive understanding of how Jimmy functioned and dysfunctioned and harboured no unrealistic expectations of what friendship involved. Connie was like that, too, and others were to come and they became all but indispensable to him, steering him round obstacles, seeing him through his emotional surges, which were many and intense, and helping him to engage with the world on broader terms than he was used to. It was Didier, I think, who fixed up our first gig, at a club, just me and Jimmy, a keyboard and some backing tracks, meant to be low-key, although word got out, and so by the time we arrived in Paris to make our debut the interest was intense. Our Communist friend Mark Ashton came along, and he took us on a tour of revolutionary Paris, which included the cemetery at Père Lachaise, best known now for enfolding in its earth the remains of Oscar Wilde and Jim Morrison. It also has a wall against which insurrectionists were lined up and shot in the aftermath of the Franco-Prussian War of 1871. These unfortunates were early pioneers of a communitarian ideal, who took advantage of the chaos of war to found the Paris Commune, hence their name, the Communards. We were so moved by their story, or Mark's rather romantic version of it, Jimmy so in love with Paris and me filled with comradely feelings of solidarity and rectitude, we chose their name for our band. It seems preposterous to me now to have chosen something so unpop music and now, whenever I have to tell people the band I was in, I feel something of what I imagine Sting feels, stuck with an unsuitably callow name in grizzled age. But Communards it was and we rolled it out to an inevitably pleased crowd, in a gay club in Paris in 1985.

Just before we went on stage, to mark this meaningful moment, I went to embrace Jimmy, but he ignored it, composing himself, I guess, for his performance rather than for my need for some gesture of affectionate solidarity. But when we came off I was full of a sort of chest-bursting triumph, so powerful and intense I was unable to cope with the crowds of people who wanted to say hello, including a man Jimmy tried to introduce me to but I walked away before he could. It was Giorgio Moroder. I left the venue and walked through the city back to Didier's in the 15th *arrondissement*. It was a beautiful night, it was Paris, the Eiffel Tower twinkled, the Seine sparkled, and I knew that life would be different from now on. I knew that some kind of triumph was mine, but I also felt, quite unexpectedly, alone. Alone, alone, all all alone, alone on the Pont de Grenelle.

London Records liked the demos and fixed a meeting with the producer Mike Thorne, who had made *The Age of Consent*. Mike was both a musician and physicist, adored technology and had a Synclavier, the cutting-edge synthesiser of its day, so advanced it cost more than his apartment, and you practically had to get clearance for NASA to take the back off if it broke down, which it did rather a lot. The Synclavier produced some of the signature sounds of the 1980s – Trevor Horn used one with Frankie Goes to Hollywood, Frank Zappa was one of the first to get one, Michael Jackson, Sting and Chick Corea used them, too – not just creating new noises but putting them together in ever more complex ways. Bronski Beat's single 'Why?' was an exemplar of its virtues, sounding like a synthesiser orchestra of Wagnerian scale sending in the Valkyries to tackle homophobia. It tells you something about the rate of technological innovation that only a decade or so later I visited the Museum of Musical Instruments in Berlin and found there, among the fortepianos and Frederick the Great's flutes, a Synclavier, venerable in a glass case.

Mike was keen, and so were we, and together with the record company we chose 'You Are My World' to be our first single to be recorded in New York. I had never been to New York – I had never been to America – and to record a single there was almost unimaginably exciting and, again, a giant step, so great I felt like one of the ghastly Pevensie children falling out of the back of the wardrobe and into Narnia.

Jimmy, Lorna and I arrived at Newark, which was beige and full of people with Toytown uniforms, who wisecracked, and 'Sir' and 'Mam'ed us, and we were met by a chauffeur with a sign saying 'Cosmonarts' who led us to a ridiculous stretch limo with a TV that didn't work and a cocktail cabinet that was empty. We drove towards the city through a streetscape that I'd forgotten about until I saw the title sequence to *The Sopranos*, went down into the Lincoln Tunnel and emerged into Manhattan, which looked gratifyingly like a film. There were yellow cabs, and the Empire State Building, and metal rims to the sidewalk, and weirdly prolix street signs (Yield To Pedestrian In Crosswalk). And there was Central Park and our hotel, the Mayflower, which was big and ugly and actually quite tatty, and not what I'd expected. I was often surprised by how expensive unlovely hotel rooms were in Manhattan, with badly grouted bathrooms and motel-level lampshades and service so surly I grew to rather enjoy it. New Yorkers all seemed to behave like they were in a film, too, aggressive and rude, yet sometimes bewilderingly courteous.

We were booked into Sigma Sound, sister studio of Sigma Sound Philadelphia where Teddy Pendergrass and the Delfonics and Huff, Gamble and Gilbert had worked in the sixties and seventies. It was above the old Ed Sullivan Theater in Midtown, and theatre it was when the lift doors opened to admit you to the lobby. Foreigner were in the main studio, not recording but *writing* an album, a most profligate way to do it, and one day we arrived to find a woman, dressed head to toe in black, sitting on a sofa with her back to us. She turned when we came in, a bit tetchily, I thought. It was Yoko Ono.

The Synclavier was installed and guide tracks put down and then the piano went on and a sort of draft vocal. 'You Are My World' began to take shape. We put on strings, arranged by Jimmy Biondolillo, and the Manhattan Horns came in and put on a punchy horn section, and then, in a diversion from uptown, we went to a studio on Flatbush Avenue in Brooklyn, a place so feared the only cabs that would take you were ones with a cage surrounding the driver and a little steel hatch for the money. There we recorded backing vocals with a wonderful singer called BJ Nelson and two of her mates, Brooklyn girls, making that hybrid church/street sound that gives so much American popular music its peculiar lyrical energy. It was exciting but also a sobering experience for me, working with New York session musicians who had not only street credibility but had also been to music conservatoires. Jimmy had street smarts to rival anyone's, but only I had Grade V piano to offer as a complementary skill.

It is a difficult moment for a pop neophyte, graduating from a four-track recorder in a bedroom in West Hampstead, to New York session musicians in a forty-eight-track digital recording studio. The session players are usually very pleasant – you are paying their wages after all – but they know what they're doing and you probably don't know what they're doing which is why you invariably find pool tables in studios, to keep the artists occupied while the producer and sound

engineers and session players get on with the job. With singers it is
different, voices being so individual, but for an inexperienced band
member with limited gifts the excitement of working with brilliant
session players is tempered by the growing sense of one's own inade-
quacy, and of having to step back to let them get on with the job at
a time when you're anxious, as a new boy, to assert your credentials.
I thought it wise, after reflection, to step back and play pool. Other
artists choose to assert their rights and in the videos which follow
you can sometimes tell from wordless glances exchanged by session
players which are which.

The track filled up, our sketchy demo transformed, and at the end
of the sessions we had a recording we all really liked. Jimmy gave as
powerful a vocal as he ever had – too powerful to my ears now – and
it had a lot of piano, arpeggios and scale passages which I think now
sounds rather like the theme tune to *All Creatures Great and Small*.
Back then I thought it showed us both off to best advantage; there
were a lot of strings and horns, it sounded different from Bronski
Beat and had the feel of a hit.

The record company seemed to like it and when we got back
to London we had to get into gear with press and promotion and
making a video. It turned out press was rather a trial for me, not
because I felt my precious privacy was invaded, but because I felt it
wasn't invaded enough. Everyone wanted to know about Jimmy; no
one wanted to know about me. Of course they did, but the repeated
slight of being ignored by journalists was sometimes intolerable and
more than once, in my self-regard and naïveté, I walked out of an
interview after half an hour of sitting in silence. One hack crossly
told me to be quiet when I answered a question I had thought was
intended for both of us. I have nursed an especial dislike for him in
my heart these thirty years.

These stroppy walkouts had an undesired effect on Jimmy, who
simply felt abandoned by his only ally. I felt let down by my only ally,
and so, from very early on in our partnership, a resentment began to
build. This increased when I was obliged to do photo-shoots. I had
to do them, it was a contractual obligation, and it felt necessary to

assert my place alongside Jimmy, who was not only the reason why someone wanted to take our picture but was also good at it. Jimmy has a natural sense of style. I have the opposite. I am anything but photogenic, anything but stylish. At one of our first photo sessions, the photographer said he was excited by my 'angles' and took a lot of shots of me in profile, which in the finished article were shown in silhouette and left me looking like Monty Burns from *The Simpsons*. The more I did of these the more I felt like the unpicked kid at school football, stuck on the outside of things, resented by those on the inside.

The indignities of making a video were worse. We asked Connie to direct the video for 'You Are My World', his first experience of directing after having co-directed *Framed Youth*. Videos were expensive to make and a lot rode on them, even the success or failure of a record, so I wondered if London Records were entirely happy to entrust it to an all but untested hand. They seemed fine, however, and I thought no more about it until we turned up for the shoot and discovered that the lighting cameraman was a veteran who worked with Roman Polanski. We rather meekly stepped aside and let him get on with it. The video was standard, Jimmy singing, me playing the piano and looking soupily at the camera in a set made of blow-ups of cartoon characters drawn by our friend Diane Pacey. Her brilliant figures, like nightmare Starlite kids, also appeared on the cover of the seven-inch single.

As the release approached Jimmy and I went to Paris for some interviews. I was staying in a little hotel the French record company recommended overlooking the Place des Abbesses in Montmartre, so cute you could almost lace onions just by looking at it. That night as I fell asleep I heard in my mind's ear an echo of the chorus to 'You Are My World', which I'd been listening to all day. But then I realised it was not in my mind's ear at all but out there. Somebody somewhere was playing it.

9. Hellooo Leicester

The Communards 2

It was Jimmy's idea to do a cover version of a great disco classic, and he suggested 'Don't Leave Me This Way', written by Kenneth Gamble, Leon Huff, and Cary Gilbert ten years earlier for Harold Melvin & the Blue Notes, and later covered by Thelma Houston. He had grown to love it on the dance floor of Bennett's in Glasgow, the sort of song that can survive just about anything you do to it (and it has been covered by a lot of artists over the years). This was the song we thought the singer – and my friend from Stratford days – Sarah Jane Morris might duet on, the contrast between her female bass and Jimmy's male treble an irresistible combination.

Back in New York to record the rest of our album, a guide track went down, a guide vocal went on top of it and it was obvious that we were on to something. We built up layer after layer of sound around them, string and horns, and then all kinds of disco magic generated by the Synclavier's mysterious circuitry. Round these Sarah Jane and Jimmy weaved almost a vocal dogfight, the one chasing the other, and coming together for an explosive chorus, which arrived after a rising aaah, altogether-now in a shameless bar of showbiz. BJ Nelson and her pals put on backing vocals and by the time we'd finished I felt we'd produced not so much a record but more a weapon for storming the charts.

We also put down some quieter tracks, a bluesy piano and vocal denunciation of Conservative domestic UK policy, called 'Bread-line Britain' – perhaps *not* a weapon for storming the charts – and another I liked, piano and vocal again, called 'Reprise', which, in a dazzling *coup de théâtre* that nobody noticed, restated the piano figure from 'You Are My World' but in mournful C minor instead of joyous C major. For this we invited a session cello player to come in to put on a track. Interestingly, he was expecting a score but we were expecting him to improvise as a sax player would. He was put out by this, the permeable membrane between art and popular music not quite so permeable, and complained, but in the end agreed.

After a thrilling summer of New York – clubbing, eating, recording, loving – back home I made a fool of myself directing strangers to a building 'two blocks' away down West End Lane, and ordering OJs in restaurants until Manhattan faded and London came back into focus and we went to meet an Irish tour promoter, who had come up with Van Morrison and U2. Paul Allen, funny and dry, began to put together a tour schedule, and Jimmy and I had to work out how to turn ourselves into a touring band. After recording 'You Are My World' we had decided we'd have a more acoustic component than Bronski Beat, so we looked for drums and bass, a sax player and a string quartet, and we looked to recruit women players as a statement of our sexual politics. I phoned up June Miles-Kingston, the drummer with whom I'd played in Pauline Black's band, and she was free and willing. We found also an all-female string quartet, alumnae of the Guildhall – as near as British conservatoires got to the Juilliard in those days as a place where popular and art music were not considered active foes. Annie Stephenson, on fiddle, came from a working-class background and brought a wildness to her playing. Joss Pook on viola was a composer as well as a player, well known now for composing the score for Kubrick's last movie *Eyes Wide Shut*. Audrey Riley on cello was more grown up than the rest of us, *de facto* quartet leader and slightly bossy, although this occasionally crumbled. Sally Herbert on fiddle was the youngest, Secretary Sal we called her, for she loved buying clothes at Molton Brown in Hampstead High Street. Jimmy came across a bass player, Dave Renwick, not a woman, but a gay Geordie so he qualified, and finally we were introduced to a brilliant sax player, Jo Pretzel, a working-class woman from Salford and a child prodigy who'd been to Chetham's School of Music in Manchester. Jo had a wunderkind intensity, although she was grown up and married to a drummer, and was one of the most exciting and sometimes demanding players I have ever worked with.

It was my job to get a set list together and to be musical director. I have folders of music manuscript paper, preserved for posterity, with all my string arrangements, dull and pedestrian, laboriously written out in ink.

Fortunately the combination of new recruits clicked, both musically and personally, and we set to record more songs. We booked into a rehearsal studio in Islington, a place where lots of bands at the spit and polish end of things rehearsed, but these rehearsals were often a time of intense frustration and stress in my relationship with Jimmy. Jimmy hated rehearsing, he couldn't read music and was an entirely instinctive and self-taught singer, so, while I was busy with technicalities, he was bored and fractious. I think I may have made this worse by enjoying my occasional usefulness too much. My usefulness and his impatience resulted in us sometimes lapsing into a parent–child relationship – this often happens with performers and I am quite capable of being the child as well as the parent in different circumstances – but in these circumstances, while I was trying to be a grown-up and he was acting out, I was frequently driven mad. I would come close to losing my temper until one day I did lose it, in front of everyone, shouting and walking out of the studio into a reception area where everyone fell silent and looked at their feet as I swept by. I went once round the block and without breaking step walked back into the studio to a patter of relieved applause and work continued.

Our first tour, in the spring of 1986, was neither fish nor fowl. Jimmy and I, after the success of Bronski Beat, were expecting that success to be replicated if not to grow. But not enough people knew that the Communards was Bronski Beat v2, a situation not helped by the two remaining members of Bronski Beat recruiting a new singer and releasing a single. Of course they did, and good luck to them, but it perpetuated the myth of Jimmy's continuing Bronski-ness and we found that our ticket sales were not all they could be. We started off in France where 'You Are My World' had done well and we got crowds at all the venues we played, I think. That leg of the tour culminated with a gig at one of the most famous venues of all, l'Olympia in Paris, the music hall in the Boulevard des Capu-cines where Edith Piaf and Jacques Brel and the Beatles and Frank Sinatra and Judy Garland and the Doors had played, and it was a sell-out, so we felt doubly exalted. But when we started the UK leg we discovered that we were booked into venues sometimes a lot smaller in reputation than l'Olympia but a lot bigger than our ticket sales necessitated. Worst was somewhere in the Midlands, where we booked into a two thousand-seater venue and sold, I think, twenty tickets, so we performed a gig to less than a front row's worth of fans. Jimmy had been drinking – brandy, I think – never a reassuring scenario, and after the gig he went into a spectacular meltdown. I had to fetch him out of the gents where he was helplessly careering from stall to stall and then he exploded with hysterical weeping and broke rather a lot of glass. It had not occurred to me that it would be so difficult for him, having effortlessly cruised to the top of the charts and the world's esteem, to suddenly be confronted by row after row of unsold seats. These issues of success and failure, of being noticed or unnoticed, pressed hard on Jimmy's most vulnerable areas and especially in drink his reactions were very often nuclear. I was all politesse, middle-class Middle Englander, and although I under-stood something about matters of life and death through growing up gay, I had never really fought for anything. When we were just friends I was there for Jimmy when the tide of rage and fight re-ceded, but working with him I became sometimes the reason for the rage and fight and our relationship altered. This was prefigured by those episodes on that first tour when my sympathy for his distress was tempered by my sense of responsibility for the show that must go on, which turned me from his peer to being his parent.

Fortunately we sold more tickets as the tour went on and Jimmy recovered his poise. It was a joy working with the band and crew and friendships began to flourish. We tried always to treat band members and crew equally as far as possible, so we travelled together and stayed together, upgrading them or downgrading ourselves when necessary, and we paid everyone the same. At least we did at first, when we were starting out. We also resolved to make ourselves available to fans, so after one particular gig we set up a table in a room backstage and invited fans to come in and we signed albums and t-shirts. However, we did this precisely once, discovering that in spite of our best intentions there were limits to what we could offer and immediately after a gig we had reached those limits.

This tension between wanting to be brilliant and wanting to be righteous besets pop stars with wonderful comedy – think of those private planes flying celebrities to climate-change conferences to express their commitment to a low-carbon world – and we too lapsed into the hypocrisy which is, as La Rochefoucauld noticed, the homage vice pays to virtue. On that tour we went to Leicester, where Toby Kettle, whom I had abandoned with hepatitis in King's Cross a year or two earlier, now lived with his partner, Steve, and played in a band of wonderfully radical credentials. Jimmy and I asked him if he would like to support us at our gig at Leicester Poly on that 1986 tour and he agreed but then went into paroxysms of gratefulness and resentment disguised by an interrogation concerning our ideological rectitude, lest he be besmirched by a capitulation to commercialism and collusion with the military industrial complex and patriarchy. We must have sorted it as later he phoned and thanked us in a rather sheepish way.

Touring Britain meant touring its gay clubs, too, for wherever we went Jimmy was feted by the gay community which we met, en masse, in venues like the Nightingale in Birmingham or Rockshots in Newcastle, friendly, with go-go dancers in cages, one of whom I discovered years later was the Reverend Giles Fraser, Canon of St Paul's and *Guardian* columnist in later incarnations. Some gay clubs could still seem thrillingly countercultural – there was one memorable place down by the docks in a northern city, where you had to knock on a door and get the once-over by a doorman who admitted you to a room that looked like a youth club, lit unappetisingly with fluorescent lights and with a pool table that was colonised by frightening lesbians who'd punch you if you knocked their pint. We stayed in hotels which every band which ever toured Britain will remember with a mixture of delight and horror, including the Britannia in Manchester, a faded tart of a place in gold and royal blue, and, most spectacular of all, its sister hotel the Adelphi in Liverpool, an even more faded and even more tarty fallen palace, where the grander passengers in the golden age of liners had stayed before embarking, and where guests of ever dwindling prestige have stayed ever since. It is the only hotel I have stayed in where I woke up in the middle of the night to find an uninvited stranger looking down at me in bed.

That tour concluded in London at the Royal Festival Hall, a venue I had first visited as a boy, and I invited my family and friends to watch my triumph. When we came on stage, instead of playing the opening to our first song I played the opening to Grieg's A minor piano concerto, as near as I have ever got to fulfilling my childhood wish to be the world's greatest classical pianist.

10. Red Wedge

After the tour, and with the album made, I began to get used to my new good fortune. I was in a band that was highly thought of if not, as yet, widely thought of. I could present a card at any cash machine anywhere and at my command it would bring forth adequate funds. I had been sprinkled with a little stardust. It is easy to get used to improved new circumstances and to believe, tentatively at first but with growing conviction, that, in the words of the slogan, you're worth it. Preposterous behaviour followed, more often than not indulged, but not always; on my regular visits to London Records' offices in Mayfair I got more and more irritated by the unwillingness of the man who sat on the reception desk to recognise me. I would arrive feeling like the belle of the ball, but he would make me wait like a gatecrasher, until once, with ridiculous hauteur, I swept past. There was little reason why he should have known that I was a signed artist, and less for me to behave so grandly, but I felt treated with less than the respect I felt was now my due. This mismatch of expectation and actuality happens quite a lot, because pop stars rise in esteem unevenly. Your fans may think you're marvellous but to others you are merely a young, scruffy stranger suddenly treading the realms of glory, and easily mistaken for an interloper.

Also, around this time you discover, if you pay attention, that your good fortune may not be as fascinating for your peers as it is for you. Before long the discrepancy between the dynamic lift of your own situation and the inertia of theirs tinges your relationship, sometimes even sours it, as you pull away and apart. I heard of two friends, college buddies and computer entrepreneurs, who made

Me, with 'clicker's hands'.

My paternal grandparents, Kathleen and Keith Coles.

Me on the threshold of literature.

My parents, Nigel and Liz, on their wedding day.

Me on my first proper bike.

Angelically, with my brothers, Will and Andy.

My favourite picture of my brothers and me.

Consenting Adults
in Public.

With my maternal
grandfather,
Leonard Davey.

At Wellingborough School. My best friend, Matthew Gammage, is in civvies.

My maternal grandparents, Leonard and Joan Davey.

My father, Second Lieutenant in the 5th Royal Tank Regiment.

Jimmy Somerville at the Gay Youth Video Project.

enormous fortunes and level-pegged for a while until the fortunes of one fell a little behind the fortunes of the other. This manifested itself when one arrived at a mutual friend's wedding in a Gulfstream V, the other in a Gulfstream IV, and they knew that at that moment their friendship was over. 'I had nothing in common with him any more,' said the owner of the V of the owner with the IV.

Private jets were a long way off, but I got a London Transport Gold Card which enabled me to travel with lordly ease on as many buses and tubes as I liked, while friends had to dodge through the barriers or look down the back of a sofa for the fare. This was the era of the Gold Card, gilded tokens of specialness for the rising new rich, symbolic of an era that was about to arrive, that of the yuppie, the personification, in double-breasted and shoulder-padded array, of the Thatcherite revolution.

With bold disregard for this brave new world, Jimmy and I committed ourselves to its overthrow. We got involved with Red Wedge, a group run by Annajoy David, a young Labour activist and former head of Youth CND, who together with Billy Bragg and Paul Weller rallied leftish pop musicians to activism, resolving to switch young people on to politics through the medium of popular music. Our logo, designed by Neville Brody – the last cool person ever to be called Neville – was derived from the Russian constructivist artist El Lissitzky's propaganda poster from the civil war of 1919, 'Beat the Whites with the Red Wedge', which showed this wedge, representing the thrusting Bolsheviks, forcing itself irresistibly into a pathetic yielding circle, the reactionary Whites. It was not only the graphics and lexicon of the Soviet era, or the bits that were palatable that were then back in vogue; we also borrowed the idea behind that image to argue that popular music and culture could work as a means of connecting young people, enervated after punk and palliated by Wham!, to the political machine and thereby to secure a Labour victory in the 1987 general election.

By now even the most romantic socialist had realised that Margaret Thatcher's administration was not just the result of another swing of the pendulum from Labour to Conservative, but an agent – or an outcome – of profound change. She and her advisers sought to restructure the economy, and the society which she was said not to believe in, according to an American rather than a British or European model. I always thought it a great irony that Margaret Thatcher and her supporters waved the Union Jack relentlessly, adopted the style and tastes of the landed gentry, and churned out the most fatigued and fatiguing rhetoric of Evensong and spinsters while at the same time systematically dismantling that Britain, turning it over to the free-market buccaneers, whose slightly too new-looking suits and imperfectly smothered diphthongs told of their origins and their aspirations, which they trumpeted but seemed paradoxically embarrassed by, too.

Well, that's what I thought. They thought they were not only going to change Britain, but *save* Britain, from the tyranny of the unions, economic stagnation, the decline of national prestige and Ken Livingstone. The left, stuck in a different paradigm, looked on helplessly as deregulation of the markets and especially the City brought opportunities to ambitious young men and women who had never had them before, and council house sales turned tenants into homeowners, Labour into Conservative. For the left, losing Middle Britons, it made sense to try to affirm the relationship with young Britons, partly because it was believed that they would more likely vote Labour than Conservative, partly because as they reached majority they got a vote, and although they may not have been too bothered about politics they were bothered about popular culture. Politicians and pop stars looked to each other, like teens at the youth club dance, and a courtship began.

Billy and Paul were really our mind and conscience. Billy was more a Party animal than Paul, a Labour stalwart, and it was not difficult to imagine him speaking to Conference, or even in a suit and tie sitting on the green leather benches of the House of Commons. Paul, by far the coolest person I had ever met, former frontman of the Jam, now of the Style Council, was more artist than politician, a star burning with a hard, gem-like flame, and with the star's odd gift of seeming to be intimate and detached at the same time. Both had been involved, as we had, in the miners' strike, but with different emphases, Billy as an activist, Paul as a fellow traveller. Paul, unlike the rest of us doctrinaire creatures, was revolted when striking miners accidentally, though only just accidentally, killed a working miner. I am ashamed to say that at the time I thought that poor man a casualty of a righteous conflict, but Paul came out and condemned it unequivocally. He also surprised me by saying that he didn't really mind who young people voted for as long as they voted. It was the first time I recall hearing someone credible say something non-partisan.

At first, the Party was in two minds about Red Wedge, but gradually grew curious to see if there was something here worth wooing. We held meetings at Walworth Road, the Labour Party's HQ, which had the feel of a branch library in a left-wing borough, and drew in people other than pop stars who had experience in education, housing, unemployment and knew how the party system worked. Our job, as the performers, was to perform and in January 1987 we put together a sort of Lefty Variety bill for the Red Wedge Tour. This was announced at a do at the House of Commons, hosted by Neil Kinnock. The artists involved had all come alongside each other as a result of playing benefits for the miners and for the Nicaragua Solidarity Campaign and a range of single issues which came into alignment as we came into alignment. It was difficult to imagine the Tories then being able to put together an alternative bill. I think there was only Gary Numan and Kenny Everett who anyone could imagine advocating the Conservatives to our demographic. So perhaps for novelty, if nothing else, Red Wedge got a bit of media attention, and Jimmy and I were phoned up by *Newsnight* one day who asked if they could come and interview us and film us doing a song. A film crew arrived at our cold little flat in West Hampstead, plugged into our already overloaded sockets and we spoke earnestly to Donald McCormick about the common purpose we as gay men felt with striking miners and the long-term unemployed. To conclude we performed 'Breadline Britain' with such aching sincerity that Donald McCormick adopted a rather solemn tone introducing it and I had to resist an impulse to laugh. I watched it with Paul Weller and Billy Bragg when it went out, both of whom seemed to pick up my unease. 'What's wrong?' Paul asked. 'I can't believe I went on television in that jumper,' I replied.

I really enjoyed the Red Wedge Tour. I think we all did. Playing our collective version of 'Moving On Up' – with the Style Council, Billy, Madness, Elvis Costello and Spandau Ballet and others – was one of the happiest five minutes I have ever spent on stage. Everyone got on, unusually for pop stars, and there was a spirit of common purpose not only between us on stage but also with the audiences, which were large and enthusiastic. At the gigs we got local activists to arrange for MPs and councillors to turn out and meet the audience, encounters that were sometimes encouraging but sometimes left you feeling that if this was the best the Labour Party could do for young voters then it hardly deserved to have any.

One of most memorable was with Derek Hatton, then leader of Liverpool City Council, who was associated with Militant Tendency. They were 'entryists', too, like us, only political power rather than cultural influence was their goal. It is not an uncommon phenomenon, observable from Weimar Germany to the Synods of the Church of England, that a small, highly motivated and disciplined group can wrest the machinery of government away from the muddled middle which can't be bothered to make a fuss. Derek Hatton had led such a group in Liverpool, which turned out to be better at securing power than administering power, and made such a mess of things they were obliged to send out redundancy notices in taxis to employees they could no longer afford to pay. He didn't lose too much sleep, I suspect, over the collateral damage that occurred on his watch, and when we joined him on the platform for a televised debate he gave me a sly conspiratorial wink. At that moment a part of me stopped believing in uncritical solidarity with the comrades.

Much more rewarding was the feel-good factor the Red Wedge Tour generated. If the show sometimes lacked polish and coherence – how very like the left – it made up for it in *esprit de corps*. It felt like we were opening up something new and that brought an energy that was infectious. A little while ago I was on a train reading *The New Yorker*, simple country parson that I am, and one of the catering managers said hello. He had been to the Red Wedge gig in Newcastle as a young teenager and it had not only awoken him to the political dynamics of the time, but also encouraged him to come out as gay. Not bad for a night out in the Toon in the winter of 1986.

We played in Bradford, at St George's Hall, and I left a pair of my favourite brown DM shoes under the bed at the Novotel; we played at the De Montfort Hall in Leicester, where my dad was mistaken for Denis Healey; we played at St David's Hall in Newport, where we met up with a crowd of former miners from Dulais who we'd supported in the strike.

There was a tension, it must be said, between what we professed and how we lived. When we played Edinburgh we stayed outside the city in an old castle that had been turned into a hotel and where we were the only guests. We were followed home from the gig by some fans who were dismayed to be barred, like marauders, at its gates. The tension is between accessibility and inaccessibility. Politicians, like parsons, are supposed to be accessible, although there are limits to the kind and duration of access. Pop stars, like potentates, are inaccessible, protected by security from the undesired attention of fans. Those left standing in the gravelled drive outside were disappointed because the message from the stage was 'join with us'. The message from the closed door at the hotel was 'don't join with us', although, safely inside, we were unaware of their disappointment. There we met in the library for drinks, an elegant room done out in Scots baronial, lined with bookcases, floor to ceiling, crammed with books. Steve White, the Style Council's eighteen-year-old drummer, walked in and said, 'What a lot of videos!'

That tension played itself out a bit on stage, too. I remember sneering under my breath a bit at Gary Kemp of Spandau Ballet, now a friend, who kindly turned up one night at a gig to accompany himself on an acoustic guitar. Spandau Ballet we thought of as a bit sold-out, in the wearying and ungenerous rectitude that so characterised the left on a bad day. That Gary was actually a working-class

Londoner whose family worked in the print trade and were active members of the unions I had overlooked; but that was the unreconstructed Trotskyist in me, so unattractively mean about those who lacked the ideological purity I claimed for myself. Also, to think that our kind of pop music could somehow preserve its political rectitude untainted by the vigorous capitalism that gave it life at all seems curiously unself-critical, but these were only vague concerns then, on the edge of consciousness. And for all that, I think Red Wedge was one of the best things I've done. It didn't really go anywhere – projects were initiated and we published a magazine, but the energy fizzled out after the '87 election, when Margaret Thatcher returned to power with a twelve-point lead over Labour – and in 1990 it was formally wound up. We hadn't halted the relentless march of neo-conservatism – I doubt if we even slowed it down for a second – and the British gig-going public was not quite as vanguardist as we hoped. We had underestimated the depth and scale of the change that Thatcherism represented in British life. It was a failure, I suppose, but all human enterprises are failures. We just arrived at that truth a little earlier than others.

What it did achieve was to help people like the man I met on the train twenty-five years later to think differently about his life and his horizons. It also helped young people in tough places to work together on projects that had some purpose and relevance. It was a rich experience of community and activism for those of us involved. Failure, modest achievements, community, solidarity: I realise now it was an excellent preparation for ordained ministry in the Church of England. That, however, lay distantly ahead.

11. Number One

We dedicated our second single, 'Disenchanted', to Jean Genet, the wildly countercultural French writer who had helpfully died some weeks before the release. God knows what he would have made of it. We adored him, he was a hero for our tribe – gay, criminal, French – and his plays and writings were referenced, if not so often read, by our circle with an almost wearying predictability. We did all know his film *Un Chant d'Amour*, thrillingly transgressive, boundlessly sexy, a black and white underground classic in which handsome prisoners in vests blow smoke through a straw, one to the other, through a glory-hole in their cell wall. Then it was the most beautiful and exciting film I had ever seen; now it looks like a commercial for Gaultier aftershave, which says little about Genet but a lot for how Gaultier turned that aesthetic to his profit in the nineties. I first saw it at a Scala all-nighter, a marathon twelve-hour film programme shown at the independent cinema in King's Cross. These all-nighters were among the most splendid entertainments of that time, offering films in these pre-video days you were unlikely to see anywhere else.

Speed, amphetamine sulphate, was our drug of choice then, which we took partly as a heightener of sensation but mostly as a way of keeping awake, sometimes for days. Speed had different effects on different people. It made me super-alert and super-garrulous, neither of which I needed much help with, and I would often talk myself literally hoarse after a weekend's indulgence. It was a great night-club drug, too, the poor man's cocaine, keeping you up with the disco beat, wide-eyed and constantly chewing, on the dance floor. It also made your concentration on, and interest in, nearly anything exceptionally intense, artificially intense, and the wondrous insights into the aesthetics of French cinema of the 1950s, or the pages of exquisite arabesques doodled in biro, faded as the drug wore off and the week began. The downsides of speed were the physical incapacity it wreaked on the body while it gripped you – pharmacist's droop if you like – and the mental incapacity it wreaked when it released that grip. A speed downer could last a week and leave you feeling the world had turned from Genet to Pinter. For me it was a price worth paying because it kept others up beyond their bedtimes, and in those after-hours provided opportunities for a kind of intimate intensity that was the best I could manage.

This changed as my stock rose. It was hardly a surprise that my allure, so faintly glowing I had not noticed it at all, burned more brightly since I'd started appearing in pop bands, and they sought me that one time would not trouble me at all. But I didn't really know what to do with them, even if I noticed their interest, and long, long evenings of smothering the possibility of erotic or ro-mantic adventures with talk were normal. Just occasionally, someone would persevere and get through.

Toby had met someone called Robert in a nightclub and brought him home to Wee Nooke. Robert lived in Amsterdam, on a house-boat, but came to London every few weeks to sell the greetings cards he designed and printed. We had become friends, and I had fallen a bit for him. He was in his thirties, stocky and handsome, and wore t-shirts and 501s and had a buzz cut, and a tattoo. He came from Wales, where he'd grown up in a working-class family in an indus-trial town, not the kind of place in the seventies with much to offer a young gay man. Desperate to escape, Robert joined the Royal Navy and that was his ticket out of South Wales and into slightly richer opportunities for sex. Nothing was more erotic to him, he once told me, than the blue static flash emitted by the swiftly removed nylon y-fronts of a fellow tar.

Robert came to stay with us whenever he was in London and as our friendship grew he invited me to stay with him in Amster-dam. There he lived in a loose but devoted partnership with Tony, a huge hotel doorman whose mixed heritage I only divined when we went to a Chinese restaurant and he ordered in Cantonese. He and Robert had met in London ten years earlier, when Robert had left the navy, and they lived in Kensington in a squat shared with some drag queens, one of whom, while dressed as Norma Desmond, stole a vacuum cleaner from Barkers in Kensington High Street, grabbing it by its nozzle and dragging it behind him out of the store, running as fast as his size eleven sling-backs allowed.

Eventually Robert and Tony relocated to Amsterdam, a city welcoming to gay people, where Tony found a seventy-foot Rhine coal barge, twelve foot in the beam, which he rented from the drag theatre company Bloolips. It was called the *Emily Pankhurst*, was basic in amenities, but was permanently moored on the Prinsengracht, a canal of tall, narrow, exuberantly gabled merchants' houses near the centre. Arriving in the city very early, I stopped to have a *koffie verkeerd met een broodje kaas met tomaat* in a pretty little coffee shop, with gingham tablecloths and orange hydrangeas in the window, and fell headlong in love with the city, the boat, the cat, with Robert, but not Tony.

This was, in its own way, a Dutch golden age and Amsterdam, most tolerant of cities, was rich in opportunities for sex and dancing and drug taking. There were discos and dungeons and rubber parties and drag parties, there was an international community of young gay men and fellow travellers, as cosmopolitan as anywhere, and with the means and the leisure to do nothing but have fun. No one seemed to have a job, and either did so well on welfare they didn't have to or made a living, like Robert, on one or two days' work a week. At night we dined out, went out, danced till dawn; by day we went visiting: to exhibitions or concerts or the flea market at Beverwijk, where a Canadian friend of Robert's had bought a Klee for twenty guilders and where you would still see farmers wearing wooden clogs. My favourite place was the Albert Cuyp Markt, not far from us, named after a painter I have since grown to love, which was then a working-class street market with a bathhouse where we went for showers. I remember one winter afternoon leaving there with Robert, smelling of soap amid the cabbagy smell of the just-packed-up market, as low-angled sunlight struck the wet street and cold wind blew in from the sea.

I was deeply smitten with Robert. He had a gift for friendship so there were always people at the boat, but Tony worked nights, so Robert and I ended up on our own and one night, to my surprise, we ended up in bed together. I think it was the first time I had ever actually attempted to have sex with someone I really cared about. The attempt was hopeless, because Rob was quite far into the S&M spectrum of sexual adventure and I was more at the Miss Jean Brodie end, so it rather misfired. But it was tender and solicitous, too, and the next day we had another go on someone else's vacant boat, but for some reason I said in the middle of it 'What are you after?' and that was the end of that.

'Disenchanted' charted modestly at number twenty-nine. For me that was a mercy because the video, for which we had concocted a narrative, featured me in acting roles, behind the counter in a café, busking in the street, and, most lamentably, as a spiv in a pork pie hat down the market selling a dodgy beat box to a young man. But it should have done better because Jimmy's vocal, in his lucky key of F minor, was one of the best he ever recorded. There's a live version from Paris in 1987 and Jimmy's singing still makes my hair stand on end. We went back to Paris to promote it and yet again I sat through another round of media interviews, silent and ignored and increasingly resentful. During a live interview on *Top Cinquante* – the French equivalent of *Top of the Pops* – I sat for very nearly an hour in resentful silence while question after question translated into English went to Jimmy, his answers translated back into French. Eventually, after about fifty-eight minutes the presenter, with evident surprise, said he had a question for me. I smiled gratefully, but the smile faded when I heard the voice of Catherine from the record company on a phone line ask me about my 'classical training'.

Our first album was due for release and we had to decide which track had the likeliest chance of becoming a hit single to propel the album up the charts. 'Don't Leave Me This Way' was the stand-out track, but it was a cover version and I didn't want our first big hit to be by someone else. However, after two modest successes the record company asserted itself and it was decided that 'Don't Leave Me This Way' was the one. It was also decided that we needed to make a grand video to go with the record, and a budget of £70,000 was agreed, which was more than the cost of recording the entire album. It was shot in London's still undeveloped docklands, and was set in a futuristic dystopia in which we were playing a clandestine gig to an excitable audience. Jimmy and Sarah Jane duetted, a female wind section stabbed away on horns, June, glorious with hair extensions, looked fantastic on drums and I looked like I'd been sub-let by Chas and Dave for the afternoon. We cut away to a handsome young blond man, coerced by a sinister man in moustache and dark glasses, actually our set designer, Ray Oxley, to snitch on this underground knees-up, the state evidently threatened by this reworking of a disco classic. Torn between conscience and fear, the young blond man chose to betray us to the authorities and in a police raid everyone scattered. It had a sort of *Mad Max* meets *The Bill* feel to it and was shot extravagantly on 35mm film with shafts of light picking out Jimmy and Sarah Jane doing their thing. The record was scheduled for release and we got a slot on *Wogan*, the early evening BBC1 chat show, on the eve of our departure for a tour of Italy.

Italy was exhausting, one of the hardest tours we ever did, partly because of the nature of working in Italy and partly because by the end of it we were a different band from the one we'd been at the beginning. Everything was late, including the gigs as they generally didn't start till ten, so playing past midnight and getting to bed at two was normal. Everything was chaos – I remember once having to come off stage halfway through a set and waiting an hour to go back on again because *Dallas* was on and everyone switching on their television diverted power from our PA. Everything was sociable; we knew some people who were involved in the Italian Communist Party, then under the charming and congenial leadership of Enrico Berlinguer, who broke with the Soviet Union after the invasion of Afghanistan in 1980 and created a version known as Eurocommunism, which we all got excited about. They booked us to play gigs at the summer festivals in Communist-controlled cities, like Cremona, where Stradivarius made fiddles and we made whoopee on those lovely summer nights. There were bands, speeches, fireworks and food, an expression of a kind of champagne socialism, or Prosecco socialism, that was life-affirming and glorious.

What really complicated things on that tour was the sudden success of the record. 'Don't Leave Me This Way' shot into the UK charts and not long after we arrived in Italy we had risen to number two, a position confirmed when the chart itself arrived at the end of the week. The video went to work on MTV and airplay increased, excitement gathered around the record, which we were oddly disconnected from, being on tour in another country where it had only just come out. On the day the chart was announced Colin Bell, responsible for our marketing, called Jimmy in his hotel room and told him the news. Jimmy came down, got on the tour bus and said: 'We're number one.' Everyone whooped while I tried not to dwell on a petty surge of irritation that Colin had called Jimmy and not me. We were due that night to do a live TV show from the Arena di Verona, a Roman amphitheatre with tiers of stone benches open to the sky. Where once Christians had been thrown to beasts, operas were now produced, but for one night only it was the venue for a line-up of international pop acts, including from the UK Frankie Goes to Hollywood, by now big stars, and the new hot band Sigue Sigue Sputnik, who had been signed for an unlikely multi-million-pound deal and had a big hit with a Giorgio Moroder-produced single 'Love Missile F1-11'.

As we approached our hotel the bus slowed to walking pace as we drove towards a big crowd ahead. Astonishingly, it was for us, a crowd of *paninari*, trendy boys and girls on scooters, screaming for Jimmy. 'Don't Leave Me This Way' had risen in the charts all over Europe, and we had gone, in a day, from a band followed by a handful of fans to a band surrounded by a crowd of screaming kids. We only just got off the bus and into the hotel safely. There in the bar we saw Frankie and said hello to Holly and Paul, the frontmen, while Jo, our saxophonist, got into a fight with their drummer and bass player and they all had to be separated. When it was time to leave for the venue, Steve our tour manager said it was too dangerous to leave by the front so we would be picked up at the trade entrance. We made our way through the kitchen, past staring chefs and pot washers, and out into a courtyard. Its gates opened and a sort of armoured car driven by *carabinieri* backed in, the back doors opening. We got in and, in a strategy which did little to conceal our exit, two motorbike outriders flicked on their blue lights and sirens and we roared off, followed immediately by crowds of kids on their scooters. The drama of this was mitigated by the proximity of the venue – about a hundred and fifty yards away – but it peaked again when the *carabinieri* dropped us off at the wrong door and left us just as the swarm of Vespas arrived. We were totally exposed and I saw, for the first time, someone literally have the coat torn from his back. Jimmy, the object of a fascination so intense it was more frightening than exhilarating. We fought our way through to the right door and security guards got us inside, but it was so disconcerting that when we went on stage we were still in a state of shock, and I was joined at the piano by Annie Stephenson, fiddle player, who plonked her handbag down on top of the Steinway, lit a fag and joined me in a mimed duet to the record that was about to become number one in Italy, too.

Next day a present arrived from Elton John, a case of Dom Pérignon. Another case arrived from London Records, and another from our US label. By the end of that week we were pissing champagne. That's what it is like when you are number one.

12. *Les Grandes Douceurs*

I have a photograph of the whole band at Rome airport looking exhausted at the end of the Italian tour. I like it because what we became after that tour was very different from what we had been before. 'Don't Leave Me This Way' stayed at number one for four weeks, so we became regulars on *Top of the Pops*, and with each appearance our fame grew. I started getting recognised in the street, turning heads and getting shouted at by blokes in passing cars, which I absolutely adored. People came out of the long grass of my life to congratulate me, shopkeepers in West End Lane patted me on the back and I achieved the great distinction of making the cover of the *Kettering Evening Telegraph*. I had lost my anonymity, a mixed blessing I was to discover, but I was too much in thrall to my new celebrity to give that more than a passing thought.

You get used to people liking you in this way very quickly – it takes about three days – but it is very dangerous because you so easily forget that this is not a state of nature but a function of what you do. As you get used to the warmth – and then deference – you find yourself aping the habits of a minor royal, tensing your face into a permanent gracious smile, or, rather, pre-smile, as you try to work out whether the person is actually looking at you expectantly. If so, full smile. If not, walk on by as if amused by a memory or passing thought. This, too, is good practice for ordained ministry, but it can go wrong. One evening, newly famous, I was waiting for a tube at Baker Street underground. A young man, handsome and cool-looking, was sitting on a bench listening to music on headphones. He caught sight of me and I pre-smiled until I was sure he recognised who I was. He took off his headphones. 'Your music pollutes my ears,' he said and put his headphones back on.

Most people, however, are pleased to see you, and some of them are so particularly pleased they want to make you their very special friend. I was ill-prepared for this sudden enrichment of my allure and kept missing opportunities for sexual adventure when they started coming more frequently. Some special friends, however, were absolutely resolute. In Paris I met a friend of Didier Lestrade's, also called Didier, a skinhead and former dock worker from what we call Dunkirk, who dodged military service by being declared P5, too gay to be sacrificed for *la Gloire de la Patrie*, and ran away to Paris where he arrived on the gay scene and almost immediately became a model for Jean Paul Gaultier. Jimmy and his Didier introduced me to him and I remember faking a swoon when he left the room. Next thing I knew we were in a nightclub and the next thing I knew we were back in my suite (we had gone up in the world by now) in the Hotel St James and Albany in the rue de Rivoli. This was the hotel made famous by Graham Greene in *Travels With My Aunt*, two hotels united by a common courtyard, and rather old-fashioned and English, but there was nothing old-fashioned or English about the night Didier gave me under its exposed beams, and when I came down to breakfast the next morning everything was in a romantic haze. In this condition I met Didier Lestrade and told him what had occurred. 'Careful,' he said. 'He's a real fan.'

The next night I went back to Didier's, two *chambres de bonne* on the top floor of a building on rue La Fontaine. Like the Hotel St James and Albany his accommodation was divided; one room on one side of the corridor had a loo and a shower, and another, opposite, his bedsit and kitchen. There was a window which looked out into a street of Haussmann-grey through one of the little wrought-iron mini-balconies big enough only for the birds. Curtains fluttered at the window. Coffee boiled on a stove. A Minitel winked in the corner. It was a fantasy come true for me, a handsome skinhead Gaultier model in a flat under the eaves of a Parisian apartment building with a big wooden door on to the street and a lady in a glassy office watching the comings and goings. Didier didn't speak much English, barely a word, and my French was not much better. Funnily enough, this was one of the reasons why we had got romantic in the first place. He said that night in the club, desperate to be understood, 'I theenk you are preety', which left no room for me to mistake his intentions. If he had been more fluent I probably would have.

After this head-spinning episode I had to leave Paris to play a couple of gigs in Ireland and Scotland. I yearned for Didier all the way from Charles de Gaulle to Shannon, sent him red roses ('not really the right kind of gesture,' said Didier Lestrade), and wrote him verses of ardent love. When I got off the plane in Ireland I was stopped by a particularly hostile customs officer, who insisted on looking through my stuff, including the black briefcase that I had as hand baggage, and in which my verses to Didier lay. He took it, opened it, withdrew them and then, and in front of everybody, read them out, slowly and loudly, mercilessly asking me for help in elucidating their meaning.

The schedule had us leaving Dublin for Scotland, via ferry, and on to Edinburgh; but unable to keep away I decided after the Dublin gig to fly back to Paris, have a night with Didier and then fly on to Edinburgh for the gig.

The Dublin gig took place at the National Stadium, normally used for boxing, and it was the first time we had performed since 'Don't Leave Me This Way' had gone to number one in the UK and Ireland. We came on stage to a wall of sound, the sound of screaming girls, who, as soon as we appeared, threw stuff at us, charms from bracelets, flowers and knickers. This was bizarre, not only because we were more likely to wear the knickers than avail ourselves of what was in them, but also because we – or, rather, I – thought a sober attentiveness was more appropriate to our dutiful performance of these anthems of solidarity with alienated gays and oppressed workers. The record-buying kids of Dublin were having none of it and shouted themselves hoarse, anticipating audiences to come, but I was unprepared for that, still less for the stinging whip of a cheap gold bracelet across the face. When we came off stage I complained about the unruly crowd to Jimmy, who was still high on the excitement of playing to them. This poorly timed remark deflated and annoyed him and we had a row, which made me yearn for Didier even more. The night passed slowly, and next morning the bus dropped me off at Shannon airport to get my flight to France and I waved the band off to the ferry terminal and the UK. When I went to pick up my ticket I discovered that I had left my passport on the bus. I pleaded with the aeroplane staff to let me fly to Paris, in these pre-EU open-border days, but they would have none of it. I could, however, fly to the UK without a passport, so I eventually found a flight to Glasgow, then took a bus from there to Edinburgh, picked up my passport from our tour manager Steve, who found this episode hilarious, stayed the night in Edinburgh, flew to Paris in the morning, picked up Didier and returned to the airport with him and we both flew back to Scotland. It was the first time he had been in a plane and he was full of childish excitement, looking out on clouds from above rather than from below, and thinking he was dying – he was a terrible hypochondriac – when his ears popped on our descent towards Edinburgh. At some point on that trip we took a train to Carlisle to appear on a pop show made by Borders Television, in the days when there were pop programmes made by regional ITV stations, and I remember it particularly because it is where I met Björk, then starting out with the Sugar Cubes, as puzzled as I was to be miming to a record next to a field full of cows. I also remember that trip because June took a photograph with my camera of me and Jimmy and Didier on the train, sitting on a bench seat like the three wise monkeys. When it was developed Didier loved it and asked for the negative so he could get it blown up by a photographer friend and framed.

Our lack of a shared language rather disguised the insubstantial nature of my attachment to Didier. It also obscured the insubstantial nature of his to me. I was a pop star. He was a model. That seemed in itself enough of a reason to get together and I was dazzled by his handsomeness and charmed by his inarticulacy. He was a model and

I was a pop star – and I was the pop star who stood next to Jimmy Somerville, whom Didier, along with half of gay Paris, idolised. Being near to me was being nearer to Jimmy, and if my preetiness seemed to wear off quite sharply, he nevertheless seemed contented enough with the status quo even though we had practically nothing in common. He became a regular on tour, and made friends with the rest of the band, especially Dave, the bass player, whom he seemed to find preety in a different way from me. I began to yearn for his presence a bit less after that and really annoyed him when I said that I would prefer him not to come when we went to Cannes for the music industry festival, Midem. I did make sure he knew I was staying in a corner suite at the Carlton, a hotel full of pop stars and those unlikely music industry people who turn out for such things, including an infamous character who had cornered the market in fly-posting in Britain, who had prospered so richly that he always stayed in the most palatial accommodation at industry gatherings in Cannes, in New York, in Montreux.

Didier went into a big sulk when I denied him access to my glamorous world. One of the worst occurred when I went to Los Angeles without him, an oversight which caused a row that began in Paris, continued by telephone in London and then picked up again in Los Angeles. I ran up a colossal phone bill, hundreds of dollars' worth of halting argument in two languages, but when I came to check out the rather queeny receptionist could not work out the tariff and I refused to accept an estimate so he had to let me off. We drove through the morning smog to LAX, tall palm trees with tiny plumes of leaf like a guard of honour.

We flew back to Paris and I thought it was time for détente so called Didier, who was also feeling conciliatory, and he invited me round. When I got there I saw on his mantelpiece the photograph June had taken of me and Didier and Jimmy on the train, blown up and framed; only he had cropped me out of it.

We didn't officially break up, not that we were ever really together, until Christmas that year, when he came on tour with us. It was not a success. After our last gig, at what was then the Hammersmith

Odeon, we drove up the Kilburn High Road in the tour bus, the last two drop-offs, together but apart, as Peter Gabriel and Kate Bush sang of the power of love to restore hope. 'Don't give up . . .' she warbled, but we did give up, after enduring a not very festive Christmas at all. I had not had time, or the desire, to arrange anything so we had a turkey pizza on Christmas Eve which gave Didier an allergic reaction so powerful we saw in the Nativity of the Christ Child in casualty at the Royal Free Hospital, waiting for hours to see the only doctor on duty, dealing with the casualties of a knife fight in Kentish Town.

In the band our nickname for Didier was Shazz, a diminutive of Sharon and not entirely complimentary; but I am happy to say that in France he went on to achieve great success in pop music as a recording artist, producer and remixer, a career he conducts under that very name.

Love finally came my way thanks to a swingeingly vindictive piece of legislation with which Margaret Thatcher, that champion of freedom, denied representation to the voters of London by abolishing the Greater London Council. For the left, the GLC was a beacon of hope in those darkest of days; and for me it was the first thing I ever voted for that had got in and made life better. A quarter of a million people gathered outside County Hall on the evening of 31 March 1986 for speeches, fireworks and the unveiling of a commemorative inscription on the building carved so deeply into Portland stone, and gilded so richly, it looked like it would last till doomsday. In that crowd I found my friends Henry McAllister, a Glaswegian who I thought the rudest man I had ever met when we first came across each other, and his partner Derek Hughes, an unreformed Stalinist school teacher in south London, and the only person I have ever known genuinely to admire Albania's Communist dictator Enver Hoxha. That night they had a friend with them from Glasgow, Russell, a handsome, red-headed man in his thirties who was wearing a jacket that looked like it was made from motley. He caught my eye. I said something friendly and he responded even more rudely than Henry had when we first met and, wounded, I retreated. We met later at Heaven and he said something surprisingly friendly and then it got a lot friendlier. We only spent a night together before Russell had to get back to Glasgow, and to his partner, which was inconvenient because after only a night we realised we both wanted to get to know each other better.

It was the distance, not the partner, from whom Russell was parting, that I found inconvenient, and we arranged an assignation a couple of weeks later. I was passing through Glasgow and came up early and booked into the hotel at Glasgow Central Station, a mournful place of solitary diners picking over a fussy menu that seemed unchanged from the 1970s. Russell came round in the afternoon, a romantic and clandestine assignation, and later, as I nudged my unyielding potato croquettes with a fork alone in the dining room, I wondered how this was going to work.

Russell was wondering the same thing. He called to say he had broken up with his partner and the possibility of a relationship opened up. It had occurred to me that I had spent the past year dating someone in a different country, and, while that was romantic, it was perhaps also a way of not being with someone, as well as being a challenge logistically. I thought Glasgow would be a bit easier to get to than Paris (not so, I discovered); but I sensed already that Russell and I fitted together neatly, without having to force anything, or suspend disbelief, or agonise at all.

I spent the next few months irritating whoever was organising our travel to reroute me via Glasgow whenever possible. I spent hours on tourist planes flying into Prestwick, or small planes serving the oil industry flying into Aberdeen, and then making complicated connections to get to Glasgow to spend sometimes only a night at his tiny flat on the London Road, in the Merchant City, then being done up as Glasgow redeveloped its inner-city neigbourhoods. The flat, though tiny, was astonishingly clean and tidy. Like Jimmy Somerville, Russell was house-proud, a trait they had inherited from their Glaswegian foremothers, although in Russell it was almost obsessional. Under the sink he kept special cleaning items that he had made for particular tasks, an old toothbrush he had adapted to dust skirting boards and detergent cocktails he made from proprietary brands to achieve 'penetration without losing viscosity'. Russell was a lecturer in printed textiles at Glasgow School of Art – hence the creativity and the motley – but that meant he worked regular hours so I had to find weekends we could take off together. I made the mistake of thinking each weekend should be a mini-honeymoon, and once arranged for us to stay at a country house hotel, formerly the home of a captain of industry, now famed for its restaurant. It was a disaster. This was the 1980s, and although hotels in London and New York and Paris had got used to gay couples, this hotel had not, especially a gay couple who looked like they should be working there rather than staying there. We had no jacket or tie, required in the dining room, and they made us eat in our room. Out walking in the grounds we were accosted by a grumpy woman who demanded to know what 'you boys' were doing trespassing. When I said we were guests at the hotel she got even grumpier, as if I had done her out of her fun. And on our last night the hotel hosted a dinner for the great and the good, in black tie and long frock, and we were practically locked in our room lest we spoil their evening. This being the last straw, I insisted on the service charges being deducted from our bill when we left.

As we sat in the train on our way back to Glasgow, Russell confessed that he hated posh hotels, hated restaurants and eating out, because, a working-class boy from Cumbernauld, he felt the whole time he was being judged and found wanting, for not knowing which knife and fork to use, for being overfamiliar or too distant with the waiters, for being a cuckoo in the nest. It had never occurred to me that someone might dislike a restaurant. It had never occurred to me that someone might not be entirely relaxed about enjoying the fruits of my success, but once I grasped it I stopped inflicting my Daddy Warbucks proclivities on him and we would spend our weekends together at home, walking the dog in the park, watching telly, meeting his friends. One of them I got to know well, Martin Henry, whom Russell had met at some Marxist summer camp in the 1970s where they discovered they were the only gays. Martin lived in Edinburgh, and Russell would stay with him when he was teaching at the School of Art there, so I stayed, too. I was fascinated by Martin. He was half Scottish, with a mother from Glasgow, and half Métis, with a Canadian father of mixed Native American and settler heritage (a Scottish tour in the 1950s by the Canadian ice hockey squad was how that happened). He grew up the only different-looking kid in a tough part of Glasgow, that sense of difference accentuated by the discovery that he was gay. He got involved with gangs and music and clubs in the seventies and things could have gone wrong for him had he not found a way, via education, into professional life. Martin became a social worker, specialising in children and what later came to be called child protection, and – most arrestingly for me – a Roman Catholic. Martin was the first person I met who was gay, on the left, cool and a Christian, and it made a very powerful impression on me to meet someone with my preoccupations and loyalties and prejudices, faithfully attending Mass every Sunday without too great a sacrifice of integrity or intelligibility. I only met him once or twice, but he made a deep impression on me, and was yet to make a deeper one.

I say I restrained my Daddy Warbucks proclivities, but with one adventurous exception. We went away to the Maldives and stayed in a little thatched hut on the most perfect beach, on the most perfect island, a little crest of white sand and green palms set in a sea the colour of sapphires. Russell loved it, even when we discovered that one of our neighbours, with whom we made friends, was the former owner of a Clydeside shipyard. Embourgeoisement, he muttered, but drank nonetheless from a coconut decapitated by a helpful boy with a machete.

I must have realised, on some fundamental level, that Russell's dislike of posh hotels was not simply an expression of class values but also of a preference for me. He was happiest when we were together doing nothing much. He never joined us on tour; I don't think he ever came to see us play. He never asked me a single question about the band or about Jimmy Somerville. He wasn't interested. Years later I was talking about this to a friend who asked me if I had any regrets in life and I said I did, and that one of them was not having really understood the value of this at the time. I was too distracted with my own affairs, too dazzled by the fireworks going off round me, too shallow and too silly to have had the confidence of what my heart and mind were telling me, that this was a man who could love me and who I could love, too. Instead I behaved to Russell as if he were not wholly there, fitting him in where I could around my inalienably more important schedule, and – worse – with a nonchalance and a lack of respect that betrayed a coarseness and unkindness on my part. While I did not exactly have a paramour in every port, there were overlaps and complications in my romantic life – not that any one of us in those days would have expected or offered total fidelity – but there was an etiquette to it that observed the priority of the lover over the playful passing relationships in the background. I failed in this once, passing through Glasgow on tour, and staying at a hotel in the West End where I spent the afternoon with a man I had picked up in the hotel in Edinburgh we'd stayed at and where he worked in the bar. He practically went out one door as Russell came in the other, not an unusual situation in a pop star's life, but a sleazy one, lacking in kindness and courtesy, to say the least, and treating Russell and the barman as if they were merely interchangeable opportunities for my gratification.

In the end my unavailability – physically and emotionally – was too much for Russell who was looking for someone to share his life with, not someone to parachute into it on all his own terms, and we broke up.

13. So Cold The Night

As 'Don't Leave Me This Way' continued to rise in the charts across Europe and beyond, the promotional circuit widened and intensified. We had been making our way round the television studios of Spain and Germany and France and Italy and Scandinavia, so when the French record company asked us if we would be interested in going to La Réunion for a week to film a summertime special, a tropical interlude in a grey winter, it seemed almost like a holiday from the promotional round. Along with a bunch of other pop stars, we were to mime to a record either while in the sea or on the beach or at a mimed concert in the island's stadium to which we were driven in absurd little buggies, like billionaire golfers.

La Réunion is a huge volcano surrounded by forest and lovely beaches in the middle of the Indian Ocean. Officially a part of France – how typical of *la Patrie* to maintain a tropical island in a sapphire sea rather than a sheep-grazed rock in the South Atlantic – there were always croissants and decent coffee to be had, but the people who lived there were a mixture of Indian and local and European and Chinese, so there was never a dull moment in its gastronomy. It was also a place where French military personnel stationed thereabouts, on Mauritius or Madagascar, could come for R&R, and in a little cottage opposite mine was a young officer, so ridiculously handsome I could not help myself and stared at him like a hopeless fan at his idol. He was dark, with black hair and black eyes, and a body that seemed about to burst with sheer vitality from his uniform. This came off and he sat on his balcony in a white dressing gown looking down at me looking up at him, unmentionable scenarios spooling in my imagination. This was my thing – looking from a distance at these icons of masculinity and slightly threatening beauty and in my imagination romancing them and them romancing me. Jimmy, no less in thrall to male beauty, actually got off with them, with infamous degrees of success, and the difference between us was so egregious that it sometimes seemed to me that his sexual success somehow necessitated my sexual failure, a quantity theory of sexual fulfilment.

This was not entirely in the mind, for Jimmy, if his blood was up, could steam in on anyone. He was often getting into trouble for having sex with someone he shouldn't have had sex with, and his appetite was so irresistible that he would without a second thought abandon one conquest immediately for another. One of the sounds I associate with the Communards was of men crying, men of many nations, whisked off their feet, summoned on tour and then abruptly cast aside. One, a trusting Geordie soldier who had, I think, run away from barracks to be with Jimmy, was literally abandoned in continental Europe, travelling with us full of excitement to France or Spain, but left behind when we moved on, with nothing but his passport and six weeks' basic training to get him back to Blighty. When Jimmy had been in Bronski Beat he was dating a very sweet and handsome man, a sticker who had been around for a while, whom Jimmy asked to play the leading role of 'surfer' in the video for 'I Feel Love'. But suddenly, without warning, this gentle and kind man found he had lost the job to a dazzlingly handsome Belgian, who had delivered room service to Jimmy in a hotel in Brussels, and got far more than a tip for his trouble. It wasn't even one in, one out; there were so many simultaneously in varying degrees of intimacy and distance that I sometimes forgot who was who. But then I have never known anyone experience desire so powerfully as Jimmy. Not just desire, but romance, too. I had a vintage jacket from the Helsinki Olympics of 1952 that I had bought with Robert in a flea market in Amsterdam and loved. I lent it to Jimmy one day and he, on a romantic adventure, gave it to someone, news he casually mentioned when I asked for it back. He did the same with a pair of silver western collar tips, too, and eventually I learned not to lend things when romance was in the air, which was nearly all the time. Jimmy, subconsciously or consciously, subscribed to the doctrine 'never apologise, never explain'. He had that degree of self-possession, fully his own person, and he did what he wanted and he paid the price. That was him, and this was me, standing chastely on my sun-swept terrace, looking helplessly at the French soldier on furlough, like a nerdy new boy gazing at a dazzling prefect and Captain of Everything.

Our schedule was getting very busy. When a record takes off, it creates an appetite for more of the same, and the record company demands new versions, twelve-inch remixes, picture discs, as many ways as possible of reselling the product to its fans. We were offered the opportunity to make a twelve-inch remix, big budget, big production number of 'Don't Leave Me This Way'. So immediately after La Réunion London Records booked us in with Mike Thorne in New York.

We left our tropical island and flew overnight, stopping in Nairobi where some guys came on the plane and sprayed us with something, and then on to Paris. I could never sleep on planes, but got into the habit of reading Agatha Christie novels instead; something about their familiarity and the England of the fifties soothed the anxiety of travelling. They also, oddly, answered the anxiety generated by the dislocations of success, and I could easily read two or three back-to-back, sometimes over and over again. It would annoy my fellow passengers on occasion, trying to sleep in these pre flat-bed days, and on that flight a soul diva, sitting alongside, with whom I'd got on rather well in our palm-fringed resort, got a bit snappy about my reading light in that way people do flying in the dead of night 38,000 feet over *la politesse*, and I had to recommend she use the eye mask provided.

On the flight from Paris to New York, we travelled first class. I had never flown first class before and was startled by the extravagance of the airline's welcome. After check-in we were led in a fawning procession to a special lounge, where formalities were completed, and then into the nose of the plane and perched on two enormous seats, like children in armchairs. An impeccable and smiling stewardess knelt at our feet and said, 'Hi Jimmy! Hi Richard! We're so pleased and proud that you have chosen us to serve you.' There was only one other person in first, a delightful socialite from New York who was thrilled to be travelling with pop stars and made us write down the name of our band so she would not forget it. People kept bringing us things, fiddly dishes and drinks at peculiar temperatures, and we watched *A Private Function* and laughed and laughed at Maggie Smith in mercilessly rationed wartime Yorkshire as we crossed the Atlantic feasting on aeroplane tournedos Rossini and grand cru Bordeaux.

We landed in New York on a freezing cold evening, and it was snowing hard as our stretch limousine lumbered towards the city. On TV in the car was another snowstorm, from *It's A Wonderful Life*, the best Christmas film of all, but again rather disorienting considering we had started our journey on a tropical island. By now I felt like we were in our third continent and third climate in a single time zone-lengthened day and I remember that night thinking that I'd had mango on a tropical island for breakfast, steak frites in Paris for lunch and a slice of pizza in New York for supper. It was December, trucks with giant menorahs were driving round to mark the Jewish festival of Hanukkah, skaters were skating in front of the Rockefeller building, and Christmas was not long off. That night we walked back to our hotel in Midtown and Jimmy had one of the new little video cameras that had just come on the market and he shot a great plume of steam rising from a pipe, striped in red and white, sticking up out of the street – you see them everywhere in Manhattan – and then these two drag queens appeared out of the shadows and started dancing around and in and out of the plume, like a steam-age Dance of the Seven Veils.

Jimmy did not much like hotels (I love them) so we moved into an apartment near Gramercy Park, a small three-bedroom duplex, and Lorna came to stay a few days with us to deal with business matters. With Christmas approaching I thought it might be good to invite some friends over, and so did Jimmy, but we forgot to check with each other and between us we invited fifteen to stay. I got into a Boy Scout fret about where we would put them and how this would impinge on work, which annoyed Jimmy, and we had a row which ended, as most of them now ended, with Jimmy refusing to speak and me complaining to Lorna that he was being irrational. We almost invariably arrived at this impasse because, when it came to the crunch, Jimmy and I were joint proprietors, as it were, and those who toured with us, our management and agents, were employees, so if Jimmy needed to be persuaded of something against his will or dissuaded from something against his will, it eventually became my job, and that just added to the resentments we harboured with one another.

Sometimes his wilful refusal to do what I thought was the obviously sensible thing drove me mad, but I realise now that I did not understand why he made the choices he made, because our assumptions about so many things were different. What gave us our distinctiveness – our difference – also, precisely, threatened our existence. Getting to know each other and working together in the alternative gay scene in London in the early eighties provided enough common purpose and common experience to bind us together. Pop music, with its particular pressures, accentuated that difference and forced us apart.

I found that row with Jimmy particularly affected me. Perhaps I was tired, perhaps I felt lonely, perhaps I saw the writing on the wall; but I remember one evening I was on my own in the apartment and on television Alistair Cooke appeared presenting Masterpiece Theatre on PBS. The snowflakes swirled outside and more fake ones swirled, too, on TV as a BBC Dickens adaptation began. I felt the strongest pang of homesickness I had ever felt. Not just, I realised, for home, but for a life that made more sense to me than the life I was living then.

We could still come together musically. The remix of 'Don't Leave Me This Way' is one of our best efforts, recorded in Mike's own studio at his apartment in the West Village. We were all up for doing something huge and symphonic and the Synclavier gave us the means to do it. We put on strings, we put on percussion, we put on voices and horns, we put on sounds sampled almost randomly. Mike was endlessly inventive with the digital editing capabilities of the new technology, so we could cut stuff up, reverse it, turn it upside down, run it any way we wanted, repeat, delete, restore and so on and at the end of our sessions had a thirteen-minute-long classic of the genre. I like it because it still fills dance floors – not that I've been on one for twenty years – but because it is very Jimmy and me, disco and Grade V theory, four-part harmony and a soaring falsetto, tenement and conservatoire.

And then our guests arrived and our little apartment filled up, fifteen then sixteen, then we lost count of who was actually staying, and it was fine; not only fine, it was a ball and we had a brilliant Christmas. I have photographs of us on the subway and we look like a squad of small gangsters, led by Jimmy and Mark Ashton in DM boots, Crombie overcoats and shaven heads. We were joined, too, by Hugo Irwin, a friend of mine, a Londoner whose father was a judge and whose mother was a posh Roman Catholic. They lived in Chelsea and sent Hugo and his brothers to a boarding school run by Benedictine monks. Hugo left and went to drama school in London, surprising absolutely no one when he revealed he was gay. He loved to sing and perform but always reminded me of Noelle Gordon in the Christmas scene of *Crossroads* when he did and we laughed rather unkindly at his party piece, 'Stormy Weather', which he performed as his alter ego, Miss Peggy Lash. He was rather grand in his own way, putting up 'two thousand pounds' worth of grey silk curtains', borrowed from his mother, in his council flat ('the home of Country in the heart of Peckham'). He was irrepressibly good fun, could turn a funeral into a party and once on a dull trip to New York on Virgin he made friends with the air crew and somewhere there's a video of me and Hugo and Jimmy dressed up as stewardesses giving out the snacks. He also completely understood Jimmy, and the two of them became close friends, a surprising closeness to me, for he was as different from him as I was.

That Christmas our gang hit the bars like we did in London, in force and hard drinking, falling over by nine in a way that horrified the more seemly New Yorkers used to less restrictive licensing laws than ours. By the time we got in, nearer dawn than dusk, things got not exactly orgiastic but there were more people than beds and you never quite knew who'd be under the covers and what would transpire. For me, one night, it was Mark Ashton, and to my surprise we ended up having rather desultory sex but not without intimacy. Mark, I think, understood the pressures of doing what we were doing, especially the pressures of working with Jimmy, so volatile and unbiddable, and we connected in a way we had not before. Because of that we slightly split off from the others and spent time together, talking a lot; and then, on Christmas Eve, he said, 'Do you fancy going to Midnight Mass?' I had no idea where the impulse for that had come from, although now I think I do, but I said yes and so we headed out into the dark, snowy night for St Patrick's on Fifth Avenue. When we got there we discovered that the sacrament was by ticket only and there was no way we would get in, but a rather grand lady offered us hers and in we went and sat incongruously beside what looked to me like the Kennedys, in furs and diamonds, us in DMs and 501s.

We had set a rule that we would shop only at the 99c store for Christmas presents that year and so, under the tree, which we stole from the lobby, were packets of Lee Press On Nails and party streamers and shower caps, but I have never enjoyed presents more. Someone must have cooked and we had a Christmas quiz, a tradition in my family, which Hugo and I delivered through the hatch connecting the kitchen to the living room, like quizmasters on a fifties TV.

It was the last Christmas before everything was utterly changed by the next and completely unexpected arrival in our lives.

14. Auntie Ada

I first read about it in *Capital Gay*, an alarming article about a suspected 'gay cancer' that doctors were seeing in New York and San Francisco. It seemed to be a sort of melanoma and it was thought that it might be caused by using poppers, amyl nitrate that was sold coyly as a 'room odoriser' but used enthusiastically as a muscle relaxant during sex. These reports began to arrive with greater frequency, and there were rumours, too, from those returning from New York and California that there was a killer bug about, released, some said, by the CIA to attack the gay community. It seemed a long way off, difficult to take seriously, but like a storm cloud on the horizon it grew closer and bigger and darker. In the newspapers, not just the gay newspapers, sinister new acronyms began to emerge: the '4H disease' – homosexuals, Haitians, haemophiliacs, heroin users its most common victims; 'GRID', gay-related immune-deficiency; 'HTLV III', human T-lymphotropic virus type three; and, finally, AIDS, acquired immuno-deficiency syndrome, a name invented by the Centre for Disease Control and in common use by the end of 1982.

In spite of these dire warnings it did not feel like a crisis about to break, even after the death of Rock Hudson, whose face, the first recognisable one to appear shockingly thinner and older, had been all over the media. In New York the clubs we frequented were as busy as ever, in Amsterdam the rubber fetish places Robert liked showed no sign of losing clientele, and in Britain, even though the first death from AIDS in London had occurred in 1982, a sort of phoney war atmosphere prevailed. We knew it was there, we knew it was dangerous but it did not seem to touch us.

Returning from New York at the end of 1987, I bought my first flat, a two-bedroom top-floor conversion in a big Victorian terraced house in what estate agents called West Hampstead but what taxi drivers called Kilburn. There was a kitchen at the back, which overlooked the railway line carrying nuclear waste by night and commuters by day, then a corridor and a bathroom, a big bedroom, a living room at the front, from which a single room had been scraped. The flat smelled of paint, magnolia, the thin oatmeal carpet it came in, and the faint adhesive smell of grout. I bought two sofas from Habitat, those big round lampshades from Oxfam, a bed, a desk in fashionable black-stained ash, and felt a bit like the man in the Halifax bank card ad, who woke up in his eighties loft conversion to Lionel Richie singing 'Easy Like Sunday Morning'. Less attractive, perhaps, it faced an identical terrace on the other side of the street, and in the flat directly opposite mine there lived a man in middle age who once in a while at night used to stand at his uncurtained window wanking.

One of the first visitors to my new flat was Mark. He had been picketing the printers' dispute in Wapping and I had joined him a couple of times. There were clashes on the picket line, once, memorably, when I was on one side and my brother Andy, then a constable in the Met, on the other. Hostilities were suspended, however, when I discovered I had a mouse in the new flat and got him to come round to deal with it. Unlike me, Mark had been there day in, day out, standing in the cold and rain, and had caught a cold and developed a bad cough that no medicine could shift. He stood hacking in my kitchen, almost bent double, feeling so ill that instead of going on to Wapping he went home to Elephant and Castle and took to his bed.

A few days later, as we were getting ready to leave for a week's worth of TV, radio and press in Spain, a friend rang with the news that Mark had been admitted to Guy's for observation. After a rehearsal the next day, I got to the hospital in the early evening carrying, incongruously, a cased soprano saxophone. I took a lift up to a high floor in Guy's grim concrete tower. Great view, I thought, and was shown into the private room where Mark was being observed. His mother was there – she and his father had flown to London from Africa, where they lived. This was not good. She said hello and then said, 'I'll leave you two alone.' Dreading what was to come, I wanted to leave too, but I sat on the bed and Mark, exhausted, took off the oxygen mask. 'How are you?' I said, hopelessly, and he said, 'Not very well. Auntie Ada's come to call.'

One of the acronyms that we all became familiar with early on in the epidemic was PCP, pneumocystis pneumonia, a form of yeast infection that attacked the lungs of people with failing immune systems. Mark had it, the cause of his unbudging cough, and he told me that, if the doctors couldn't halt it, 'it's curtains'. I didn't believe him. He was in his twenties, young and fit, and a golden boy, full of promise, precious to so many – surely nothing could hurt him? I sat beside him and he talked about his life, about its great regret, a relationship that had failed, and he tried to say goodbye, but I wouldn't have it, and stood miserably at the door, saxophone in hand, and said I would see him when we got back from Spain.

We left the next day for Madrid, and checked into the splendid Palace Hotel near the Ritz and the Prado, a huge white stucco building with a glass dome, the sort of place you could imagine Edward VII meeting his mistresses. We were surrounded by journalists, who were fascinated by Jimmy, and spent a few days going from venue to venue almost without stopping. It was in Madrid that we met two Spaniards – Álvaro Villarubia and Jesús Vázquez – who were to become great friends. Álvaro was a photographer commissioned by a magazine for a session with us and, I don't know why, but we crossed the divide from professional to friend, and we met him later at a nightclub with his boyfriend, Jesús. Jesús was perhaps even more striking than his namesake, I think the most handsome man I have ever seen, a model so alluring people would stop still and drool at him as he passed by. They became our mates in Madrid and whenever we were in town, which was often, we would meet up. This friendship endured beyond the band's life, and in time beyond their relationship's life. When they broke up Álvaro told me: 'I cried for a day, and then it was done and I do not look back.' Jesús did not look back either. He became a television presenter and is now one of the most famous people in Spain and still astoundingly handsome.

We went from Madrid to Barcelona, booked on to a television show that was shot in a studio in what looked like an industrial estate on the edge of the city, windowless metal boxes set down beside a road, to which the teenaged audience was bussed in from the less desirable suburbs of the city. Jimmy had done it before, in Bronski Beat, and hated it because the children were delinquent and threw things at the artists on stage, even shooting at them with catapults. While we were getting ready for our performance, a woman from the record company came up and said there was a call for me in the office. It was our friend John Crossland, in tears, needing to speak to Jimmy though he didn't say why. I told him to hang on and went to fetch Jimmy, who was sitting in a make-up artist's chair in a big bib with half his slap done, and said that John was on the phone and he needed to come. He followed me back to the office, took the phone and listened, and then wailed, a howl of grief, and a wash of tears spread across his face.

I went back into the dressing room. Jimmy's wail had been heard, and my white face seen, and everyone was silent as I told them that Mark had died. Jimmy came in and everyone was crying and the poor woman from the record company said, 'I'm sorry, you're on', and we walked on to the stage into a wall of children's screams and mimed our way through a song called 'Don't Leave Me This Way'.

We were scheduled to fly on to Paris later, but the record company cancelled that and tried to get us on a flight to London, but there weren't any. They even tried to hire a private plane to take us home but it was too late, so we were booked on the first scheduled flight in the morning. Our rooms had gone at the hotel and they weren't all available for one more night so Jimmy and I were booked into a twin. I hope I disguised my disappointment when we were told this, but I did not want to be with Jimmy because I didn't think his grief and my grief were compatible. I didn't think I would get comfort from him and I didn't think he would get comfort from me. We had gradually become wary of each other, grown distant from each other, and that unacknowledged reality was suddenly right in front of us. So he disappeared after dinner and I went out with June Miles-Kingston and we found a cinema showing *The Name of the Rose* in English with Catalan subtitles and I was fascinated by Salvatore, the misshapen idiot, who spoke in an untranslatable gibberish and made, that night, the only sense anyone was making. Later, in the hotel room Jimmy told me he had picked up a bloke down by the docks and spent most of the night with him cavorting among containers; a stranger's comfort.

When we got back to London the next day we all met at Mark's. This was to become a common experience over the next few years, meeting in a dead man's flat for the distribution of their effects, or the concealment of things which needed to be concealed from their families, and sometimes, most awkwardly, negotiating funeral arrangements with a middle-aged couple who had only just learned that their son was gay in time for him to die. Mark's parents, however, were anxious for all his friends to be as involved as possible, and Jimmy travelled with them in the cortège at his funeral. We all waited outside the crematorium for the arrival of the hearse, and that weird pantomime of Victorian solemnity with which we dispatch our dead. The funeral directors were called Ashton's and their sign was everywhere and it made me feel that Mark's death had become a public as well as a private event: whose is this funeral? Ashton's.

There was a public dimension to it, we discovered. Somehow the papers had got to hear of it and there were some photographers there, who rushed to get shots of Jimmy and the grieving parents. But the sight of the coffin was so devastatingly pathetic that their heartlessness seemed negligible. The funeral passed in a blur, everyone crying, including me, who never cried, the unsleeping, self-regarding part of me noted.

A couple of weeks later a journalist from a tabloid contacted us and said that if she didn't see proof that Jimmy was HIV negative she would run a story saying he had AIDS. She was told to fuck off

and die. In due course there was a story, which, instead of claim-
ing Jimmy had AIDS, coyly referred to his attendance at Mark's
funeral in a way which suggested they were more than friends and
that Mark's fate might also be his.

We all felt Mark's fate might also be ours. It was devastating not
only because we had lost a close, loved friend and – to use a word
Mark used without embarrassment – a comrade, but because it
meant that Auntie Ada had indeed come to call, and her dark and
dreadful presence was close beside us, now calling time on a brief
and beautiful interlude of hope and joy and grace.

In a photo album from 1984 I have a picture of a concert we put
on at a party in the back garden of a friend's house in Belsize Park
during which I performed a music-hall version of The Internation-
ale with two friends, a rallying cry for the international proletariat
in the style of *The Good Old Days*. I took this picture at the picnic
afterwards, my friends sitting round a rug, men and women, gay and
straight. All the gay men in it are now dead.

Mark's death overwhelmed us, and we did the things people do
when they suffer such a loss, forming a Trust in his memory and
putting on a benefit to raise funds to help people diagnosed with
HIV. We got involved with the newly formed London Lighthouse,
a centre dedicated to care and support for people with HIV. And we
wrote two songs in Mark's memory, in tribute to him, an attempt to
give voice to the shock and grief caused by his death, rather clumsily
turning pitiless loss into pop music.

Mark had been working with Red Wedge, and just after he died I
attended a meeting at Walworth Road to discuss political priorities
for young people. I thought AIDS should be one of them. Looking
at the doomsday scenarios suggested by the rate of transmission and
the potential destructiveness of a virus indifferent to the sexual orientation of its host, it seemed obvious to me that young people in
particular were going to be at risk and we needed to alert them and
plan for the impact the epidemic could have. But no one else saw it
that way and I sat looking at a sea of puzzled faces, thinking, one of
your colleagues has just died of AIDS in his twenties; this is a virulent

and incurable disease that has the potential to kill a generation, and you don't think it is relevant? But, then again, I hadn't thought it affected me until it did. In an era when plagues were all but lost to living memory, at least in the places people like us lived, most young people feel immortal, invulnerable, it's-never-going-to-happen-to-me.

Back then the hatred of homosexuals was commonplace and often unselfconscious. I was struck by the nonchalant cruelty of a leader in a broadsheet: 'The problem with AIDS,' it pontificated, 'is that it is not confined to homosexuals.'

Some people – surprising people – did get it. Norman Fowler, the Tory Health Secretary, got the seriousness of what was happening. He was responsible for the doomy 'Don't Die of Ignorance' campaign, which put ads on television and posted leaflets through doors, showing falling gravestones and funeral wreaths to shock us into paying attention. It may seem clumsy to us now, but he understood and was respectful to the response of the gay community, an inconvenient truth for a tribal lefty like me. That political tribalism was to recede in the coming years as I began to see that the defining issue for me was not going to be class or economics or the imminence of the revolution, but a much deeper fight against ignorance, indifference, hatefulness: a fight against AIDS.

It was a peculiarly isolating experience, the first years of the epidemic, so selective in its choices, subtracting so precisely the gay men from the picnic. Not long after Mark died I was on a crowded tube and a man who had spent that crowded Christmas in New York with us hugged me extravagantly. 'How ARE you,' he boomed. 'And how's MARK?' I didn't know what to say, so mumbled something about him having died, adding pointlessly and truthlessly, 'but it's OK'. He didn't hear me properly, or couldn't hear me properly, and I had to explain while a dozen strangers listened in, and then, as he began to cry, I had to get off at my stop and leave him on his own.

Our isolation also produced solidarity. Christopher Spence was raising funds to buy and convert a building in Ladbroke Grove to provide services for people with HIV, specifically a place for them to be treated and to live to the end with understanding, care and dignity.

He showed us round the building, then a dripping, semi-derelict shell. Jimmy and I immediately agreed to put on a fundraiser, and become patrons. We were on tour when it was opened and returned to find it transformed, with meeting rooms, a small garden, offices, a residential section and places for medics and, of course, a mortuary. The Lighthouse, as a dedicated facility, soon became expert in caring for people with AIDS and was able to share that expertise with others. As a result the care people with HIV received from the National Health Service, at St Thomas's, St Mary's, and the Chelsea and Westminster in London, was very good.

It was not the same story everywhere. One morning Tony called from Amsterdam. Robert was seriously ill. He had collapsed one day and an ambulance had taken him away, unconscious, to a general hospital, but then he was transferred to a special hospital where Tony was not at first permitted to visit. Eventually a doctor called him in and told him that Robert had AIDS. Tony had to put on a gown and mask and gloves and was taken as near to his bedside as he could get. Robert had had a terrifying experience. When he first recovered consciousness he did not also recover his senses, so he was blind and deaf and dumb, unable to work out where he was and what had happened, self-aware and able to think, but without any sensory information to help him work out where he was. This had gone on for days, and he thought he had been damned and was in hell.

After a while his senses returned, and he discovered that his hell was a hospital where he was in isolation and that he had toxoplasmosis, a parasitic infection of the brain which normally affected cats, not humans, certainly not young, healthy humans, and not to the extent that it affected Robert. He was recovering and if he continued to recover he would be discharged, so Tony decided he wanted to return to London, where he thought Robert would receive better care than in Amsterdam. They asked to stay with me.

I was there to welcome them. Robert was very weak and suddenly much older and shakier and Tony and I pretended everything was fine. I left them to it as I had to go to Europe for a few days on a promotional trip and when I got back I could see they were awkward.

I asked if everything was all right and Robert said he had had an accident with some hot chocolate and it had made a bit of a mess but they had cleared it up. I knew it was not hot chocolate, and I could tell from what would not shift that it had been more explosive than a spill, but I said not to worry, it didn't matter. And it really didn't matter to me, but it mattered to Robert, suffering the merciless indignities of opportunistic infections. Robert got treatment, and they found a flat, but he was too weakened by the infections to survive long. He died a few months later.

I came home from a leg of our tour for the funeral, which took place at a church in Camden Town. Rob's family was Salvation Army and the funeral was a very strange mix, with Salvationists in their caps and bonnets at one end and fetishists of many nations in their caps and accoutrements at the other; and in the middle his family, his friends, trying to make sense of who he was and why he had died. I thought the service itself, led by a Salvation Army officer, might be a nightmare, either ignoring his sexuality and his partner entirely or acknowledging them so awkwardly everyone would be put out. But he did it without any embarrassment at all, acknowledging how difficult this might be for people for all sorts of reasons, but with gentle assurance insisting on the irreducible value of love and care wherever found.

It was not always love and care; it was sometimes ignorance and fear, but back then it was not so surprising that someone with HIV, and the host of bizarre infections they were prey to, would excite such alarm and caution. It can still happen. Only last year someone I know was admitted to hospital for surgery and was visited by the hospital chaplain wearing a gown and a mask and gloves. When one of the other patients asked why he was dressed up like that, a nursing auxiliary announced to the ward, 'He's HIV.'

AIDS is so pitiless, so unlike anything we had encountered before, that no wonder people's reactions were and are inadequate. One of the most telling and, for me, painful moments in this period occurred when we were asked to participate in a television documentary about the AIDS crisis, filmed for some reason at the Groucho

Club, the then new celebrity and media private members' club in Soho. We were seated and introduced by an interviewer who then showed a video of someone pretending to be dying in a hospital bed while singing a song. It was ghastly, awful, but instead of complaining I sat trying to think of clever things to say, diligent, detached cultural commentator in the making. Jimmy suddenly said, 'Stop it, I can't stand it', and got up and left, a far more honest and honourable reaction, I realised with shame, than my own.

15. The Best of Times the Worst of Times

There was also work, 'the great therapy'. We had a single out, 'So Cold The Night', in which Jimmy sang in the persona of a voyeur looking at the object of his soon-to-be-fulfilled desire, to a wobbly Arabian-sounding accompaniment and a disco beat. We thought perhaps the success of 'Don't Leave Me This Way' would ensure it a place in the top five, but it didn't rise that far. Following a big success is often tricky, even more so with albums than singles.

Second albums are notoriously difficult. Your first album comes out of your experience, being young, discovering things, making up your own life. Your second album also comes out of your experience, but by then it is sitting in a car on the A40 early in the morning, making videos, checking into hotels, not quite so rich a seam to mine. And by the time you get there, if you do, the relationship between band members can already be difficult, and Jimmy's and mine was sometimes very difficult.

No man is a hero to his valet, it is said; and no man is a hero to his band either. You spend too much time together for that, experience too much pressure, too much competition for light and air, and in my case jealousy too awkward to admit and deal with. I hated it that Jimmy got more attention than me, more credit than me. I hated it that everyone wanted a piece of him, that hotels would book him in a suite and me in an ordinary room; I hated it that when I was signing an autograph the fan would see him and pull their book from my hands leaving a zigzag of biro where my name should be. I sulked about being ignored in interviews. I sulked about a helicopter nearly taking off without me because no one remembered I was there. I sulked about a security guard not letting me into a venue when I forgot my pass even though we were standing next to a poster with my face on it. I hated it when Lorna, trying to sort out a Norwegian journalist backstage at Wembley Arena, asked to borrow my Access All Areas pass for him, thereby confining me to the dressing room because security didn't know who I was. I am embarrassed now at the grossness of my vanity and the triviality of the offence, but it did not seem like that at the time. In one especially unguarded moment we were caught outside a venue by an excited group of fans who pushed me out of the way to surround Jimmy, gushing how much they loved him, how brilliant he was and I snapped, 'WHAT ABOUT ME?' There was a silence and someone sniggered and then they went back to bothering Jimmy. And of course it *was* bother for Jimmy, bother I was excused and the luckier for it, if only I had had the detachment to see it, but I did not and seethed with resentment and self-pity.

These outbursts became more frequent as the resentments accumulated and pressures grew. One of the worst occurred at that hotel I loved, the Palace in Madrid, when we were on tour and top of the charts, and being chased by fans wherever we went. We had asked Jesús and Álvaro to arrange a dinner for us on a night off in a restaurant that was quiet and private, in what looked like Madrid's answer to the Bishops Avenue in London. We met in the hotel bar for a drink first and Jimmy came down wearing some new trousers by Jean Paul Gaultier that had wide braces. I laughed and said they made him look like a trawlerman and he did not take it kindly, turned on his heel and went back upstairs. Oh dear, I thought, this is going to ruin our evening, so I followed and knocked on the door of his suite and he came to the door. I said I was sorry, but he was having none of it and tried to shut the door on me. I wedged myself in the door and he pulled on it even harder and in an instant the accumulation of frustration and humiliation and sheer spite erupted and I lost my temper spectacularly. I remember screaming at him 'YOU DEMENTED LITTLE TROLL!' and him screaming back at me and we made so much noise a waiter appeared, and Jimmy said, 'This man's trying to break into my suite' and the waiter called for security who frogmarched me away, despite my protestations that I was actually staying in the hotel. They marched me through the lobby, out of the door and literally threw me down the steps outside, like in the films. But humiliation was added to humiliation because I had nowhere to go but back in the hotel, only every time I tried they came for me again. In the end our tour manager came by and rescued me, and the status quo was restored, with a bit of huffing and puffing from me. I went straight to my room and wrote Jimmy a long letter about my frustrations, and how difficult I found it to be dependent on him, so volatile and capricious, yet so essential to the success of the band and my own success. I put it under his door and the next day he was fine. 'Thanks for your letter, doll,' he said, 'that's one for the memoirs.'

Another danger with second albums is that the band may think it time to produce themselves. I thought it was time for us to do this and in the end London Records agreed we could be responsible for half the tracks – the acoustic half of the album – but for the more commercial half of it they put us in touch with Stephen Hague, who had just produced a brilliant track for New Order, 'True Faith'. We invested a lot personally and professionally in this album, which we called *Red*, for a reason I can't remember now, and throughout the recording AIDS both united and divided us. We wrote 'For A Friend', in memory of Mark, and I wrote – both the music and words – 'Lovers And Friends' about the losses that were by now becoming a common experience for our friends and peers. It was a simple little song, a vocal over a backing of piano and string quartet. The trouble was Jimmy and I were so distant with each other by then that we passed it between us and worked on it more as individuals than as a duo. When we came to record the vocal I discovered that B major, a key I love, was not great for him and he sounds a bit forced and uncomfortable on the album. With Stephen, we recorded another big cover version, this time 'Never Can Say Goodbye', for which I wrote some string arrangements and a horn section was hired and Jimmy's vocal was one of his best ever. But the bulk of the track was computer-generated and I have never felt more fraudulent than when miming to a keyboard break, which was invented, programmed and played, in so far as it was played, by Stephen's programmer.

The album recorded, we were booked at the Montreux Pop Festival. Unlike our first time, when Jimmy and I were on the brink of coming together, this time we were distant, strained with each other and doing our own thing. To mask the tension, I took along the man I had started seeing, handsome and younger than me, along for the ride. One day we went for a walk into the hills around Montreux. We kept walking and talking, getting higher and higher until we were suddenly above the snowline and on a crag, me carrying a copy of the *Observer*. The romance of the moment, the wildness of the scene, took us over, and we fell on each other, but the spell of the moment was broken when I looked up and saw a man a few feet above us looking down aghast from his hang-glider.

Two legendary stories derive from this visit to Montreux. One, much put about, was that one evening, in a smart restaurant, Jimmy, a vegetarian, demanded that the live lobsters kept in a tank for diners to peruse and select for their entrées were all bought by the record company, freed, and liberated into the wholly unsuitable waters of Lac Léman, where they almost immediately died. I think I may have made this story up and released it, like a liberated lobster itself, into the world. But I'm not sure. There was also a food fight in a fondue restaurant with the Beastie Boys, a food fight engineered by their PR, or our PR, or a tabloid journalist, but, again, I'm not sure if it actually happened or if it was something that was just put about. Bands are much mythologised by others and by themselves, and twenty-five years later it is sometimes difficult to distinguish between real events and fictions, memory being, as Mary Warnock has suggested, the same thing as the imagination. With bands the mythologising is particularly intense because we so readily project our fantasies on them, or not necessarily fantasies. I have always liked stories that reveal the vainglory and silliness of pop bands, stories about ridiculous demands on the rider, or terrible behaviour. One of my favourites came from the Red Wedge Tour when someone said they kept bumping into members of the Smiths' road crew clandestinely eating burgers in McDonald's because Morrissey, a strict vegetarian, did not permit his employees to consume flesh. This probably just meant that the tour catering was vegetarian but it was a good story and suited the myth of Morrissey's high-handedness and grand manner. I don't know if it was true or not, but I did see how quickly these stories got around.

We could behave grandly, too. Jimmy once made a stagehand take off his t-shirt because he didn't like the Confederate flag motif on it. Another time we were doing a gig at the Hammersmith Apollo, which was being filmed by the BBC. For some reason Jimmy got in a rage and at the camera rehearsal refused to be lit by a spotlight because 'it gets in ma eyes'. I could be grand, too, of course. I once insisted an executive fly from London to New York, where we were in the studio, to discuss a disagreement about a video or a record cover or something, but when he arrived we refused to see him and he had to go straight back to London with nothing but Duty Free for his pains. On another occasion, when things were really getting to me, we missed a plane because a guy from the record company was late getting to the airport and I lost my temper and shouted at him. He's now an artist himself and when I bumped into him a couple of years ago he brought it up. It still rankled.

Sometimes the artist or indeed the whole band is just in a bad mood, on an off-day, and snaps at someone or shouts or is unkind, like everyone else. But you are not like everyone else, you are a pop star and people have expectations of you which you may confirm or you may thwart and what may seem trivial to you may seem important to them. Fame, like beauty, elicits ambivalent feelings in people, of desire and resentment simultaneously. They want you but they do not like wanting you because they give you power and you may not use it as they would wish.

After Montreux we had to pick a single from *Red* for release. We chose 'Tomorrow', a densely layered track backing a song, typically, about domestic abuse (I wrote for it a big string arrangement which quoted, though no one ever noticed, *Don Giovanni*). Alas, the record did not do as well as we hoped, charting in the twenties, which was where nearly all our original songs charted. I think now that there they found their own level, but at the time I was really disappointed that 'Tomorrow' didn't do better. I had been disappointed, too, when our first release from the first album, 'You Are My World', got no higher than the twenties, so we re-released it with a new video to see if it would do higher, as it had in other territories, but again it stayed in the respectable, but not exciting, twenties.

The promotional round began again and the record company decided that the next release would be 'Never Can Say Goodbye', our second disco classic cover version. For this we again decided to spend some money on a video, which was shot in one long day in a nightclub in the East End of London. We chose it because it had a light-up floor, like in *Saturday Night Fever*. Dancers were hired and a choreographer and even I, in a Gaultier suit behind a keyboard, make a brief and rather regrettable excursion on to that floor, looking like a line-dancing archdeacon-cum-blitz kid.

In spite of that, it breezed through the twenties and once again we were back at the top of the charts in Britain and Europe. Hotels got grander, our venues got bigger, the distance between us and our fans grew greater, and the distance between us grew, too. Jo Pretzel, our brilliant but not always easy saxophonist, could sour in drink and by the end of a tour there were often tears before bedtime. I remember her once having a go at Sarah Jane as we sat on a plane at JFK and I lost my temper with her and she ran down the aisle chased by me until an air steward intervened and peace was restored. Annie, one of our fiddle players, turned up one day to get on the tour bus, with characteristic scattiness, had been unable to get a babysitter, so we ended up with her six-year-old son, Pete, on tour, which actually turned out to be great fun. Pete, by the way, grew up to become Pete Bennett, the man with Tourette syndrome who won *Big Brother*.

Jo was getting more and more detached by now and this reached a horrible climax in The Hague where we were booked in to do a big concert broadcast live on Dutch television, our only gig in Holland on that tour. It was attended by the great and good, whom we invited backstage after the gig. Jo was in a bad way that night and started playing wildly on stage, as a protest, or a subversive gesture, or to get in trouble, and when we came off Jimmy completely freaked in the dressing room. At that moment the dignitaries arrived outside so I went and explained that unfortunately Jimmy was not very well, while the sounds of screaming and crying and shattering glass raged behind the door. The dignitaries dispatched, I went back into a scene of devastation. Jo had fled, Jimmy was bawling and everyone looked on aghast. I said – typically – 'It'll all be all right' and June snapped, 'No, Richard. It won't.'

She was right. We were in trouble and the prospect of another big tour was too much for Annie and she bailed out. Sarah Jane had already left to pursue her own career, not without some unfortunate coverage in the tabloids – 'those bitchy Communards' – and Jo, we felt, was ready to take on new challenges in life and work. We put together a new line-up and returned to London to rehearse for our next tour, three months round the UK and Europe.

While we had been locked into promoting the album – travelling, making records and performing – our friends back home had been dealing with the deepening crisis of AIDS. Henry had died and then Derek, who I saw at his wake, reduced to flesh and bone. People were being diagnosed all the time now. Medication was getting better and the pneumonia that had killed Mark would not kill so readily, but as drug therapy improved so the virus developed, too, wrecking its way round people's bodies, and the dreadful lexicon of unheard-of diseases grew longer. The gap between diagnosis and dying was widening, but it was still, with one or two very rare exceptions, a disease that killed you within a couple of years.

The response to AIDS, however, had become more organised, medically and therapeutically. There had also been a shift in the public's response since Princess Diana, with no hesitation, had shaken the hand of an AIDS patient – an image that went round the world. The Terence Higgins Trust was now well-funded, professional and internationally recognised. All this engendered a sense of encouragement in the gay community but it was still a hostile world. Ronald Reagan did not even mention the word AIDS until 1987, six years after it was first reported. Nearly forty thousand Americans had been diagnosed by then, half of them dying, and as long as he was silent on the subject it could hardly be called a priority. Even in Kettering my mum, rattling a tin for the Terence Higgins Trust, was told that we should be thankful for AIDS for wiping out gays.

It all took its toll: the helplessness we felt when a friend got iller and iller, the dark shadow it left across our lives, the sense of isolation from others untouched by it, and our exclusion from a circle of compassion other illnesses were seen to 'deserve'. The gap between the darkness of the AIDS crisis and the brilliance of pop success opened up in us, too, the best of times the worst of times, vindication and condemnation, a fanfare of triumph and a passing bell, all simultaneous. Work, in the end, only masked the destabilising effect of this, or delayed its consequences.

We were in Switzerland, halfway into our long tour, when I began to feel unwell, exhausted after months of being on the road, and one morning I woke up with a pain in my lower back. I couldn't remember having hurt it, and it was dull rather than sharp, but it was persistent so the tour manager got in a doctor. He gave me a B12 vitamin shot and a packet of morphine suppositories but it didn't get any better, and by the end of the week I was limping and having to play the piano standing up. I also began to feel wretched, not just in pain, but low in spirits. Next I became aware of a burning pain on my thigh, a pain that felt like it was on the surface, though I could not see anything. Then one morning I could. Blisters appeared and someone said, shingles. Shingles sounds faintly comic, like dropsy or gout, but it is anything but funny. I felt dreadful, and also full of dread, because shingles is an indicator of HIV infection.

It sounds ridiculous now, but it had not occurred to me that I could be HIV positive. I knew I was in a high-risk group. I knew I had been exposed to others who were infected, but I did not think it would touch me. Now I had to face the possibility that it had. I was too ill to continue on tour so it was arranged that I should return to London when the band was next on a couple of rest days, give a session player a day's crash course in the set and send him out to Switzerland to pick up the next leg of the tour until I was well enough to return.

On the day I left the tour I felt very sorry for myself and was so unwell that at the airport I had to be driven around on the back of one of those little carts. Sitting alongside me was another passenger to London, Sir Keith Joseph. He was one of the architects of Thatcherism and ranked with Enoch Powell in infamy as far as I was concerned and we sat in silence as we drove with a faint whining sound to the gate.

In London it was arranged for me to go and see a doctor much used by touring bands for his – how to put this? – sympathetic attitude and broad diagnostic approach towards those who worked in the music industry. I sat miserably in his consulting rooms while he examined me and diagnosed what I expected, shingles. He also, as I expected, suggested a test for HIV and took my blood. I can still see the dark red phial he took, and its unanswered question.

At home, as I opened the front door one of the neighbours appeared and asked me in for a cup of tea and I was grateful for the offer of company, the company of someone I didn't really know. We sat and made small talk companionably and then the doorbell rang and we were joined by a jolly man who said, halfway through his cup of tea, that he'd had a client call in to see him who had told him – and here he adopted a camp voice – 'I'm gaaaay, and I've got AAIIDS.' He laughed and laughed about it and I said I had to go.

All I wanted to do was go to bed, but the session player filling in for me on tour was waiting for a crash course on our set. I took my Zovirax and tried to be patient and spent two days revealing the mysteries of the key changes in 'Don't Leave Me This Way'. I then slept until I was ready to rejoin the band in Switzerland. I was still feeling wretched but everyone was in mid-tour mode and my state of health, amazingly, was not at the top of the agenda. I limped around the stage and stood half-heartedly at the keyboard and I think my morose mood irritated Jimmy because one night we had an argument and in the thick of it I said, 'I'm ill, I've just discovered I'm HIV positive – get off my back.' Jimmy was taken aback. 'I'm sorry, doll,' he said, and I discovered that this terrible news brought benefits, sympathy where there had been none, status of a peculiar kind, a part in the story.

And then I got a message to call the doctor. 'Good news,' he said, 'I have your test results. They came back negative.' And that is how I became the only person ever to be disappointed to hear he was not HIV positive.

16. A Song at Twilight

I am not the only person to have pretended to be HIV positive. The disease drew all sorts of people to its darkness, some because they wanted to be part of the excitement, some because it worked to their advantage, some because they got off on death. I wasn't in that last group. I came across one man who was a volunteer death organiser, who made himself indispensable to the dying and in this role rather colonised the last days of someone I knew, acting as a self-appointed gatekeeper. I was not permitted to visit him *in extremis*, but at his funeral this man, a stranger to me, told me with obvious enjoyment how much I had meant to the departed.

It did work to my advantage in the sense that I was treated more considerately than I had been and it did mean I now had a leading role in the drama. I liked this so much, and so vehemently dreaded having to admit the truth, that I told no one I was in fact negative. On the contrary, word got out and I sort of found myself on a roll, enjoying it so much I told even more people, including my oldest friend, Matthew, and my closest buddies, Kevin and Hugo. It did not occur to me that this was a terrible thing to do. It did not occur to me that people might be distressed by the prospect of my death, apart from in the highly dramatised funeral service I ran in my head.

I went back to work and we continued our progress round the parts of the world that were pleased to see us. Sometimes they were not so pleased to see us. In Dijon one night, on the way to a restaurant, half the band, including Jimmy, were attacked by a group of skinheads who called them faggots and whores until June and Jimmy managed to beat them off. Another time, back home in London,

someone phoned me to say they'd heard on the radio that Jimmy
was in hospital having been attacked by a queer-basher. I went to
see him and arrived at the same time as a bunch of flowers from
Neil and Glenys Kinnock was being delivered, which, he grumbled,
he thought he'd send back because of the Labour Party's unequal
response to Clause 28.

Jimmy and I may have been in bad shape but the Communards had
never been in better. The second album sold very well, at home and
abroad, and the tours got bigger and more industrial as we moved up
the league. Now, instead of buses and scheduled airlines, we would
fly out to gigs in a private plane, actually an economy when you fac-
tored in the swelling retinue we took on tour, of laundry operatives
and under-caterers and Shiatsu masters. We played the Glastonbury
Festival, helicoptered in from our posh hotel in Bath, looking down
on the thousands squelching in mud, before taking to the stage. All
successful bands have to get used to living in the widening distance
between what you say you are about and what you actually become,
but for us this was particularly acute because we had said so much
about what we were about. We were offered a *Top of the Pops* during
a strike by BBC technicians and had to decide whether to cross the
picket line to promote the single or not to cross the picket line and
stall its rise. We crossed the picket line, in a limousine with darkened
windows, pretending not to notice the placards and shouting.

And it is easy to lose sight of your commitments in the sheer pressure of keeping up with the demands that fall upon you. Lorna had
known John McCarthy before he was kidnapped by Lebanese militia
so we were happy to agree to play a benefit for the Friends of John
McCarthy at the Camden Palace in London. We flew in from New
York to be there and were driven straight from the airport to the
venue. John, now a colleague and friend, worked then for ITN, so
there was a TV crew and Trevor McDonald just inside the entrance.
We were taken straight to him, sat down, mic'd up and interviewed.
Unfortunately we were in such a rush that for a moment I couldn't
remember what the gig was for and just tried to give open answers
to his questions – 'We think the government should do more'; 'We

hope for a quick resolution to this problem' – until someone with a Free John McCarthy t-shirt walked past.

Then we were off on tour again, including a six-night residency at l'Olympia in Paris and a tour of Spain where we were joined by Álvaro and the divine Jesús, with whom I was so smitten I used to dedicate songs to him with meaningful looks from the keyboard. We were so popular in Spain at this time that we were once chased through the streets of Zaragoza by children and had to hide in the cathedral for sanctuary. We played the Fallas in Valencia, the noisiest and most spectacular festival in the continental calendar, which culminates with an enormous concert in the main square followed by the burning of giant effigies. We went to Germany where I got into a scrape with a man who managed to get past security and into the dressing room after the show and then back to our hotel. He followed me into a lift to make his intentions plain and I ended up, hours later, going back to his flat in a nondescript block on the outskirts of whichever city it was. There, as romance unfolded, I noticed he had a scar on his arm. 'How did you get that?' I asked, and he said, 'He gave it to me', and a figure appeared out of a dark corner. I gathered as many of my clothes as I could and got out of there. It was dawn, I had no idea where I was, there were no shops or taxi ranks, so I flagged down a night bus and then realised I could not remember where I was staying. The driver very kindly took me on a tour of the hotels in the city centre until we found mine and I arrived in the lobby just as everyone was checking out.

I needed to spend some money. Tax arrangements – how unTrotskyist – made it sensible for me to buy a house, but being on tour made it difficult for me to go house hunting so someone did it for me. Faxes arrived, in Los Angeles and Munich and Dundee, and I made a little pile of those I liked. One, not far from me in Kilburn, was a big Edwardian house in red brick overlooking Queen's Park, but it seemed extravagant at £200,000. Today it would fetch about £4 million. Eventually I saw a house in Islington that seemed all right, end-of-terrace, two bedrooms, study, dining room, sitting room and kitchen, with a garage and a yard and roof terrace. It was right next door to the entrance to the GPO sorting office off Upper Street and the Georgian windows had been replaced with ugly metal-framed tilting windows, but I liked Islington, and the price was under £200,000, so I bought it. It was done up by a friend, Sue Winter, rather an eccentric whose own flat in south London looked like Sir John Soane had been let loose on a Peabody Estate. Sue did not so much do it up as create a theatrical experience, each room in a different colour, with extravagant painted effects, and tiles and tie-dyed fabrics and a glazed front installed on the original unrestored fireplace in the sitting room on the first floor. Work dragged on and went over budget and I was mostly away but eventually I moved in and dreamed that night that the house was built on sand and it swayed and tipped beneath me and fell into ruins. More prophecy than dream.

I saw some letters a while ago that I sent to Russell in Glasgow while I was on tour, written on ever-more luxurious notepaper from ever-grander hotels, with Edwardian names in copperplate script, from Paris and Rome and Hamburg and New York. I wonder now how it felt to receive them, sitting in a flat he could barely afford as a cold, wet wind blew up the Clyde. It did not occur to me, with characteristic self-absorption, that my success might not be as delightful for my friends as it was for me. One day Matthew called and said, a bit thickly, that he needed to see me and could he come over. I said of course and thought, in a reflex way, that he was about to tell me that he'd realised he was in love with me, and had been for years, and that it was time for us finally to fulfil each other's deepest desires and exalted destiny. In fact he had come to tell me that I had grown so insufferable in my success that he had started to hate me and needed to get that off his chest.

Jimmy and I were getting on particularly badly. His stubbornness and contrariness, as I saw it, made me behave more and more manipulatively. If I thought he would say no to something because I wanted to do it, I would pretend I didn't want to do it so he would say yes. It sort of worked, but at a cost, the erosion of a friendship without which nothing would work. My impatience with him turned me into someone I would rather not have been. One day a car turned up to take me to the airport, having already stopped to pick up Jimmy and Sally en route, but when I got in only Sally was there. She told me that Jimmy had heard that our friend Kevin Murphy had died and he was too upset to come. I blew my top again and cursed him, concerned only with the interruption to our schedule. Sally, very gently, wondered if I might be a little more sympathetic, but I could not be more sympathetic and said, 'He doesn't care about Kevin Murphy, he's just being a little shit', a remark which drew a look from the driver, who you would think had picked up enough pop stars to be unmoved by their outbursts.

AIDS' catastrophic progress had been unrelenting, and hospital visiting and news of a death had become daily realities. We continued to support the London Lighthouse and to agitate for better understanding and treatment for those with HIV, but the effect of being at the heart of an epidemic of this scale and dreadfulness took its toll. It demanded so absolute a commitment that all other commitments began to pall, and I found my patience for the political process, and my confidence in it, diminished. AIDS was not a theoretical problem and the need to withstand it was literally a matter of life and death for many. For me, trapped by the myth of my own HIV status, there was also the persistent shame of being falsely credited with a combatant's honour, a shame that was greatly intensified when I discovered one day, sitting with Kevin and Hugo in the Bell, that Hugo had been diagnosed HIV positive. Again, this should hardly have been a surprise, but it came as a shock because it is unremittingly difficult to accept that something so terrible could befall someone so dear. With the realisation that it could, and had, to Hugo, I felt for the first time the true awfulness of having lied about it.

But work, the great palliative, intervened and the appetite for our music, recorded and live, meant we were either on tour or away promoting records almost constantly. Like a couple trapped in a dying marriage, Jimmy and I managed this by meeting as little as possible. He kept to his circle and I to mine, although there were plenty of people in both, including Hugo, who had become such good friends with Jimmy that they were flatmates; not entirely easy for me. Song-writing had been abandoned and it was clear to me, and I am sure to Jimmy, that we were end-stage. There was no joy, or little joy, in the music making by now, and in YouTube videos of us playing live at this time the songs have become almost ridiculously fast, not because we wished to display our virtuosity but because we were bored of them and wanted to get to the end quicker.

In the absence of enjoyment I found I took pleasure at least in money. By now the large royalties were arriving, the record company having finally extracted all they could, and I remember paying in six-figure cheques at the bank and getting stared at by cashiers. I liked getting richer. It was an unarguable plus in an ambiguous world, and I found I could spend hours thinking about my riches. Indeed, I found a tour itinerary the other day from 1987, and the back of one of the pages was covered with detailed calculations, which I realised were me working out just how rich I was. I once or twice shared this news of my good fortune with others until one day Lorna told me that the rest of the band would appreciate it if I didn't go on about how much I was earning. I flashed my Gold Card around in the vain belief that it would inspire the admiration of others, but I never really understood money. I saw it not as a means to realise a prosperous and secure future but as an end to demonstrate my prestigious place in the world, an attitude so at odds with our manifesto commitments that it was no wonder the comrades looked askance. We were both silly with our wealth. Stuck at an airport once, waiting for a delayed flight, Jimmy went mad and bought a pile of kit from the hi-fi shop. When he discovered that he would have to pay duty to bring it into the UK, he couldn't be bothered and left it at the airport. I liked to be Father Christmas and rather assaulted people with unasked for largesse, so enraptured by my own munificence I did not think that these gifts might produce uncomfortable obligations. But money, on the whole, is wasted on the young. Good fortune is really only for the over-forties; in your twenties it overwhelms you, puts you at an awkward angle to your peers, and spoils you for a future in which you will earn less, not more.

Our real good fortune was to have Lorna for a manager, who tricked us, really, into starting pension schemes. She put documents in front of us, which we signed without looking, that put a large chunk of money away. Such a chunk, invested in your twenties, produces in your fifties the warm assurance of a viable retirement, a prospect so remote at the time neither of us would have given it the scantest consideration. Now, ten years from my annuity, I give grateful thanks for her foresight and guile. Pop bands, Clive James observed, make either more than you think or less than you think. We were in the less than you think category, but it was sufficient to buy a house and a pension scheme, which, thirty years on, puts me in a very small and very grateful minority.

We released two more singles from *Red*. First, 'There's More To Love Than Boy Meets Girl', our disco mariachi anthem in praise of non-conventional relationships, and then 'For A Friend', our lament for Mark, the video for which gave a pretty accurate representation of reality. Jimmy and I talk in a café as the saxophone wails. To me it looks like the sort of conversation people have at the end of something, a marriage or a partnership, and that's what it was, for by now we were trying to work out how to end things.

I had strong views on how we shouldn't do this. I didn't want to announce a split, with the opportunities for media mischief and recrimination that might allow. I didn't want to then announce solo projects so the record company could keep deducting costs from royalties yet to arrive. I didn't want to pursue solo projects, because I didn't want to be in a band any more. I had never wanted to be in a band – it had just been an opportunity too good to miss and, while I regretted that the moment in the sun was to pass, I had never thought it would have, or should have, been more than a moment. In the end we agreed we would announce that we were stopping for a while, taking some time out, when the album and the tour were done.

The two singles rose no higher than the twenties and the mammoth tour – which felt like it would never end – drew to its close. The distance between us had now widened to the point where I spent more time with the crew than the band, not because I didn't want to be with the band, but because that's where Jimmy wanted to be. I joined the crew in endless, addictive hands of nine-card brag, an accumulating pot that rose to more than £5,000, the last rounds so exciting I was coming off stage and going straight into the game, which continued whenever we had a few spare minutes on the bus, backstage, in a hotel bar. In the end John, the band bus driver, won it, a triumph far more memorable than anything on stage.

Our last gig in Britain was in Brighton, and got off to a shaky start when Jimmy went AWOL between sound check and show time. I tried to enlist some help from the entourage to find him, but they all refused and we were just mustering a search party from the crew when he turned up. The gig passed in a haze, though the demob-happy fun and games we played on the crew and the crew played on the band remain vivid. With regret, I chose to travel back to London on the train with our agent, rather than in the band bus with everyone else, not because I wanted to be arsey, but because I found endings unbearable and did anything to avoid them.

It wasn't actually an ending. We played one more gig, in Barcelona, and that was that: the lights faded, the crowds went home, we sold our last pair of Communards boxer shorts and my career in pop music was over.

17. Not Raving but Drowning

I was at the end of my twenties, I had more money than I could count, the fine-grained Filofax, for the first time since 1984, was empty; but I was not entirely idle. I started reviewing films for a late-night programme on London Weekend Television, where I showed my mettle by interviewing Kiefer Sutherland and not asking him a single question about his father. I made three good friends there: Emma Freud, whose interviews with celebrities, conducted in bed, would have been grist to her great-grandfather's mill; Rowland Rivron, the comedian and drummer, who once fell off my piano attempting an act of congress with a famous starlet; and one of the production assistants, Rosie Thornton, who came from Kettering and was eccentric even by the standards of Kettering. She and I were to become close friends and housemates.

But what really diverted my attention in these days of fading glory was ecstasy. I had encountered it before, in New York, but during the summer of 1990 it became a staple. It was the second Summer of Love, and all over London, especially on the gay scene, little white and yellow pills were suddenly available in clubs. I went out one night with some friends and we bought some and took some and it was like an explosion of delight going off in our heads, and we all ended up entwined, chastely, on the floor stroking each other's faces and pledging undying love until morning gilt the skies.

The next year of my life was taken over by E. I had the opportunity – money and leisure and Access All Areas; and I had the motive – yet in spite of these privileges I was wretchedly unhappy, my self-pity boundless, the dreadful onward march of AIDS pitiless, but these little white and yellow pills could dispel troubles like dawn dispels the night.

E very quickly generated its own subculture, because it made being with other people such a fantastically enjoyable experience. Pumping serotonin into your system would have made the trenches of Passchendaele an enjoyable experience, but we had clubs and the arrival of the drug precipitated a whole new scene, peopled by what *Time Out* described as a 'Day-Glo fun-loving crowd'. I discovered Troll, a club that happened on a Saturday night in the Soundshaft in Charing Cross, a smaller sibling of Heaven, to which it was joined, but accessed differently, down an alleyway behind the station, which looked like something from Dickens. There was nothing Dickensian about the club itself, a pleasure dome, throbbing with the beat of Acid House, jumping with creatures of the night dressed as fantastically as King Lear in his mad flowers.

In its short life Troll became famous, the hottest club in London. Those of us who were regulars were a tight little gang, but every week, as its reputation grew, celebrities would loom out of its unearthly black light; Imran Khan, Rupert Everett, and once an unlikely appearance from the man who played René in *'Allo 'Allo*.

Less widely known, but no less celebrated, were its inner circle, who had earned their places by extraordinary devotion to duty, which might mean dancing all night on a rostrum with fluorescent fans in tie-dye pyjamas, or organising post-Troll parties, when to the tune 'Promised Land' by Joe Smooth we would wander out into the dawn to find double-decker buses waiting which drove us to Margate or Alton Towers, or once to a clearing in the New Forest where we built a fire in dawn's early light and were then shooed away by forest rangers who threatened to call the police. I remember once sitting on the top deck of one of these buses talking gushingly to people as the E surged, subsided and surged again, offering to buy them a car, or educate their children at Eton, then coming downstairs to find someone on a back seat carefully injecting himself with amphetamine.

Troll was also a gateway to raves, then taking off in places like

Hackney Marshes or the semi-derelict industrial stretches of south-east London. Long after dawn, still crackling with pharmaceuticals, we would go back to someone's house, or sometimes to my house, and play music for as long as the drugs kept us, and everyone else, awake. The drugs were potent and in their euphoria prudence withered, so it was open house, and over the year I must have given away my pop memorabilia and now I have only one gold disc to hang on my wall.

Another characteristic of this culture was its indifference to sexual orientation. Gay and straight came together, a model for a post-sexuality obsessed culture, or just a less inhibited evening out than usual, but also a field of opportunity for a gay man looking for a straight man and a straight man looking for a gay man. I remember disappearing with a Cockney builder into the remoter parts of Chislehurst caves at a rave, not quite believing what was happening; but we were followed by a panicky caretaker who caught us in the beam of his torch before that particular fantasy became a reality.

One particular fantasy, however, was to give me a lot more regret than a missed opportunity in a cave. I met a man called Billy.

He was as different from me as you could get. Straight, working-class, from a North London Irish background, where he, like his father, had learned to box. He had a boxer's lightness and fitness, but played with what looked to me like effortless masculinity by a sort of straight version of camping it up. He had long and lustrous brown hair, which he was vain about, and cared for diligently because after he got fed up with working as a scaffolder he retrained as a hairdresser in West End salons. There he got used to the company of gay men, which he took to with enormous relish, before starting his own salon in the East End while attempting to settle down to family life. He had married at seventeen because he 'wanted to see what it was like to have a ride in a Rolls-Royce'. There was no settling down, of course, and before long he was spending more time in clubs than at home. I had noticed him around the place and we had spoken a few times, but on one of those bus trips we talked and talked and by the end of it became friends. He was good fun, he stayed the course

– last to bed like me – and he became part of the gang that would end up at my house in Islington, crashed out on the roof terrace, from which we would look down on people in real life walking along the street: neighbours, friends, my MP Chris Smith, once, surreally, Esther Rantzen.

I have no idea how we managed it, but that summer a trip to Ibiza was arranged. We rented two villas on a hill not far from Ibiza town and the nightclubs, which were to Acid House what Mecca is to Islam. Among those left behind was Billy; but the lure of a trip to Ibiza was irresistible and funds were obtained, I don't know how, and one afternoon while sunbathing by the pool I heard my name. There he was, coming up the hill, with another of our number who managed to blag his way onto a flight without a passport by pretend-ing his mother was dying in hospital on the island and was hanging on for him.

In our villas we formed a mixed group in the flat social structure of ecstasy, drawn from worlds which would not normally overlap, mysterious people who attached themselves without seeming to know anyone, and the Troll inner circle, of which I was now a part, a pop star on the slide, and generous to a fault especially in the sympathy-enlarging pulses of MDMA. And there was Billy. In the Ibiza sun his hair went a bit golden, his upper body browned, and glistened with the sun-tan lotion I was quick to offer to apply as my curiosity in him began to turn into something else. It was not just that he was beautiful, it was not just that he was a straight working-class East Ender – hardly an original focus for a middle-class gay man's desire – he was also a person of complexity, not entirely at home in his persona and angled to the world differently from the people around us, an angledness which I found answered something in me. He was also, like Jimmy Somerville, extraordinarily sexually charged, helplessly in thrall to his desires, which were not directed, I knew, even at the vastest tangent, towards me. But I think he was fascinated by me too, a public school gay pop star so different from him, so interested in him, and I suppose we started having a bro-mance before bromances were invented. And he was great company too, rude and funny and a bit dangerous, and after the pressures of success, and AIDS' grim progress, I was ready for stupid fun, and we would play like boys, making up our own jokes, talking in a private language, which must have been irritating for everyone else. Billy and I had a thing about singing everything in Cockney style, like Chas and Dave, and we used to belt out 'Nessun dorma', theme tune for the Italia 90 football tournament, poolside at dawn. 'Ha-Nay-sssun dAW-mAAAAH, Ha- Nay-sssun dAW-mAAAAH! A travel rep was soon sent round because of complaints received from neighbours half a mile away. I let her in and she stepped lightly past the roaches and the fag papers and the tobacco and the unfolded sachets scattered round the living room and if she noticed, she didn't say anything, but standing on the terrace she did say something. 'One of you an artist?' A mural had appeared on the sparkling white wall beside the swimming pool, a psychedelic fantasy, which coiled and unfurled in a strange narrative which made me think of Thomas de Quincey. 'It's only crayons,' I said, as she made a note on her clipboard.

Crayons and speed, the foundation drug in our drug-taking. You would think it would be ecstasy, the defining drug, but ecstasy, along with acid and everything else, was laid on a foundation of amphetamine, heightening and intensifying and lengthening everything, enabling us to stay awake for two or three days. Fatigue hallucinations followed, much more dramatic than acid hallucinations for me, and in one of our party, an amateur muralist, it produced an insatiable desire to draw. He once did some lovely arabesques in Tippex on a glass vase I bought in Venice, and I quite often found an unauthorized painting on a wall, or a patchwork of motley stitched on to a favourite coat.

Through music business connections I managed to get us passes to all the nightclubs on the island. Amnesia was our favourite, and there, after a preamble through the bars, we danced and fooled around in our kit, printed t-shirts, baggy shorts, and the most peculiar fad of the summer, undone trainers with the tongues hanging out. We did not so much arrive at a club, in our clownish footwear, as take it over, twenty of us *en bloc*, dancing with a certain house style

which marked us off from the rest; energetic, slightly comic, and full
of jerky movement, unlike the more sinuous and rhythmic style of
the Latins, barmy army to their Brazil. The staff kept trying to stop
us dancing in the water feature and bothering strangers, but we were
far beyond that, again caught up in the drugs and our exclusive enjoyment of each other.

One of our gang was approached in a very friendly way by a
famous pop star in Amnesia one night and invited back to his villa,
but the mere thought of having to go through the subtleties of disclosure that this would entail had him hooting with laughter – and
all of us hooting with laughter because he immediately reported this
to us, humiliating the famous pop star. No one got a look in apart
from the anonymous, who seemed to attach themselves without any
sense of pull or friction. One guy, I think he was Portuguese, stayed
with us for the whole summer without saying a single word, as far
as I know. Billy asked him who he was after a day or two but he just
refused to speak and he stayed. I took a photograph of him standing
by the pool in swimming shorts, the very picture of male beauty, but
he held out his hand towards the camera to obscure his face as if he
didn't want to be identified.

After the clubs closed, after dawn, we would go to a café in the
town and order coffee without drinking it and breakfast without
eating it. Then we would go exploring. At some point we were
banned by the car rental company. We hired, and crashed, and re-
hired, and crashed, their jeeps and their mopeds, and I think I may
have bought a speedboat from someone. Did I buy a speedboat? I
remember being in one and trying to go very fast, and I remember
asking to rent a plane and a pilot at the airport, but not being allowed to because Billy was not wearing a shirt and the bloke at the
counter, who obviously hated us, would not countenance this breach
of etiquette. I don't think the plane can have happened, and if I did
buy a speedboat I have no idea where it is now.

I do remember going into town and buying an Armand Basi
t-shirt because it looked nice. In a fit of generosity I then bought an
Armand Basi t-shirt for every one else and we paraded around the

pool wearing them, but they only really looked nice on the beautiful boys and I looked like von Aschenbach on the Lido leaking hair dye and staring at them with desperate generosity.

After our fortnight we went home, psychedelic gypsies on a rampage, stumbling through the airport, passing out on the plane, and playing music on huge beat boxes on the Gatwick Express back into London, annoying everyone else, but that's ecstasy for you.

There were people on the edge of our world who spun out sometimes and were lost and disappeared. One had a serious speed habit and would disappear from time to time to sort himself out. One day, back at mine after a long weekend, I came down to find him sobbing in the kitchen trying to find somewhere to inject himself. Half his toes had been amputated. Another time we were sitting on my roof terrace after a marathon weekend, when a girl I knew a little suddenly burst into tears and wept and wept as we looked on caught up in the surges of ecstasy. Someone tried to comfort her and clean her up but instead of passing her a bar of soap to wash her face passed her a bar of Vanish stain remover instead.

I had odd moments when I thought 'this will be me'. Not toeless, but hopeless, not raving, but drowning. Those anxieties crept up on us sometimes, as they had crept up on the toeless man, and in the gaps between ecstasy binges, when our biochemistry returned to something like normal, terrors would come in the night, terrible dreams, or half waking up to find you could not breathe for a moment before your body systems restarted themselves. The classic solution to this problem is to take more drugs, but the more you took the more you had to take to achieve the same high, and because I had the means and the leisure to take as much as I liked, I added quality as well as quantity, taking all sorts of pills and powders and some sort of industrial solvent which you squirted onto a J cloth and held over your mouth and nose, like a Victorian seducer subduing his prey . . .

The odd offers of work came in but I was really too busy falling apart to make much of them. One day Malcolm McLaren phoned, having read a piece I had written about opera, and wondered if I might like to do something with him? Malcolm McLaren, manager of the Sex Pistols, a hero of mine. But I had nothing to give and nothing came of it. Someone called on behalf of Sir Michael Tippett. He was writing an opera for Glyndebourne: would I be interested in participating? I was so flattered to be asked I made some sort of coherent reply, but as the conversation progressed it became evident that the caller thought I was Jimmy Somerville, whose voice and presence the great composer was after, and not, inexplicably, my mediocre keyboard skills and the call ended in embarrassment for both of us. And I got a call from the playwright Noel Greig, one of the leading lights of the Gay Sweatshop theatre company, who suggested collaborating on an oratorio about gay identity and gay protest. This struck a chord and I agreed, setting and scoring a piece called 'Paradise Now and Then', although I was in such bad shape that I was slow delivering and had to rush pages of still wet manuscript to the rehearsals.

It turned out that this manuscript saved my life. I had become friends with a man called Dan Wood, who I had seen out and about in clubs and talked to a few times. He lived in a tiny flat in Old Compton Street, the gayest street in Britain, in a block where all the other tenants seemed to be gay, too. One of his friends and neighbours was a banker, Antonio, and through Dan I was invited to his birthday party one summer night on a boat on the Thames. A couple of days before the party I came in to find my water tank overflowing, water cascading through the house from the bathroom on the top floor to my piano on the ground floor, on which the fresh score for the Gay Sweatshop piece was strewn. It was ruined and I was on a deadline, so I cancelled with Dan and arranged to go to my parents for the weekend to write it all out again without interruptions.

My grandmother came to Sunday lunch and I told her about the water tank and the party I'd had to miss and she said I must be glad that it hadn't been on the pleasure boat that had sunk on the Thames during the night, killing so many young people. I don't know why, but it didn't occur to me that of course it was the same boat, the *Marchioness*, and it was only later when I was watching the news and saw a friend, in shock and a blanket, that I realised it was Antonio's party. I called Dan at once but the phone was engaged but I kept trying and eventually he answered. He was in shock and ill from having swallowed so much Thames water, and did not know who was dead and who was alive, but told me, over and over again, that he had lost his favourite pair of trainers, and that the police had amazingly detailed descriptions of the missing because so many people worked in fashion and knew exactly what people were wearing.

I came back to London and went to see Dan the next day, taking a pair of trainers to replace those he had lost, but got the brand slightly wrong and he could not disguise his disappointment. He was still a bit hysterical, especially after his father, a Church of England bishop, had come to see him from the House of Lords, arriving in a purple shirt and pectoral cross, an unintended gift to the photographers gathered ghoulishly there in a street of Soho sex shops. I arranged to take Dan out to dinner a few days later at the new restaurant I knew he wanted to visit in the Festival Hall and found him trembling at the foot of the Hungerford Bridge, which I had thoughtlessly obliged him to cross.

A fortnight of funerals followed, once the coroner had released the bodies, or the ones they found first. One of the regulars at Troll had also died on the *Marchioness* and that cast a shadow across the club that we loved precisely because it offered, paradoxically in black light, a shadow-free night out. So we took more drugs, and as our consumption rose friends who could not, or would not, keep up fell away, and we moved into a different circle, graduating, as it were, from civilian to military use. Billy too had graduated, so he and I were in a more or less permanent orbit now, round drugs and the club and staying up all night.

Our weekends began on Thursdays and continued until Tuesdays, a druggy blur of nightclubs and then my house, where people slept and danced and took stuff, curtains drawn against the dawn, or was it dusk? One day Lorna, my old manager, and her flatmate Jonathan were in the neighbourhood and came to call. I let them in. The house was greyish yellow with cigarette smoke, someone had passed out on the kitchen floor, I was woozy, but lucid enough to notice their alarm at the sight of me.

Billy and I were by now inseparable, but in the narrowing gyre of our relationship, things began to change. The asymmetry became daily more acute and tugged at the balance of our friendship, and there were moments when we were suddenly not so friendly. One night I confessed my passionate love for him, and made something unspoken explicit, and he made a joke about it and made me laugh, but he began to move away from me. I would pursue him nonetheless, on a confessional roll, and bleat of my unhappiness and rail at my fate.

We cannot bear too much reality and when the reality is particularly unflattering we do anything not to have to look at it. But on my way down I found I began to miss Russell, terribly at times, and he would emerge in my thoughts and even in my dreams, and I longed to be out of this spinning catastrophe and back in his flat on the London Road, watching *Brookside* in bed amid the faintly resinous odour of customised Flash. But I had walked away from that, and there was no going back, and he was in Glasgow with a new partner and a drawer full of attachments to vacuum Venetian blinds and dog baskets and architraves.

Then, one day, I was in Soho and someone called my name. It was a friend of Russell's from Glasgow. He said how sorry he was to hear that Russell was ill. I didn't know, so I wrote to him, but he didn't reply. When he died, the new partner, Robbie, who had nursed him and been by his side to the end, called and I went up to Glasgow for the funeral, his coffin carried by friends who did not have much to lift by the time the virus had finished with him. Afterwards we went to a wake in the city and I saw Martin Henry, with whom we had stayed when we were in Edinburgh, and he and I talked properly and exchanged numbers. A little while later Robbie got in touch to say he had a pile of my letters and asked if I wanted them back. I don't know why, but I said no, they were Russell's, and now his, and he should do with them what he thought fit.

Perhaps I was trying then, in retrospect, to be more a part of Russell's life than I had actually chosen to be when I had the chance. What I had chosen was Billy, with whom I had no chance, although in my derangement I sustained the hope that somewhere, deep deep down, his unacknowledged desire for me would rise and flower. One night, after days of drug taking and dancing and fooling, we got back to Moon Street and ended up chastely sharing a bed. I lay in his arms, which I made sure were around me as he slept so deeply it would have registered on the Glasgow Coma Scale.

18. Teeth

Another moment of clarity. I remember catching sight of myself reflected in the window of a tube train. I was wearing a long-sleeved t-shirt, black with dirt, and a pair of baggy shorts and trainers that looked like the shoes Boris Karloff wore in *Frankenstein*. I had what looked like blood coming out of my nose and I stank. It was a Monday morning, early, and I had gone out on Friday and I had no idea what had happened or how I had got there or who I'd been with, and I knew that I had to stop or I would die.

The first sign of the resolve to change was fixing my teeth. Ever since I had broken them on Jason Everard's bedpost I had tried to shield them from public view, so assiduously that it fed my sense of myself as faintly tragic, for I never smiled and the world reacted to me as the song suggests with a proportionate lack of warmth. Not only were they broken they were crowded, my jaw too narrow to accommodate them neatly, and so they grew this way and that. Andy Lipman, a man who did not shirk telling uncomfortable truths, once said to me when we were alone, 'Get your teeth fixed', seeing correctly in this small change a large difference. Now I was rich enough to do something about it and I went to see a celebrity dentist, Vik Advani, at his Kensington practice. He looked at my teeth and declared them, with great relish, spectacularly bad, so bad that he would like to include them in his folder of before-and-after shots when the work was done. He advised eight crowns, crafted from platinum and porcelain, the finest money could buy, and created by the most skilled crown-maker in London. The cost reflected this, a grand a crown, or eight thousand pounds for the smile I had never had. I agreed and spent twenty hours, on and off, in Vik's chair, a delightful place to be even for someone with a fear of the dentist, because he was also a sculptor and his studio and his surgery were pretty much the same place. And he was related to the composer Kaikhosru Shapurji Sorabji, who came, in spite of the name, from Chingford and had died a year or so earlier. Sorabji had composed one of the longest and most difficult pieces for piano in the repertoire, the *Opus Clavicembalisticum*, four hours or so of densely complex piano which I would never have listened to in its entirety had Vik not played it as he worked.

He first filed down my offending original teeth to pegs and fitted me with temporary crowns while the genius crown-maker went about his work. I liked the temporaries so much I almost told him to forget the others and leave them in, but Vik was a perfectionist, working like Fabergé on an egg, and so diligent in my care that injections were given at body temperature rather than cold from the fridge.

The work was done, so beautifully it felt like there should be an announcement in the newspaper and private view, and I did indeed become the star of Vik's before-and-after picture folder. Not long after the new teeth were installed I received a letter regretting to inform me that Vik had died of AIDS-related complications, and offering a free HIV test.

I got rid of my specs and tried contact lenses, but they did not work well with the astigmatism in my right eye, and friends would walk past in the street without recognising me. And I started going to the gym, with Billy at first, who I nagged to give up smoking and get fit, and I guess he must have felt under obligation, because he did, until I caught him one night having a fag. He tried to hide when he saw it was me and I felt a pang of betrayal. I felt another when one morning a friend came to pick up Billy to go to the gym. It was more than a pang. I felt shocked, incredulous that Billy could make gym arrangements that did not include me. He saw my distress and it made him angry and I saw where the boundaries lay and how far I had overstepped them.

You might think eight grand's worth of new teeth, the amputee's tearful struggle to find a vein, and my own blood-stained reflection underground, would be enough for me to Just Say No, but it wasn't. I remember an all-nighter at which I was so far gone I didn't notice that the blender I was using to make shakes was giving me electric shocks. By now I had an arrangement with a dealer who I could pay by cheque for enough gear to keep me and my circle drugged for days on end, but another disappointment was to discover that the more I took the more indistinguishable their effects. Ecstasy no longer produced in me the intense feelings of euphoria, so I tried to make up the deficit with everything else, speed, acid, cocaine, some new stuff that had come in from New York, a clear liquid that one of the more hard-core clubbers gave me, which was said to make you feel like you were in purgatory; but it was all the same, producing a sensation which I remember as a sort of painless migraine. The ecstasy was not always reliable; often it was cut with heroin, which made me nauseous. In the grip of speed and heroin-adulterated ecstasy I would talk incessantly to anyone who would listen – gay skinheads who were mysterious regulars at Troll, fierce black drug-dealers (one of whom stole my Chevignon leather jacket), a repairman who had just called to fix the TV, breaking off only to be sick in a bin and then carrying on where I'd left off. In spite of this, there were people who liked me, some who wanted to know me a lot better, as people do with pop stars, even scooped-up, hollowed-out, pop stars. But I was still backing away, even from the two men I fancied like mad. The first invited himself back to mine, the second tried to kiss me, but the fulfilment of my desire was not in the script.

I was too absorbed in the unfulfilment of my desire for Billy, so overwhelming that it dictated everything else. Every word, every gesture was interpreted in terms of whether it got me closer to him or further away and I fell on any opportunity to press nearer. One day there was a commotion outside. Billy's dog was on heat and she had got out onto the roof terrace and from there saw another dog walking down the street, a temptation so irresistible she jumped off the terrace to fling herself at him in a moment of pheromonal madness.

She hit the ground and howled in pain. Billy and I ran out into the street to be confronted by a familiar predicament in four-legged form, disabling pain following the reckless pursuit of an unsuitable attachment. Billy, whose emotions were understandably more stirred by the dog's predicament than by mine, grabbed her and we took a cab to the vet where astoundingly expensive veterinary treatment was recommended. Anything, anything for the dog; so I paid with a credit card, and Billy had to mumble his thanks, and we came home silently in the back of a cab.

Emma Freud came to the rescue with a trip to New York. Her then partner was in the Cambridge Singers on tour in the United States, a tour that culminated with a concert at Carnegie Hall, and she decided to surprise him by turning up for it and asked me if I wanted to come too. I was thankful for a chance to get out of the house and off we went. We checked in to the hotel where the singers were staying and did our ta-daa, which did not seem to disconcert Emma's partner too much. It coincided with my twenty-eighth birthday, which I celebrated by buying a bag of cocaine, and behaved disgracefully at the after-show party, offering lines to nineteen-year-old undergraduate sopranos in taffeta dresses, like Sid Vicious backstage at the BBC Choir of the Year Competition. Later, in a 24-hour diner in Times Square, I talked to Emma about my situation. It was obvious to her, and to me – it would have been obvious to anyone – that it was only going to get worse, so when I got home I called time, I bailed out, and told Billy that this couldn't continue. He replied with a very acute account of my self-absorption, dishonesty and weakness, no less excruciating for being deserved. Billy came close to punching me, and even in that moment of humiliation I felt an ignoble thrill because at least it would mean some physical connection with him.

I stopped going to Troll, I stopped taking drugs, I stopped smoking, I started trying to get healthy, but then I crashed, falling into a depression as bad as the one I had suffered when I was seventeen. What was different was that I knew I could survive it, and that I had the means to sit it out at home. I did go to the doctor and got some antidepressants but never thought they did me any good. So I found a therapist and started to go to see her twice a week in a house in Archway, in a room at the top of the stairs, where I entertained a fantasy that she lived permanently, quietly knitting in the 166 hours each week I wasn't there talking about Billy, Billy, Billy, who I once described like a figure in an icon, transfigured with light, walking towards me on Upper Street.

Billy, Billy, Billy; in my disordered state I decided to make an effort for forgiveness and reconciliation, which I somehow thought we owed each other – but really I just couldn't let go. I hung around where I thought he might be, and once thought I saw him going into the Post Office in Upper Street, so I waited to see if he would emerge but he did not. I suppose it wasn't him at all, though I could hardly blame him if he had insisted on being smuggled out in a van rather than have to deal with me stalking him outside. I talked about him to anyone who would listen, one evening to my very patient friend Matthew, who I met for dinner in a restaurant round the corner. As I talked, the door opened and Billy came in. I trembled but went over and asked how he was, but he wouldn't reply, and rather than beat a retreat I pulled up a chair and tried to explain why he should talk to me, a conversation overheard by others in the restaurant and the waiting staff, all of whom we knew. Matthew, with typical grace, came over and made me come away.

Billy, Billy, Billy. For months and months he occupied my thoughts and focused my longings and tortured my sleep. Why? I think now it was because I saw or sensed in him something that I thought I lacked – masculinity, potency, fatherhood – the sense of being deficient that had agonised me since I was a teenager. At first, for me, it was just fun, feasting with panthers, and Billy enjoyed playing up to that for as long as it was fun. But he was not a panther, he was a person, and not there to focus my fantasies, behind which a dark and desperate desire was looking for satiety, like a vampire after a neck. Like a vampire I thought he had what I needed, and that I could suck it out of him and be made whole; but I met a vampire's end, with a stake through the heart.

19. 'Tis Mercy All

What should a man make of remorse that it might profit his soul? – a line from a poem by Geoffrey Hill that I wrote on a Post-it note and stuck on my desk.

There were always new people. My friend Rosie from *Night Network* days moved in. I had got closer to Daniel Wood, survivor of the *Marchioness* tragedy, and introduced him to Jon Turner, with whom I walked the dog, and they got together, a move which I did not see coming and was rather put out because neither had sought my imprimatur. But I got over that, and got used to it, and we three, now neighbours in Islington, started seeing a lot of each other. We would meet at the café round the corner from my house on a Saturday morning for cappuccino and to read the papers. Glitter Club we called it, my friend Adam Mars-Jones occasionally joining us, too.

But I was thirstier for more than a cappuccino, hungrier for more than a croissant. I had no appetite for that which had nourished me before – gay liberation, the politics of the left, being in a gang. What could nourish me now?

It was around this time that I first felt twinges towards religion. I brought this up in therapy, thinking them symptoms of mental crisis, but they were in fact intimations of what it might be to be better. I felt, in crisis, an almost overpowering yearning for the feeling of peace that I had experienced sitting in chapel when I was young. I had already started listening to a lot of Renaissance polyphony, finding in its transparency and lift an expression of that feeling, too, the lifting up of mine eyes unto the hills, from whence cometh our help. I sometimes used to play it to people back at mine

in the long sleepless nights after Troll but they didn't get it. One unfortunate girl, to whom I played the whole of *Spem in alium*, Tallis's
magnificent forty-part motet, remarked at the end that it made her
'fink of def'. Sober, I was playing a lot of piano music by Francis
Poulenc, a French composer of the twentieth century, cheerfully gay,
devoutly Catholic, 'half monk, half naughty boy'. His piano Noc-
turnes and Sonatas and Improvisations were pure boulevard, but his
sacred music for choir austere and powerful. If I felt there was a
tension between the two it was a tension I wanted to explore myself.
In southern Europe I was drawn to the imagery and kit of popular
Catholic piety, the kitschier the better, and I remember buying a
giant rosary made from wooden beads the size of golf balls in Ibiza
town, which I wore round my neck to go to nightclubs. And I loved
the work of Pierre et Gilles, fashionable photographer-artists in
Paris, who also used that imagery, worked, very incarnationally, with
gay erotica. But this was in the background, a backwards look at the
religious tradition we were forgetting, not an invitation to stand on
its threshold and look in.

I knew, or intimated, that I did actually need to look in, so one
Sunday morning, walking past the parish church, I did. I sat at the
back as others worshipped, connecting with nothing. After it finished a man offered me a cup of coffee, but he was wearing grey
slip-on moccasins and I thought, as Nathanael thought, that nothing good could come from that. I made my excuses and left.

It was not only that I disliked the aesthetics of that place. The
Christian Church was the enemy; in a general sense, the defender
of reaction, obfuscation and distributor of opium to the people; in a
specific sense, the most implacable enemy of gay liberation, the most
consistent in opposition to the liberalisation of law and culture, and
not a place of welcome. How I hated, and still dislike, those signs
outside churches saying All Welcome, when actually some of us
were, and are, as welcome as Typhoid Mary at a parish lunch. How
could I have any part in that? Rationally, none; but I was hungry and
I was thirsty and I could sniff food and drink.

I was working again, thanks to a producer from *Night Network* who was now with BSB, the forerunner to BSkyB. To enhance their cultural credentials, BSB was covering the Edinburgh Festival and asked me to go to present some of its coverage and also to play live for a Festival Special for broadcast. I got together Sarah Jane Morris, the singer Ian Shaw and trumpeter Chris Bachelor and we came up with a version of 'My Funny Valentine', a song I loved, which suited Ian and Sarah Jane, and as I played it I thought 'Billy Billy Billy', whose birthday was Valentine's Day.

I stayed in Edinburgh for a day longer than the others. It was a summer afternoon and I was walking along Palmerston Place past the Anglican cathedral with its three spires punching above its weight in that Presbyterian town. Inside Choral Evensong was under way, that quintessence of Anglican worship. I sat at the back again, but this time recognising what was going on, the choir sing-ing the versicles and responses as I had done when I was a chorister, the Evening Canticles in praise of Mary and beseeching the Lord for a quiet night, the hymns so deeply printed in my memory that my lips moved involuntarily. The words from the Magnificat that I had not heard in twenty years, 'he hath put down the mighty from their seat and hath exalted the humble and meek', seemed espe-cially significant, seeking me out in my dark pew, but I dismissed that as a trick of the subconscious mind. Of course the choir was singing the Magnificat, it was a Sunday evening when Magnificats are sung.

The next day I took the train south for home, but got off when it stopped at York. I wanted to spend some time alone, away from familiar places and the people I knew, because I did not want to feel constrained by loyalties to others or embarrassment by being watched. I headed for the Minster and looked at the Seven Sisters window and tried to decode what the building was telling me about the human angle to heaven and the ways in which we seek, or sought, to know in this life the mystery of the life beyond. I couldn't crack it, couldn't get a sense of it as anything more exalted than a museum of how we used to think and feel. In the shop I intended to buy only a postcard as a souvenir, but I bought instead a little silver cross on a chain. In retrospect this was one of the most significant moments of my life, for I went in a tourist but came out a participant. 'You must sit down and taste my meat,' says Jesus Christ to George Herbert in his poem 'Love': 'So I did sit and eat.'

But I did not sit and eat, or not at first. I came back to London and decided, at my therapist's suggestion, to talk to a priest. But I didn't know any priests and ignorantly assumed they would not know anything about someone like me. I only half remembered the civilised and kindly priests I had known when I was a boy, but these were overlaid with less civilised and less kind priests denouncing homosexuality and, worse, talking about homosexual people as if we were less than they were, less than fully human. A friend of mine's flatmate in south London had just died of AIDS and on his death-bed, asked to see the vicar. When the vicar came round he bullied the dying man into renouncing his homosexuality and his partner before he was able to offer him the consolation of the Church. I don't know if that was quite what happened, I suspect it was not so straightforward, but that was the version that was circulating and it fed my mistrust and dislike of the Church. Also, to be truthful, I did not want to get involved in the Church because it was so hideously unfashionable. It was more than a matter of grey moccasins; it was to do with a dislike of the body and the things of the body. Being gay was, in contrast, all about the body, discovering its loveliness, its fallibility, its way of articulating who we are and what we're for. Christianity, all religion, seemed to me to be the opposite of that, a repudiation of the body, all those flagellants and penitents, mortifying the corruptible flesh to put on incorruption. That's Gnosticism, actually, not Christianity, but it is an easy mistake to make, as many Christians and non-Christians have done, but I did not then know the difference.

I thought of my therapist's advice and asked around to see if anyone knew a kindly vicar I could talk to. Adam said he knew someone married to a vicar and perhaps I could talk to her. This sounded much more agreeable, especially when I found out she was the novelist Sara Maitland, like Adam a winner of the Somerset

Maugham Award. She had been at Oxford in '68, was a feminist and a supporter of gay rights – well, she would get me, I thought – and lived in the East End of London, where her husband was Vicar of Haggerston. A date was arranged and I cycled to their vicarage from Islington on my new blue mountain bike, another effort towards health and sobriety, through progressively meaner streets. The church, dedicated to St Chad (patron of disputed elections), was as incongruous in the district as a Spanish galleon on the Manchester Ship Canal, built in the Victorian era of Anglo-Catholic expansion in the London slums, but surrounded now by tower blocks, optimistic replacements for Blitz-damaged streets. The vicarage, which adjoined the church, looked like a Scottish laird's house that had run away to Hackney and had a Victorian Gothic makeover, with a turret and a tower and a massive chimney stack – but this must have seemed quite familiar to Sara who, I discovered, came from an aristocratic Scottish background and had grown up in the sort of house where you find a dead stag on the hall table. Sara had warned me not to leave my bike unattended outside, but I ignored this and chained it up to scaffolding, and rang the doorbell. A bell sounded distantly in the house and then there was Sara at the door, shorter than me, with long, long hair and a fag on.

We talked for hours. She was completely unfazed by homosexuality, pop stardom and drug taking. I responded to her intelligence and intensity and directness, and when I left took with me a copy of Angela Tilby's *Won't You Join the Dance?* and the telephone number of the curate of St Alban's Holborn, a church Sara felt would suit me more than my own parish church. I returned after two minutes to report that my bike, chained up outside, had been trashed by parishioners, frustrated in their efforts to steal it by the forged-steel bike lock.

Won't You Join the Dance? was a revelation. It was about the Christian creeds, those dense summaries of doctrine recited Sunday by Sunday in churches all over the Christian world in one way or another, and by me without knowledge or understanding through my childhood, full of mystifying creatures which proceedeth from the

Father and the Son, in holy, catholick and apostolic ways. Some people can think their way into faith. I couldn't, but I did know I wanted to be part of this; I needed to join the dance, an image I found as attractive as a banquet to which we are all invited.

I had to find somewhere to sit and eat, somewhere to take my first uncertain steps. I called the curate at St Alban's Holborn, Fr Peter Baker, and found myself at another slum church, with a house for its clergy next door, situated in a backstreet, in the nineteenth century as rough a city neighbourhood as any. By 1990 it was no longer rough, the few people still living in council flats or Peabody blocks outnumbered by the tens of thousands who worked in banking and insurance and the law. I rang the bell by the Clergy House door and Fr Peter answered. He was a few years older than me, with a doctorate in church history from Cambridge and, I discovered, a partner called Keith. Another hour-long conversation followed. I must have seemed particularly tactless to Peter because I spelled out slowly and clearly my sexuality and recent history as if I were speaking to a deaf grandmother rather than to someone not lacking in experience of life, but he was patient, as priests have to be, and made no issue of my clumsiness. He invited me to Mass, as he called it, on Sunday.

Mass, this mysterious enterprise, took place at eleven, a civilised hour on a Sunday morning for most people, but for me then nearer to going to bed time than getting up time. I did get up and got there, chained up my repaired bike and entered the church, which revealed itself in an entirely unexpected vision of glory. I later learned that the original, built by Butterfield in the nineteenth century, was almost destroyed in the Blitz. A side chapel, dedicated to its first vicar and ritualist pioneer, Fr Mackonochie, is a survivor of the bombardment, though there was an ominous crack running through the wall that made me think of the veil of the Temple torn in two. It was dark and Victorian and rather sepulchral, and had been prayed in by an ardent young Gerard Manley Hopkins before he crossed the Tiber to Rome. Fr Mackonochie had been deprived of his living for 'ritualism' and he and others were persecuted and indeed prosecuted for wearing vestments, placing candles on the altar, behaving towards the bread and wine as if they were indeed the body and blood of Our Lord. Anglo-Catholicism, as the movement came to be known, was in its day, roughly the 1850s to the 1930s, the most energetic and exciting movement within the Church of England, which since the Reformation – some would say before the Reformation – has been pushed and pulled in the opposite directions of High and Low, Catholic and Protestant. St Alban's Holborn was one of the highest of the High Churches, and Mackonochie, one of its most celebrated vicars, not only endured humiliation and reproach, but died spectacularly of hypothermia lost in the winter snows of Scotland while on holiday with the Bishop of Argyll and the Isles.

Beyond the chapel lay the huge surprise of the church, full of light and colour and sound. It looked like it belonged to Catholic Europe rather than the City of London, and was dominated by a huge frieze on the east wall of *The Trinity in Glory*; in Technicolor, I thought, for it was almost too bright, Hans Feibusch at his most exuberant. And the church was full of sound from the organ in the gallery at the west end, where a professional choir sang, too, and the nave and chancel were bright with candles, six big ones on the altar, and red and white and blue shrine lights burning in front of statues of St Alban, the first martyr in Britain, and Our Lady. Someone gave me an order of service, as incomprehensible as instructions for flat-pack furniture, and a hymn book that was green rather than the dark red of my recollection, and I found a place in a pew near the back, hoping that no one would try to befriend me.

I sat and looked around and felt like I had walked into entirely the wrong place. I certainly stood out. I was wearing a scarlet puffer jacket, jeans and a pair of very complicated trainers. Every other single male I could see was wearing a sports jacket, polished shoes and the air of a connoisseur. I had no idea what I was doing, but hoped this was not too obvious, as I did not want anyone to try to help me through the service.

No one did. The Mass got under way with a mysterious clanking of chains and rustling of damasks, and wheezing of organ, and we stood and sang as the clergy and servers formed up and processed in from behind me, led by a thurifer swinging a silver pot of smoking incense. The effect was extraordinary. It was Panavision, it was Grand Opera, it was as odoriferous as Christmas, sound and colour and smell and scale conjuring a sacredness and mystery that was both awe-inspiring and moving. We sang, we stood, we sat, we bowed our heads in unpredictable places, we knelt, and then something extraordinary happened. Three robed men stood at the altar, and the one in the centre lifted with both hands a small white disc. The thurifer raised his smoking silver pot, a skein of smoke began to rise in the sunlight slanting through a window, and a chime rang out unexpectedly. I think it was the chime that roused me, like the dinner bell roused Pavlov's dog, or maybe it was the scent of the incense, straight into the limbic system like the madeleine on Proust's lips; but I was pierced to the soul at that moment.

And then it was as if iron bands, constricting my chest, broke and fell away and I could breathe; and a shutter was flung open, and light flooded in and I could see. And I wept and wept.

Sometime later, familiarising myself with the breadth of English Christian experience, I came across Charles Wesley's thumping Protestant hymn 'And Can It Be': 'I woke, the dungeon flamed with light; My chains fell off, my heart was free, I rose, went forth, and followed Thee,' we sang, and I realised that the imagery of the dungeon flooding with light and the breaking chains have a longer heritage than what happened to me that Sunday morning in Holborn in 1990. Indeed, I was to discover that it goes back further, to the New Testament itself, and another witless man in a mess.

And I realised, too, that I was one of the very few people in the Church of England to have gone to a Solemn High Mass at St Alban's Holborn and there experienced a classic Protestant conversion.

20. Roman Fever

What I had encountered in that moment at St Alban's Holborn was the gift of Jesus Christ in the Eucharist, the gift of himself in bread and the wine – food and drink for me at last – and an invitation to sit at his table. But in the first rush of conversion it was all about feeling, feeling with an intensity that took me by surprise and dispelled any anxieties or reserve I might have about joining in. I prayed so intensely in those first months that I had a sensation of colour and movement rather than words or pictures. Perhaps that was because the words and pictures had yet to form, or perhaps that I was in a mental and spiritual crisis, but God was extraordinarily forthcoming, and had I come across a burning bush or a voice from a cloud, like Moses, I would not have been so surprised. God, as I have gone on, has become more elusive, or indirect, more R. S. Thomas than J. H. Newman; but back then my experience of the mystery of God was as vivid as anything I have ever experienced.

It was not only the mystery of God I encountered, but the person of Jesus Christ also, this enigmatic figure who I have never been able to shake off, who haunts me still, encountered in the echo chamber of Scripture and the feast of the Eucharist, and as someone who has just left the room, but whose vanished presence still alters the temperature and the currents of circulating air and leaves a fading music. Perhaps that does not sound like much, but in him I discovered forgiveness for my sins and my silliness and my hard-heartedness – forgiveness for more than my sins in the fathomless riches of his grace.

In the Sermon on the Mount Jesus teaches us how to pray. Go to your room, he says, and shut the door, and there pray to your Father who is in secret. In all of us there is such a room, with a tightly closed door, windowless. We want it that way, because in it we keep those things that shame us, the humiliations we endure, our foolishness and cruelty, the very worst of us. That's exactly where Jesus wants to meet us, and we dread it because his grace falls on us like a judgement; but in his revealing light we find not a misbegotten horror, like the Monster of Glamis, we find ourselves, nothing special, nothing dreadful.

The door opened on my airless room and I saw my obsessional attachment to Billy, the heaped-up grief and dread at the rampage of AIDS, the distorting effects of success and celebrity, the mess I had made of things. It was long past time to put things right, and I did not know exactly how to do that, but I did know that church was the place to do it so I set about entering more fully the life of St Alban's Holborn. The vicar at that time was Fr John Gaskell, a remarkable priest in his sixties – tall and beaky and quite bald, in a black cassock with the scarlet piping and buttons of a Prebendary of St Paul's, and a black biretta with a scarlet pompom. He looked forbidding but was extraordinarily kind and compassionate, and had, at cost to himself, worked out how to reconcile Christian faith with an inconvenient sexual orientation. He made it look possible.

I wonder if I could have made my leap of faith had it not been for others making it look possible. Lorna had, without fanfare, started going to church herself, information I received with immense surprise. After the band stopped working, she took an MA in leisure management at Sheffield, an odd choice I thought, but all choices are odd after you stop being involved in pop music. Returning to London, she found a job working for an organisation that brought together arts groups with businesses looking to fund them, and bought her first flat in the Elephant and Castle. It was tiny, and it was urban, but she colonised it for Laura Ashley, filling its little rooms with lace, the front door practically bursting open in an explosion of frou-frou. Lorna, whose commitment to the radical and unlacy politics of the eighties was always a little strained, released the cavalier within, and started going to the parish church round the corner from the flat. When I had first heard of this I denounced it, naturally, as a sign of mental collapse, but now, as I pondered this thing in my heart, it made my own leap look a little less impossible when I had to leap.

St Alban's was actually full of people making faith possible but I did not have the wit to see it at that time, stumbling into a world I thought would not recognise me. Anglo-Catholic churches have traditionally been a place of refuge for the odd and the damaged – one of the tradition's best features – and eccentricity was not only tolerated but cultivated. Sometimes that could be a little forced and there were those for whom it offered almost too readily an opportunity to indulge in panto. But there were also genuinely off-centred people who found a congenial orbit around St Alban's. One woman, I assume from an Irish Roman Catholic background, sat on her own, wreathed in rosaries and lucky charms, joining in the congregational responses just a bit out of time with everyone else and sometimes, in moments of ecstasy, soaring to heights of piety, adding exalted phrases to the Lord's Prayer and rattling her rosaries like chains.

It was also a place of die-hards, tense young men and fierce old ladies, for whom Anglo-Catholicism was a religion rather than a way of doing religion. These were the stalwarts of the Parish Pilgrimages and Parish Retreats and Parish Lunches, who remembered the Anglo-Catholic Congresses of the 1920s, or said they did, the high point of the movement within Church and society, when platoons of priests in complicated kit processed militantly, like Act II of *Aida*, but in Birmingham rather than Thebes. Most in the congregation were local people from the Peabody Trust and council housing, whose names were remembered on the sick list, prayed for each week for recovery from whatever ailed them. There was a peculiar poetry to those names and I still remember Pearl Needles and Doris Norris, adjacent in the litany of the poorly. And there were gay men, quite a lot of gay men, but most had not been radicalised in the alternative scene that I had come through. I thought they were un-radicalised, dwelling in the churchy High Tory gay cliques of Oxford and Cambridge and the London choral circuit. Actually they were just as courageous as those of us who were more confrontationally gay, and their quieter activism did much to bring about changes in society over the next twenty or thirty years. And I would not like to suggest that Anglo-Catholicism was not a serious discipline for men and women of any age or sexual orientation – it is – but its worship can be particularly resonant for people who like drama and things done just so and the kinds of codes that campery delights in. When a new curate arrived in the sanctuary, in a cotta – the short white pleated surplice worn over a cassock – one server turned to another and said: 'Hmmm, FIVE pleats'.

St Alban's Holborn fielded a crack team of servers, sometimes a dozen on high and holy days, from the thurifer, swinging the thurible, the silver pot of smoking incense and traditionally a star role, to the acolyte, basically a candle holder on the move. Our company of servers was drilled by Simon Jones, the Master of Ceremonies, who soon recruited me to the ranks of acolyte. My job was to accompany the Gospel book when it was taken down from the High Altar to be read by the deacon, and to kneel in front of the altar when the bread and wine was offered and blessed by the priest, and to raise and lower my candle as a sign of the activity of the Holy Spirit in its mysterious transformation into Christ's flesh and blood. This happened every Sunday, but on special days the drill was more showy. At the feast of Corpus Christi it was spectacularly so, with a procession of the Blessed Sacrament, a disc of consecrated white bread in an elaborate holder, carried aloft and attended by the clergy in gorgeous vestments led by little girls scattering rose petals before them, one server carrying the ombrellino, a little umbrella of golden cloth on a long stick held over the Blessed Sacrament as a sign of its sacredness. There was prose among the poetry. On Palm Sunday, which marks the beginning of the week that culminates with Easter, there was a procession round the parish, everyone carrying palm crosses as a reminder of Christ's triumphal entry into Jerusalem. Our triumphal progress round Holborn was led by the Master of Ceremonies,

who used a special stick to indicate piles of dog shit imperilling our
seemly progress.

Anglo-Catholic worship, in its complexity and drama, is actually
a great way to learn the rudiments of doctrine and practice, the traditions of the Church, the peculiarities of the Anglican end of it.
I learned also from the great Feibusch mural, *The Trinity in Glory*,
which I would sit in front of for hours, distracted from the drone
of words by the brilliance of its colour and imagery. I say the drone
of words: they came not from the pulpit where we were extraordinarily lucky to have John Gaskell as its principal occupant, one of
the finest preachers of the Church of England at that time. I knew
next to nothing of doctrine but never felt left behind, for John, holy
and learned and wise, knew how to be simple. He could be quite
frightening at first, but I gradually got to know him, over sherry, inevitably, in the Clergy House after Mass and then in his study, which
looked down the street to High Holborn, and had on the wall one of
those oars painted with the names of rowers, his among them, from
what looked like a surprisingly sporty university career.

John was of a different generation from mine but he had a knack
for closing gaps, and once at St Alban's, after a service, I found him
at the west end of the church talking to a man I recognised from the
music industry. He looked at me and I looked at him, both equally
surprised to see each other in that place, but John had a long list
of surprising friends, from John Betjeman and his coterie to the
leathery-cleated mustachioed men of the Vauxhall Tavern. John, I
was delighted to discover, liked the same things as me, *Middlemarch*,
'the greatest novel in English' according to him, but we disagreed
on Wagner, his great love but utterly lifeless to me, until he opened
it up when we went to see a Ring Cycle at Covent Garden. In the
intervals I was surprised at the number of times people approached
him to say hello but he never greeted anyone himself. I thought this
was a little grand on his part, a little aloof, but when I mentioned it
to Peter he said John never approached people because he could not
be sure if he knew them from everyday life or from the confessional.
His punctiliousness in preserving the confidentiality of that sacred

encounter was so rigorous he would rather be thought rude or forgetful than threaten it.

Converting to Rome – jumping the Tiber – was like a hereditary disease in High Church circles, subtracting people from the pews at a fairly consistent rate. In reality this is the effect of attrition – those who insist on the Catholic identity of the Church of England ask for a fight with those convinced of its Protestant identity – the Low Church faction – and much of the heat and energy of the C of E, where you can find it, derives from this tension. That can get boring. Also there is a risk that the more Catholic you get the harder it becomes to resist the gravitational pull of Rome, original and best.

Around this time I got friendly with one of the waitresses at the café where we met on a Saturday morning. Her name was Rachel and she came from Devon where her mother lived at Buckfastleigh, the village in the lee of Buckfast Abbey, one of the great Benedictine monasteries of England. Rachel's family was Catholic – that was the reason they lived there – and we started talking about Roman Catholicism. My endless questions were perhaps overwhelming, for she suggested I write to Fr David, one of the monks there, a housemaster at the pre-school the monastery ran. He invited me down to visit.

I was completely captivated by Buckfast. The monastery stands on the edge of Dartmoor, not far from the A38, where the Little Chef is reputed to belong to the Abbey, famous for its enterprise. It produces Buckfast tonic wine, drunk in Glasgow by people who are looking for a higher percentage of alcohol than a structured bouquet, and so successful was Buckfast in paying its way that the other Benedictine monasteries nicknamed it Fastbuck Abbey.

I was greeted by the Guest Master, who showed me to a room in the guest quarters, when I was left to settle into a room appointed with the peculiar discomforts of a monastery. Fr David had left instructions for me to make my way to one of the boarding houses of the prep school, a feeder to the Benedictine public schools of Ampleforth and Downside, where he was housemaster. He was ten or so years older than me, one of the plumper sort of monks, shy and very welcoming. After the boys went to bed, we talked until the bell for Compline tolled and we made our way down to the Abbey. I sat in the nave in a pew in darkness, save a couple of candles on the altar, and then heard a rustling as the monks, in gowns and cowls, silently and slowly processed into their stalls. Compline is sung and read in darkness, the texts and chants do not vary much, and concludes with a hymn to the Virgin Mary as the community settles in for the night. Hoods up – like black-vested druids – the monks processed out again into the Greater Silence, which prevailed until matins and lauds on the following day. It left a deep impression on me – the silence, the suppleness of the chant, the extraordinary feel for its rhythm and pulse, the awareness of the other, the commitment of the brethren to serve one another and God. Fr David and I returned to the house, where we carried on talking and talking until after midnight. I said goodnight and made my way back to the monastery via a side door to the church. I stood in the great empty building in pitch darkness, so dark I could not see anything, and inched my way along the Choir, like a blind man lost in a hangar, until I saw, very faintly, the shrine light burning in the ancient chapel where the Blessed Sacrament was reserved. It was tiny in all that darkness, but it guided me through the darkness to where I needed to be.

I was immediately drawn to the monastic regime – prayer, to a pattern I could not yet discern, monks facing each other in their stalls, chanting psalms and hymns, hearing Scripture, offering prayer. As I watched I noticed something that mystified me. During the psalms a monk would occasionally turn to the Abbot and bow, the Abbot would make a gesture, and the monk would continue with the chant. I asked Fr David about this and he told me that when a monk made a mistake in the chant he would turn to the Abbot and wait for a sign of his forgiveness before continuing. This habit of confessing and absolving ran through their lives, individually and corporately. One of the community's regular meetings was Chapter of Faults, when monks would one by one confess various infringements of the Rule of St Benedict, which they tried to live by, or of the rules of the house, hear the community's judgement, and receive God's forgiveness.

I stumbled. I loved so much about the monks' life but I didn't love this. Indeed, I recoiled from it. It seemed so totalitarian, and the only parallel I could think of was Stalinism, where judgement and forgiveness could be summary and sharp. I could understand submission to God's judgement and forgiveness, but as long as it is mediated through God's fallible servants circumspection seemed and seems only right to me. Fr David said in the old days, before the reforms of the Second Vatican Council, life was much stricter, and when he entered the novitiate in his teens on Fridays in Lent the monks were expected to go to their cells with a flagellum, recite a psalm of penitence and whip themselves in an exercise called the Mortification of the Flesh. The novice master would stand at the end of the corridor listening to make sure they did it, but, he confesses, they actually whipped their bolsters instead.

The coldness of some of the monks mystified me. New to Christian faith, I was rather gushy and zealous and expected monks to be wreathed in serenity and holiness as they went about their monkish lives. I did not find this to be so. On the contrary, some of them were bad-tempered and supercilious and rude. They were just being real, of course; and in a world where the serious practice of a life of faith seems at best picturesque, at worst utterly incomprehensible, monks are going be mystifying. Actually, picturesque is worse, because it implies that the commitments are no more than ornamental, a modern version of the hermit paid to live in a rich man's grotto. Incomprehensible is better, because only when we stop trying to understand faith solely by the standards we bring to the world in front of us can we begin to get it at all.

I went to the monastery shop and took home to Islington a breviary, a monastic prayer book, which I began to use daily, sitting at my desk in my study, getting in rhythm with the pulse of the monastery's prayer as the buses and the car alarms and street clamour swelled outside.

21. Perestroika

John Gaskell had been vicar of the Grosvenor Chapel in Mayfair where, at the end of a confirmation class, he said to a well-heeled lady from that poshest of neighbourhoods that he looked forward to seeing her the following week. 'Next week?' she said. Yes, and for the following five said John. 'Oh,' she said, 'I didn't realise there was quite so much to it.'

There is indeed, and the further I advanced into its mysteries the more keenly I felt that I needed to make a deeper commitment to the life of the Church and a public commitment, too; but I rather shied away from coming out as a Christian because I thought it might disappoint and dismay my friends and – worse – I could not bear the thought of people looking pityingly at the wreck of my life.

One day I was at the gym underneath Centre Point in Tottenham Court Road where my friend Rob was a personal trainer and, as I hung from a bar at his behest, I saw him looking at me curiously. He had noticed the little silver cross under my t-shirt and asked, 'Are you a Christian?' No one had ever asked me that before and I answered yes for the first time.

That yes was significant, for if I had been hovering before making a formal commitment to full participation I realised I could not any longer. I had not been confirmed, which meant I was not able to join in sharing the bread and the wine with the community at St Alban's, so when Peter asked me if I wanted to I again said yes, and joined a small group for confirmation classes in the curate's flat at the top of the Clergy House. There was another man about my age there, too, Maurice, also a server, who came from Northern Ireland

and a Presbyterian background and wore stripy shirts and was quite fiercely Tory. He was also gay, but that to him did not come as part of a bundle of liberal political values. I found this difficult to grasp, but I had stepped beyond the orthodoxy that had been so much a part of my life for nearly a decade, and was in a new place.

Also new was the serious study of Scripture. Peter, to get us going, recommended that we do some homework and read the Gospel of St Mark, the shortest of the four. I couldn't get on with it. The stories were so peculiar, the parables so unexpectedly difficult, the strangeness of it so strange that the intense experience I was hoping for did not flow. *Tolle, lege* – take, read – came the mysterious childish voice over the wall to St Augustine as he stood on the threshold of the Bible and of faith in the fourth century, but no mysterious voice came to me. It was coming, actually, in the very words of Scripture, strange and peculiar and difficult, but I did not yet have the ears to hear. But the bishop was booked and I slightly nervously told my friends. Some were dismayed, some looked pitying, my parents looked long-suffering, but the response that most surprised arrived in the post. It was a book of prayers for the lesbian and gay community sent by Jimmy Somerville. The last time I'd seen him was at Heaven, the nightclub, when I had to introduce him on stage at a concert, but I was off my face and walked away holding the microphone he needed to sing and annoyed everyone. How he had heard of my confirmation I don't know, and I would not have relished telling him, so I was touched by the generosity of his gesture, especially, as he noted in the dedication, 'I can't say I get it, doll.'

The day of my confirmation came. I went to church in an Armani suit and a waistcoat I had bought at Paul Smith, silk, but painted in bright colours with a sort of Keith Haring motif. The Bishop of Edmonton, the last of the grand old Anglo-Catholic prelates, remarked on its vibrancy, before invoking the Holy Spirit to confirm me in the faith and I went for the first time to the altar rail to receive the bread and wine.

In the congregation I saw some invited friends, those not too freaked out by having to be in church, with my brothers and Mum

and Dad. The last time I'd been home was in the thick of my obses-
sion with Billy and as I told them what had happened I was unable
to prevent myself breaking down. My father, with typical understate-
ment, recommended a diet of Weetabix and perhaps to try smoking
a little more to get me through this crisis. My mother looked drawn.
Now, in the church, they looked much happier, if a little uncomfortable in the flamboyance of an Anglo-Catholic shrine on full power,
my mother perhaps wondering if this new enterprise of mine came
under the gay umbrellino. My older brother, Andy, brought his own
drama with him. He looked like he had just walked out of the woods,
his hair long and shaggy, with a straggly beard, his ears rattling with
piercings; but his disarray was not like mine, an outward sign of
internal distress, but suffered in the line of duty. He had joined Special Branch and was undercover, living a double life, infiltrated into
some sinister organisation while his wife and baby daughter made do
with unpredictable visits. Afterwards we went for lunch, the Coles
family gathered again, not for a wedding, like Andy's at St Bart's,
with 'I Was Glad' and morning suits, nor Will's that was yet to come,
but it was the nearest I had got thus far to a life event they, too, had
experienced and shared and had solemnised. What I remember most
clearly was the confirmation present I received from Dan Wood, the
bishop's son: it was a tin duck riding a tricycle and when you pushed
it along its hat went round.

After my confirmation I began to see a further horizon, undiscovered country lying ahead, and for the first time an intimation
that my vocation might be to priesthood. I was rather hoping that
someone else would say something to that effect: 'Have you ever
thought? . . .' But no one did.

I can quite understand why. In spite of my new Sunday pastime,
my life did not entirely conform to the pattern of authentic Christian living. I had stopped doing drugs but I was still hanging out
with people who were, or who had, although as I emerged from
their dominion I saw how strange a dominion it had been. I had a
friend who was dating someone who lived a slightly mysterious life,
the son of a Nigerian prince and a French mother. Throw a bottle

of Evian in any gay nightclub in any city in the world and you'll hit half a dozen people with similar tales to tell. We got friendly and he invited me and my flatmate Rosie to join him and his boyfriend for a week's holiday at his Majorcan villa. Great. As we drove there from the airport, he announced that due to a washing-machine accident we would not be able to stay at his villa but at his mother's villa instead. Fine. We duly transferred to another villa, which had a nice view and nice pool, and while it was very comfortable I thought it oddly masculine for a Frenchwoman married to a Nigerian prince, the bookshelves lined with military histories and men's suits in the wardrobe. Just as we were settling in, the phone went and he took the call speaking in a language we did not understand. It seemed a little tricky, and after he hung up he said he was sorry but we could not stay there, his mother had promised it that week to the world-famous flautist James Galway. I remember thinking 'no one would make that up' and although our host seemed stressed and a little strange, reciting Shakespeare sonnets to the indifferent night by the pool, I booked without complaint a couple of rooms at a hotel in Palma and he called a cab. As we were leaving I noticed some LPs in a rack, at the front *James Galway's Greatest Hits*.

We ended up having a brilliant week, because on our first day in Palma I ran into Jesús and Álvaro, my friends from Madrid, on holiday themselves, and they took us everywhere, from cafés for breakfast to restaurants for lunch, to clubs at night. Leaving one at dawn, having taken a capsule of God knows what as a holiday treat, as I walked along the harbour front the sun came up in those peculiar ice-cream colours of pink and pale green, reflected in the perfectly still water, which suddenly rippled and broke and cleaved to the arriving prow of the arms dealer Adnan Khashoggi's yacht, its helicopter, with drooping rotor blades, parked on the deck.

I was in the fortunate position of not having to work and, rather than let the devil find anything more for my idle hands to do, I decided to look at university degree courses in theology. I wanted to know more about Christian history and doctrine and Scripture, and I think I also wanted to test myself in an academic environment, which I had deserted ignobly after A levels. I didn't want to leave Islington so Sara suggested King's College London, which had a renowned theology department on the Strand that in the past had not only taught the subject but trained men for ordained ministry in the Church of England. By the nineties it was just another university department, but something of its vocational identity endured, its corporate life centred on the chapel. It also had a distinct identity of its own: those who graduate from it are often awarded an AKC, as Associates of King's College, though unofficially those initials are said to stand for Another Kinky Clergyman. It was a place of toleration in the broadest sense, and I thought I would like to be part of it. I got the documents to prove my paltry achievements at O and A level and put them in an envelope with an application form and a reference from Adam Mars-Jones.

I was invited to an interview with Colin Gunton, Professor of Theology, a minister in the United Reformed Church as well as an expert in the work of Karl Barth, the greatest theologian of the twentieth century. He must have found me a *rara avis* but offered me a place to study for a BA honours degree in Theology, starting in October 1991. Just after this I met an old friend from Consenting Adults in a pub in Islington and told him I was going off to college. 'What are you studying?' he asked. I said, 'Theology.' He said, 'Geology?' I said, 'Theology.' He said, 'Geology?' It took me three goes before he got it.

The rest of my life now had a start date and I had an excuse to take some time out before it began. I have always loved travelling by train and found a company that arranged the longest rail journey in the world, from London to Hong Kong, via Warsaw, Moscow, Irkutsk, Ulan Bator, Beijing and Guangzhou.

Trailing my Globetrotter suitcase – perhaps the most expensive thing ever made from cardboard – I met with a group of fellow travellers at Liverpool Street station. There was a retired army officer and his wife, an American couple from Vermilion, Illinois, who looked exactly as you'd expect an American couple from Illinois to look, a mysterious and slightly nervous Englishman and a couple of

American nurses who worked in Saudi Arabia and took half the year out to go travelling. I gravitated to them and to the tour leader, who looked like a party girl, and we set off, unromantically, to Harwich. There I was outed by someone on the train, who would not back down when I said I was not in a band, strictly speaking true, so my story came out, along with everyone else's, as we rumbled through Europe, to Berlin and on to Warsaw. This was still the Soviet era, but only just, and we were reading in the international newspapers, picked up as we went along, about the gathering crisis in the USSR. There were even stories of an attempted coup by the old guard against Gorbachev, summering in his dacha.

In Poland, in spite of its own recent political turmoil, it was business as usual, with streets full of soldiers and nothing in the shops. It was the first time I had been to a Soviet bloc country and I thought that while the graphics might have a certain élan little else did in a city so grey and wretched. When I went to see the Palace of Culture and Science, an enormous and overbearing and unpalatial chunk of architectural bombast that Stalin gave to the people of Poland in the fifties, I felt a peculiar sense of bathos that followed me on my journeys in the Communist world. But I also went to Mass in Warsaw, in a church with a mural that depicted a Jew with a nonchalant anti-Semitism that shocked me. We knelt at a rail for communion, very Church of England I thought, and a server held a golden plate on a stick under our mouths as we stuck out our tongues to receive the wafer – not very Church of England after all.

We rumbled eastwards and arrived in the middle of the night at Brest-Litovsk, on the Polish/Russian border, a name from history lessons at school but a place not often visited. Two exciting things happened there. We rose from our couchettes (hideous word) to find ourselves in a huge shed, its walls painted with pictures of happy and heroic workers industrialising Mother Russia, to make the switch from Polish track to Russian track, which required a change of bogies. The compartments we stood in were jacked up and the bogies released and rolled away. We were then slowly winched, still in our compartments, to new tracks where new bogies were rolled in

The Communards at Rome Airport. We had just gone to number 1.

In Rome.

Jimmy and me with my mum.

KEY MAN IN BAND'S HIT

KETTERING'S Richard Coles is riding high today . . . at the top of the pops!

His group the Communards have reached No 1 in the charts with their record Don't Leave me This Way.

Richard, 24, is the group's keyboard player and worked in London as a session musician before forming the Cummunards with ex-Bronski Beat singer Jimmy Somerville.

Richard was educated at Wellingborough School and his parents, Nigel and Elizabeth Coles, live at Top End, Pytchley.

Mr Coles is sales director of the Kettering removals firm Pink and Jones and this year was chosen as president of Kettering Chamber of Trade.

● Top of the pops . . . Richard (left) and Jimmy.

From my mother's scrapbook – the *Kettering Evening Telegraph*.

Jimmy in New York,
1985.

Billy with my dog
Foggy, 1989.

Jesús Vázquez, Jimmy and Álvaro Villarubia.

Celebrity holiday.

Martin Henry in Edinburgh.

Hillsborough Castle, Mo Mowlam and friends.

Billy and me, friends again.

Shenanigans at Mirfield, 2005.

Helen Fielding in Los Angeles.

Ordination at Boston Stump, 2005.

and attached. Then Russian border guards came on board and passed through the train checking our passports. One spoke English and I asked what was happening in Moscow. He said, 'We don't know. Do you know?' and carried on. Our guide from Intourist, the state travel agency, without whom you could not go anywhere, was not able to tell us much more. She spoke fluent English, but seemed harassed and said we would make our way to Moscow before making a decision about whether we could continue, and we all complained about geopolitical change interrupting our itinerary. At every stop teen-aged Russian boys would get on with bags of ex-military tat to sell as souvenirs, more and more of them, until by the time we approached Moscow the corridors were like a bazaar. I remember thinking if you could release this entrepreneurialism the USSR would be like the USA in a generation.

At Moscow we were directed to a coach and driven to our hotel, the Rossiya, which looked very like the Palace of Culture in Warsaw, another concrete block with a spike on top. Our guide checked us in and said we were to stay in our rooms until dinner when she would make an announcement about our itinerary. Back then in Russian hotels a woman sat at a desk on each floor by the lifts – purpose obscure – noting every coming and every going, but I decided not to wait in my room and walked down the steps in front of the hotel and waited at the kerb. Within ten seconds a man in a Lada stopped and I gave him five US dollars and said 'Bolshoi', the first place I thought of. He dropped me off there and I sat in the park by the theatre thinking of Mussorgsky and Diaghilev and Chaliapin and suddenly realised I was not alone. A man had come and sat next to me on the bench. 'Are you Jewish?' he asked. I couldn't think why he would ask this and said 'no', wondering if the Chevignon jacket I was wearing might have some kosher significance. It started a conversation. His name was Ivan, he was in his late twenties, he was blond and hand-some and very Russian-looking, and was on leave from the army's special forces. 'Spetsnaz, Spetsnaz!' he said. As we carried on talking, I realised he wanted to do more than brush up his English. So we went for a walk on this summer evening, and came across a crowd.

It was in a square dominated by a vaguely recognisable building
– 'Lubyanka,' said Ivan, and grimaced. It was the notorious headquarters of the KGB, not only a headquarters but a prison where the
victims of Stalin's terror were tortured and murdered. A statue of the
secret police's founder, Felix Dzerzhinsky, stood on a plinth outside,
and this was the focus of the crowd's attention. Ivan, excited by the
mood, discovered that someone had sent for a crane to pull down
the statue, an extraordinary gesture of defiance. We stayed there all
evening, talking to young Russians on the threshold of a new world,
watching the crane remove the statue rather delicately compared
with the more aggressive topplings that were to come – and plant in
its place the flag of the as yet unborn Russian Federation. An epochal
moment, I realised at the bar of a hotel nearby full of western journalists watching what we had just seen on CNN – the end of Soviet
Communism. I celebrated by sneaking Ivan back to my room, past
the woman on the desk outside the lifts, and in the small hours of
this new world I discovered that while the gay scene in Moscow was
like that of Wigan in the late forties I did not need to explain the
merits of safer sex; and that while he had served in the army as a
conscript, Ivan was actually an antiquarian book specialist.

I had a surreal few days in Moscow. You would see tanks in the
streets in the morning as the city's mayor, Boris Yeltsin, began to rally
support, and then have an ice cream outside the Pushkin Museum
in the afternoon. I went to Red Square and visited GUM, Moscow's
famous department store, which looked like it had been abandoned,
so few were the goods on sale, and then to Lenin's Tomb to see the
murderous tyrant whom I had once admired in the arrested decay
that was so commonplace in the Soviet Union. It, like him, was on
the turn. As I queued, a fleet of Zil limousines departed the Kremlin
at speed, taking their passengers I thought into retirement as the
coup collapsed and Gorbachev made ready to return to Moscow.
We, too, were making ready to leave, aboard the Trans-Siberian Express, bound for Irkutsk, east of the Urals. I said goodbye to Ivan
and promised to send him contact lens fluid from the West. He gave
me his old army hat (I still have it) and I kept my promise, sending

him litres and litres until he was able to buy his own as liberalisation arrived in Russia and enriched even antiquarian booksellers.

We then spent a week on the train rolling slowly east through Russia and into Asia. At every stop more boys got on with goods to sell, metal holders for tea glasses, hat badges, Sputnik souvenirs, bottles of Georgian champagne with plastic corks and tins of caviar – half a kilo of beluga in a blue tin with a rubber band fastening the lid to the bottom, for twenty-five dollars. I bought a case of the champagne, and a couple of tins of caviar, and made friends with the 'Chief of the Train', as he grandly described himself, and 'hired' the restaurant car after dinner one night for a party. We drank and sang and shouted, as Russians love to do, and chugged towards the dawn with the odd bouncing roll of the Trans-Siberian. At every station we would see people waiting for trains dressed in unimaginably drab clothes that smelled of mildew, holding gorgeous bunches of flowers. And when we went through the Siberian steppe and the train came to an unscheduled halt, everyone climbed down and ran towards the woods, returning with handfuls of mushrooms.

I loved the country and the people, the different calibration of their warmth and coldness. A nun in a monastery I visited snarled and snatched from my hand a couple of candles I wanted to light; one of the entreprencurial boys on the train smiled a lot, and rather invitingly, but our Intourist guide shooed him away. Unexpected smiles, revealing rows of stainless steel false teeth, would catch you by surprise, as would the unparalleled standard of customer service. At one restaurant we were presented with a menu that ran to twenty pages. Eventually we heard the slow slap-slap of the waitress's mules on the tiled floor, faintly at first and then more and more loudly as she approached our table to answer 'Nyet!' to every request. She went away, returning with a trolley laden with plates of dry black bread and a bowl of a sickly Soviet version of a Heinz toast topper.

We arrived in Irkutsk, one of the biggest cities in Siberia, where we were due to change on to the Trans-Mongolian for our next leg to Ulan Bator. We were taken to see a hydro-electric power station

– one is enough for me – and I bunked off and found a market where ladies in scarves piled red currants and white currants on tables and where I heard a familiar sound, one of my own records, played on a bootleg cassette.

We left the collapsing Soviet Union behind and on our way to China passed through Outer Mongolia, where I visited a Buddhist monastery, the one left standing by the Communist puppet regime, and felt immediately at home there, finding monks in the temple facing each other in rows and chanting from sacred scriptures, so close to the western monastic tradition you would assume they shared a common origin. Another unexpected moment of familiarity in this vastly unfamiliar place occurred when I met a local who one evening took me out on to the steppe. We drove through a rolling landscape covered with a pale green lichen in which creatures that looked like gerbils would bob up and down in the failing light. We drove on as night fell into what seemed like the middle of nowhere until some lights appeared ahead. An extraordinary building emerged, white and tiled with a sort of spacey minaret and a glittering red dome, dropped on to the steppe as surprisingly as the Holy House in Loreto. It was the clubhouse for a chip and putt course, a gift, I think, of North Korea, and inside we found a party of Chinese Communist officials on a jolly. It was the strangest thing, to imagine them in Outer Mongolia standing at a tee overlooking the steppe hitting golf balls into its emptiness.

After Mongolia, Beijing, where the hotel had room service and movies on the TV and I had a long bath and ordered a beefburger with fries and watched *When Harry Met Sally* and thought of the melancholy, long, withdrawing roar of Communism. I made friends with someone who worked there and one night he invited me through a door on the guest side into the service side of the hotel and I discovered a vast space, as plain as the hotel was not, thronging with workers, like bees in a hive, so I could lie in perfumed waters and squeeze Heinz tomato ketchup from a sachet eight thousand miles east of Pittsburgh.

We took another train and headed south, through a country that also seemed to be changing very fast, with tower blocks, shops, shiny cars in the streets, and kids making the V for Victory sign, although wherever we went men in uniforms would shout at you, and you sensed the state's muscle behind the economic reforms.

Hong Kong, however, had trams and Union Jacks and a cathedral that looked unchanged since the 1930s, with ceiling fans listlessly moving humidity around to the sound of Anglican chant. I took the Star Ferry across the harbour to Kowloon at night, one of the loveliest sights in the world, and spent hours haggling for a state-of-the-art Minolta camera with a man in a tiny shop. When I got back to London I found it on sale for less in Jessops.

But I did not go straight back to London. I said goodbye to the group and went to Thailand for ten days, checked into the Shangri La in Bangkok and had the longest and most luxurious soak of my life in a bath you could have swum horses in. I dined alone that night in a restaurant built on a teak platform over the river and had a tom yum kung so delicious I burst into tears.

Less appealing was Patpong, the sex district of Bangkok, where middle-aged European men sat dead-eyed in bars watching waitresses and kick boxers, some of them barely teenagers, if teenagers at all, dancing or kick boxing or offering 'MASSAGE?' I flew north to Chiang Mai, near the Burmese border, and went for a walk round town and within thirty seconds a young man appeared in front of me. 'You wanna fuck my sister?' he asked. I said no. 'You wanna fuck me?' I said no, but began to understand that single male Europeans travelling in Thailand were probably interested in more than the vibrant culture and scenery of the region. I called in at the Catholic church in the city and found a form outside the confessional which listed in English certain sins of the flesh and gave each one a number so the English-speaking penitent could just say the number to the Thai-speaking priest and all would be understood and, one hopes, shriven. It was well-thumbed.

I was, however, genuinely interested in the vibrant culture and scenery and went to visit the Buddhist monastery at Doi Suthep, which required a climb, but I found there, to my great surprise, some miniature short-haired dachshunds which I would dearly like to believe are sacred to Theravada Buddhism.

Foggy, my badly behaved wire-haired dachshund, in Rosie's care while I was away, would not be sacred to any tradition, but nevertheless, with mystical foresight, his ears pricked up and he barked at the door for twenty minutes before I arrived back at Moon Street. I was home, having seen the Soviet bloc crack before my eyes, having stood in Tiananmen Square, overlooked by a giant portrait of Mao, while around it bank HQs and chain hotels were beginning to rise, having been shyly pursued round Ulan Bator's one hotel by a lady determined to sell me a cashmere sweater for twenty-five dollars. A new world order was forming as I took up my Greek New Testament, a present from Sara Maitland, and set off for the Strand.

22. *Fides Quaerens Intellectum*

I supposed I was the only person in the entire department with a background like mine, the eighties pop star-turned-theology student, and while being noticed is not normally something I shy away from, on my first day at King's I wanted to be like everyone else. I picked up my fresher's pack and followed a crowd to a room where we were to be inducted into the peculiarities of our course. I sat next to a black guy about my age. His name was George and he was a Pentecostal minister and, as I answered his questions as to what I had done before, I wondered how he would cope with me and my background. He seemed completely unfazed. 'Actually,' he said, 'I wrote "So Macho" for Sinitta in 1985.' I had sat next to Britain's only ordained gay-disco-anthem writer-producer.

I had also worried that I would be spending the next three years in the company of teenagers, but actually we were about a third mature students, including a few who were ordained in one tradition or another. Maggie was a URC minister from Islington and looked exactly what I thought a woman URC minister from Islington should look like, from dangly earrings to a beatific smile, but confounded my prejudices by being super-bright and drily funny, and funny without ever being unkind. Also there, about my age, was Chris, a former Royal Marine Commando and member of the SBS, who had left the army to do his degree in the expectation that he would return to uniform as a padre. He had that devil-may-care attitude that you often find in soldiers and he was undoubtedly the fittest person I have ever known, radiating health and physical self-possession, and we Anglo-Catholic bachelors became rather flustered around him.

The school leavers, who I thought I would not get on with, I did get
on with, of course. I became friends particularly with two, Nick, a
former chorister from Hereford Cathedral, posh in a stripy shirt and
the sort of hair matrons like to ruffle, and Suzy, whose father, the
broadcaster Robert Robinson, I had seen around the BBC. In class
it was Maggie I spent most of my time with but outside class it was
Nick and Suzy, both singers, and with them I joined the choir. The
choir was run by Ernie Worrell, a great personality on the London
choral scene. My musical CV rather surprised him, but he offered
me a place as a bass, thin that year, and that was my reintroduction
to choral singing, and I fell in love with it again.

For theology students life at King's revolved around, or was meant
to revolve around, chapel, where we had a weekly college Eucharist
at which the choir sang, and a number of special services through
the year, culminating in an annual carol service on three consecutive
nights. Because of its history as an Anglican foundation and as a
theological college it had a full complement of clergy, a dean, traditionally theological high-flyers, and under him an Anglican chaplain
with an assistant; and part-time Roman Catholic, Orthodox and
Free Church chaplains. If that sounds like religion was secure in the
life of the college it was not always. The chapel, in a secular age, was
looked on enviously by other departments and there were constant
efforts to reduce it, or turn it into a library. By now, the early nineties, a new kind of atheism was emerging, more confrontational and
less respectful, mostly because of the cultural wars in the US, where
the religious right were trying to enforce the teaching of Creationism
in schools. This was to dominate the discourse of sacred and secular
in the years ahead. It had its adherents in college, who would set off
fire alarms during college services, or insert inappropriate comments
on the board where the pious could pin their requests for prayer. I
always felt they were my natural allies, far more than conservative
Christians, and on one occasion I, too, turned the prayer board into
an ecclesiastical battlefield with the chaplain. High Church people
tend to mark the anniversary of the death of Charles I – Charles
King and Martyr in the Calendar, or a version of it – with particular

ceremony. I felt this lacked circumspection, so on that day I put up a prayer for the immortal soul of Oliver Cromwell, Lord Protector of England, which the chaplain, in a rage, tore down.

King's had a very active Islamic Society – it met for prayers in a room visible from chapel, and as we bowed to sing the Sanctus we could see them bowing, too, but for a different reason. In those days, before the attacks on the World Trade Center, activism could be very intense and confrontational. One who never shirked the confrontation was the Roman Catholic chaplain, Fr Derek Jennings, known to all as Dazzle. He looked like a cross between A. N. Wilson and Dr Evadne Hinge, cycling round town on a sit-up-and-beg bicycle wearing a homburg. Not always blessed with an even temper, on a bad day he reminded me of a bird pecking at worms, and he could be quite high-maintenance, snappy and difficult. He had been an Anglican, and an ordinand, studying in Oxford at St Stephen's House, one of the High Church theological colleges, but had been diverted to Rome, as a layman at first, in which estate he became Secretary of the Historic Houses Association. For this reason he was adored by aristocrats the length and breadth of Britain, because he could help them satisfy the requirements to get grants to fix their ancient and expensively maintained roofs. He and I became friends almost immediately, recognising in each other, across the divides of confession and allegiance, a certain sympathetic attitude.

Dazzle lived at the Catholic Chaplaincy in Bloomsbury, in a room in the basement, but maintained a grander billet in the vicarage of a friend from his Anglican days. He was very intelligent, and loved a row but he was also, like so many High Church men, damaged, with a mysterious childhood which he loathed being reminded of. He was of course gay, although – incredibly – he thought this was a secret known only to a few. He found intimate relationships impossible or very difficult, so the celibate state he was obliged to adopt by the discipline of the Roman Catholic Church quite suited him. Also he liked the clarity and rigour of the Roman Catholic system; it was better suited to his temperament than the indistinctness of Anglicanism, though, like many Anglican converts to Roman Catholicism, he did rather reserve the right to do whatever he wanted when it suited him. 'It sufficeth me to live in truth principally, and not in feeling,' he would quote approvingly, as if feeling and truth were always mutually exclusive.

King's was a fertile place. I loved the communal life based round the chapel, and the liturgical year and singing in the choir. And I discovered I loved learning. A theology degree is really three fields of study, Scripture, philosophy and history. The history I knew I would like, the philosophy I knew I would find more difficult; what I did not see coming was falling in love with Scripture and the study of Scripture. New Testament Greek was compulsory and for the first time since school I had to sit down with a book – Wenham's *The Elements of New Testament Greek* – and conjugate verbs. I found it came quite readily and soon I was reading, slowly, the gospels in the language they were written in, the common Greek spoken around Asia Minor in the first century. The real impact, however, came when I started reading the epistles of Paul in the original. They came alive, those dense, endless sentences suddenly flowing like rivers through a wilderness, bringing a sousing freshness to my thinking, like a total immersion in baptismal waters. Around this time I saw *The Piano*, in which a woman entangles her foot in a rope fastening a piano on a boat, which she then shoves over the side into the water, dragging her with it. That image stayed with me powerfully.

Church history and philosophy were more closely entwined, especially in the history of the early Church, the writings of the Latin and Greek fathers and the work of the great councils that took place in the first centuries of the Church's life and sorted heterodox from orthodox belief. The distinctions seemed at first very fine, matters of angels on pinheads, and it was often frustrating to get stuck in arguments about sameness or likeness, about the weird dynamics of the trinity, about the fleshliness of flesh, but really these specifics arose from the extraordinary comprehensiveness of their intellectual schemes. I found myself drawn more and more to the details, not for their own sake but because they offered a way into the comprehensiveness, like the tiny door to the great church of the Nativity in

Bethlehem – strait is the gate. I became fascinated by the history of the text, by the big story, and the intellectual drama, captured, however imperfectly, in this net of readings and variant readings.

Alongside the study there were opportunities to get to know the breadth of the Christian tradition around us. Dazzle took us on a trip one weekend to stay at the Benedictine monastery at Prinknash, pronounced 'Prinnidge', in Gloucestershire, where they make the choicest incense for use in liturgy – Sanctuary, Basilica, Rosa Mystica, lovely smelling stuff sold in lovely boxes – in a modern monastery that stands next to the Tudor house the community originally lived in. Dazzle was on excellent form and in the course of a lecture on the topic of English monasticism gave his falsetto version of the 'Vissi d'arte' from Puccini's *Tosca* lying on his back. I cannot remember what it was supposed to illustrate. The monks there seemed shyer than the monks of Buckfast, and wore white rather than black habits, the Abbot's tiny wooden pectoral cross very different from the great gold and enamel cross of the Abbot of Buckfast. I loved Prinknash; I loved the daily round of the offices, the prayers of the church, the quietness, the rhythm, the seclusion. I don't think I was discerning a *vocation* to monastic life, which would probably have been to a place rather than a system, but I was beginning to imagine myself doing it. Not the same thing at all, but I loved it, and still do.

I had thought that I would, in a semi-cloistered way, lock myself up in learning for three years as a preparatory to ordination; but as is so often the way, resolving to do one thing seemed to make other things happen. Not long after I started at King's I got an evening job. The BBC had launched a new station, Radio Five, with a magazine programme that went out on Monday evenings called *The Mix*. The incumbent presenter was leaving and I was asked if I wanted his job. Did I want it? Yes, provided it fitted in with the rest of my life and did not hurl me back into the world I had left behind. 'No danger of that,' said the producer, aware of the modest profile of both show and station. The programme was, for Byzantine BBC reasons, made by the schools radio department, which was housed in a dreary building opposite Broadcasting House. There, in what felt like an interview for a civil service post in the 1950s, I was offered the job and accepted it. From the following week on Mondays a car would pick me up from college at five, drive me to Portland Place, where I would write the script, have a curry and be on air at nine.

There was a problem. I didn't know how to present radio programmes. I assumed someone would show me, but nobody did, and it didn't occur to me to press the point until about half an hour before I was due to go on air for the first time. 'What would you like me to do?' I asked. Presenting, I was about to discover, is not a profession but an aptitude, like being comfortable at cocktail parties. From the moment the green light came on I found I was comfortable in the presenter's chair, able to talk to strangers, to be interested in anything for five minutes, and to feel I could rise to the occasion if things should go wrong.

The Mix mostly went right, although any live broadcast two hours long is vulnerable to the mood of the guest, the vagaries of the technology, the live band delivering. I was lucky in having brilliant regular contributors, among them John Wilson, Mark Kermode, Andrew Collins, Stuart Maconie and David Quantick, who all went on to greater things, which tells you something about the producer Jane Berthoud's knack for spotting talent, and mine for being in the right place at the right time, when something is beginning and nobody knows the rules yet. I settled in and soon got into a patterned way of working, part organisation and part propitiation of the fates. Live broadcasting makes you superstitious even if you are not superstitiously inclined, and I confess that even now, a quarter of a century later, I touch the sower's toe every time I pass the Gill sculpture just outside the ground-floor lifts in Broadcasting House on programme day. There was a break during *The Mix* for the ten o'clock news, and in it I would go for a pee. Derek Jameson was in the studio next door presenting his programme on Radio Two and he stopped for the ten o'clock news and went for a pee, too, and every Monday night at 10.01 we would stand at opposite ends of the row of urinals relieving ourselves and he would look at me and say in that deliberate way of his 'another day, another dollar'. If one day he had not shown up I'd have been worried that Broadcasting House would burn to the ground or be struck by lightning.

A magazine programme has an extraordinary appetite for guests and as the months turn into years you pretty soon have met everyone with something to promote. After a while they come round again, higher or lower in the pecking order than the last time, and the famous faces blur a little, but it is the same six dozen or so who fill the sofas and studios. I cannot always tell why some stick in the memory more than others. Justin Fashanu, trying to please everyone, the gay footballer who committed suicide; Jeff Banks the fashion designer, immensely impressive and likeable; Paul McKenna who semi-hypnotised me live on air, which was a bit tricky considering I had to present the programme; and I particularly remember the American comic Greg Proops, who was then well known for appearing on the improvisation show *Whose Line Is It Anyway?* I had been told by a producer to ask him to improvise something live, which he had been warned about; but when I asked him he appeared not to know about it and took umbrage at what I guess must have seemed to him like an act of sabotage.

In spite of these infelicities – or perhaps because of them – I was nominated for a Sony Award, the radio Oscars. My category was New Broadcaster and one Friday lunchtime we made our way to the Grosvenor House Hotel on Park Lane, me in a suit, and joined the throng of people dining noisily while Ludovic Kennedy handed out the prizes. When the New Broadcaster category was announced he stepped aside, and the prize was given out by Jeremy Beadle, a notch or two down from Sir Ludovic, I thought, but that passed when my name was announced as the winner. I went up to receive my trophy and the congratulations of Mr Beadle, who turned with me to the photographers, firing their flash guns, and said, 'You'll get used to it, son.'

After the lunch I walked back to the BBC with a couple of the producers and we stopped in the little park in Farm Street Gardens, just by the Connaught Hotel, and I smoked a nostalgic joint. I remembered when the band was at its height being picked up one night by a driver at Heathrow, and as I sat in the back and we went east along the A40 he asked me questions about the band, how we were doing, who we were working with, but his questions had an edge which I found a little unsettling and this edge grew sharper. By the time we got to Hammersmith he was saying things like 'Do you think you've been lucky, to do as well as you've done?' and 'It's not talent people are interested in these days, is it? No offence?' I was trying not to bridle, but then he told me he had been in a well-known band in the seventies, and ten years later he was driving a minicab, picking up from the airport people who were enjoying what he had lost, and it pained him. I wondered then, with dread, if his today would be my tomorrow.

Maybe not; I was New Broadcaster of the Year 1992, and I was thirty, and I had survived being a pop star, I had not died of AIDS, I had not entirely gone under with drugs and hopeless attachments, and maybe I had crossed without stumbling too much, the threshold of a new life.

23. Crossing the Tiber

I had fallen, like so many Anglo-Catholics before me, for Rome.
Enchanted by its mystique, its counter-cultural appeal, its glamour,
I found myself drawn to the banks of the Tiber, and looking over
to the other side I fancied I saw myself as a Benedictine monk, a
vocation extraordinary in itself, but particularly difficult to explore
within Anglicanism. There are monks and nuns in the Church of
England but very few compared with the Roman Catholic Church,
which in England alone could turn out dozens for every one of ours.

The timing was awkward; the ordination of women priests in the
Church of England was about to arrive and had provoked some of
the more conservative Anglo-Catholics to cross over to Rome in protest. I was, and am, very much in favour of women's ordination and
did not want to be seen as part of that protest at all; but the Eternal
City is the Eternal City for a reason and I found myself drawn in opposite directions, towards its unfading allure and to the home I had
made, even if not for long, at the Anglo-Catholic end of the C of E.

In the end it was Dazzle who got me over, made explicit what
others did not, answered my questions as efficiently as the catechism
of the Catholic Church, and made me think it might be possible. I
said nothing to anyone at St Alban's Holborn but after a retreat at
Buckfast, where I had become a regular visitor, I finally decided I
had to cross over. Dazzle offered to prepare me for this, to take me
through the necessary elements of being a Roman Catholic, but first
insisted that I stop receiving communion in the Church of England.
That Sunday at St Alban's instead of going up to the rail for the
bread and wine I held back, a tiny difference in the choreography,

but one that was noticed, and after the service I went to see John Gaskell. I stood in the doorway of his study, embarrassed, and he sat at his desk and I told him I was poping, as the expression goes. He looked wounded and said, 'I think you have much to offer the Church of England.' I said I did not really believe in the Church of England, and he winced again. 'Has Derek Jennings anything to do with this?' he asked. 'Yes,' I said, 'he's been very helpful.' It was one of the more painful exchanges of my life, and I did not have the stomach to prolong it, so I said goodbye and left, leaving my cassock and cotta hanging up in the huge vestry. I called Peter, by now running his own parish, and told him, and he was kind about it, but not everyone was. It was a difficult time in the Church's life, a time of the parting of friends, and some saw it as an abandonment, some as a betrayal. It was definitely ungrateful. I had learned much at St Alban's, and I had been very well cared for by Peter and John, and tested their patience greatly, too, but I chose to submit to the impulse to leave it all behind and step forwards into something new, such a recurring trope in this tale.

There were difficulties. The Church of England, for all its lack of enthusiasm for gay rights, in its breadth and equivocation provided some room for gay people to be gay. But in the Roman Catholic Church no such latitude existed, in spite of the equally surprisingly high number of gay men, some actively so, around. The Roman discipline was clear: homosexuality was disordered and sinful and intrinsically evil. I did not believe that for a moment, and wondered how I could belong to a Church that so explicitly stated I should not belong to it. Dazzle tried to reassure me that the condemnation was of the sin and not the sinner, but it seemed to me that was a distinction which made no difference when it came down to it. I did not care much if I was being loved or not by the person condemning me to exile, disgrace, prison or psychiatric intervention. Dazzle, too, in his tense, celibate state, seemed to me to have paid a high price for his priesthood and I had moments of dread when I saw myself in his shoes. My parents were down in London one day so I took them to lunch at the Ivy and Dazzle came along, too. I suppose he thought it opportune to reassure them about my move, but he managed to talk about 'homosexuality' with such clinical detachment, as if it were epilepsy, that they just looked more and more worried as the waiters came and went.

But I thought, too, of Martin, Russell's friend from Edinburgh, who seemed to me to be gay and a Roman Catholic without becoming invisible or preposterous; and I knew in the pews that many faithful Roman Catholics were less exercised by matters of sexuality than the clergy. The Church's view on contraception, for example, was routinely ignored by millions, and if it angered God, he showed no sign of it. So I went to see Dazzle once a week in his room at the Catholic Chaplaincy and he took me very diligently through the catechism, the highway code of the Catholic faith, in which every conceivable question is answered with a thoroughness that could fatigue St Thomas Aquinas. Much of it was familiar to an Anglo-Catholic, and I had no problem with the Real Presence or transubstantiation, but the management structure, so to speak, was very different, much clearer and direct than the Church of England's, and the tone was different, too, rather legalistic and – well – Roman, which I found less congenial. I wrote to my friend Fr David, now Abbot of Buckfast, to ask if he would be prepared to receive me formally into the Catholic Church. After a tellingly long pause, and a prod from Dazzle, he agreed to receive me at Pentecost; but before he did I had to make my confession for the first time, as far as the Catholic Church was concerned, to seek absolution for the freight of sin I had accumulated so far, which was substantial. If I were obliged to do that now I would call in at the nearest church and kneel and get on with it, but then, like a bride who wants the bishop for her wedding, I sought out a clerical celebrity. I went to see Monsignor Alfred Gilbey, former Chaplain of Cambridge University, well into his eighties then, a priest so old school he wore the same sort of hat as Chesterton's Fr Brown, and who had known the glamorous converts in whose footsteps I thought I was treading, Evelyn Waugh and Graham Greene and Muriel Spark. The monsignor lived then at the Travellers Club in Pall Mall, where I went to see him, and if I had thought Catholicism was really an interesting if minor tradition in English literature the exchange I had with him in his little chapel upstairs rather put paid to that. He was searching, and shrewd, and he was kind, and afterwards gave me tea and anchovy toast and we spoke about Northamptonshire, where his gin-making family once had its country seat.

Pentecost arrived and I went down to Buckfast with Dazzle and one other witness, my younger brother, Will. I have a photograph of us all, Dazzle in his dog collar looking rather mischievous, Fr David in his habit and gold cross, looking abbatial, and Will, not especially religious, looking like the best man at a wedding in his suit and tie. Will is welcome company anywhere, but I think also I wanted someone with me who knew my whole story, from childhood and adolescence, my years of glory and catastrophe, and someone who was not so thoroughly fatigued by my restless chopping and changing he would not begrudge too much giving up another weekend for it. Fr David, in the mitre and crozier of a Lord Abbot, duly received me into the Roman Catholic Church in the Blessed Sacrament Chapel at the east end of the abbey. It's a modernist extension to a building which, although not old, looks old, its eastern wall a giant stained-glass window showing Christ at the altar blessing the bread and wine. I was now able to receive what Christ blessed, not a doubtful version of it, the best the Church of England could provide since it had separated itself from Rome in the sixteenth century, but the real thing, in its fullness. According to Roman Catholic teaching, the bread and wine I had been eating and drinking so far was just that, bread and wine, blessed not by priests but by men – and *women* – in fancy dress. Now that I was one of the flock a monk let me into a little joke, and showed me the altar in the abbey which they allowed visiting Anglicans to use. It was dedicated to the English martyrs, Roman Catholics who had been executed for their faith by the Protestant Queen Elizabeth. Was the sense of deliverance that I had felt that Sunday morning in St Alban's not really genuine? Was the faith and the priesthood of John and Peter and so many others a risible mistake? *Roma locuta est, causa finita est* – Rome has spoken, the matter is closed. But I wondered if the assurance of exclusive authenticity was really the last word.

These ecumenical concerns soon faded at the parish church I had started attending since leaving St Alban's. St John the Divine served the north London Irish community in Islington and the gentrifying converts of Barnsbury and Canonbury. I liked the mix, with kids in Arsenal shirts on high and holy days alongside former Anglicans like me with whom I would occasionally exchange glances during the more appalling hymns of modern Catholic worship. People were perfectly polite, but not anxious to make friends, and in this denominational honeymoon one of the things I liked most was not being asked to do anything. Nobody even asked me who I was, and I sat quietly at the back trying to learn the basics. I knew the Roman prayer book and Mass already, because we had used them at St Alban's, but the culture took a bit more getting used to. The clergy were simply too busy to maintain the one-on-one relationship I was used to in the less densely thronged C of E, and its clerical culture kept them not distant from the people but separate from the people, the better to do the things they had to do. Another difference I noticed was there was no ecclesiastical connoisseurship of the kind I was used to, going to churches where you could tick off the pukka things that were done, like the music, the choreography, even the handwriting of the vicar.

There was none of that at St John's. It was a big parish with lots of families, many of whom were connected through the primary school. I did not really figure, I think, in the parliaments after Mass on the pavement outside. I would have been left alone entirely had I not known one of the women who worshipped there through her husband, a builder who worked on a friend's house, and through her I began to get nods of recognition, and eventually an invitation to become a reader at Mass. One of my neighbours saw me read one day and began to say hello when we passed in the street. Another time when a Catholic neighbour died I stopped and made the sign of the cross as the hearse came down the street on the way to the funeral. This mark of respect was returned by the family, who were said to be involved in organised crime, and one of them told me that my car, if I'd had one, could henceforth be parked in the street without any danger of being broken into.

At college, now halfway done, my conversion meant that I fell out of the semi-official feeder system for the Anglican priesthood. If I wanted to explore a vocation to monastic life, rather than a parish life, that meant becoming part of a monastic community, and the opportunity to do that was still a long way off. I started going to the weekly Catholic Mass at college, and got closer to Dazzle, for whom I became a sort of unofficial assistant, but I did not think for a moment of no longer attending the college Eucharist, or keeping up with the choir, so I never really left Anglicanism behind. The academic course, too, was a very Anglican sort of syllabus, and I was at home in it, and was again a little dismayed to see in Buckfast's library some of the books which we were using as texts marked with a white P for Protestant as a warning to the reader.

I was also now an award-winning broadcaster, and that perhaps made me think, not really consciously, of the possibility of a different future altogether. I loved doing *The Mix*, my programme on Radio Five, and after I won the Sony I was encouraged to receive a letter from the then Chairman of the BBC Governors, Sir Marmaduke Hussey. In it he thanked me for reflecting such credit on the organisation and expressed the wish that we would continue to work together long into the future. I began to wonder if my photograph might one day appear alongside Robert Robinson's and Ned Sherrin's and Sue Lawley's on the wall of heroes outside the Board Room at Broadcasting House.

And then they cancelled the programme. This was a very good lesson for someone starting out at the BBC. We think it is all about the programmes, and in the end, if it gets it right, it is. But it is also about the politics, and the strange economics of licence fee-funded public broadcasting, and about paperclips and who's in power and who's not, and the *Daily Mail*, and charter renegotiations, and all the other numberless pressures that affect the life of a big and venerable public sector institution, even one that dresses itself in a bit more glamour than the NHS or the Department of Education. I was a victim of a reorganisation at the top, which took some of the glitter off my prize.

Soon after, someone I had worked with at *Night Network* asked if I wanted to do an ITV God-slot programme called *Divine Inspiration*, made by LWT to satisfy, I don't think it is too cynical to say, its charter obligations. It was, unusually, a quiz show, subtitled 'Have I Got Good News For You?', which made me the equivalent of Angus Deayton, although a very cut-price one. Like him I sat between two teams of three, which might include a bishop, a Sufi, or Claire Rayner, asking them questions about the Bible, the tradition and religious things in the news. It wasn't very well received at all; indeed, two of the reviews were the worst I have ever received – one a particularly excoriating piece in the *Church Times* from the Rector of Cogenhoe and the other in a national broadsheet, which denounced me, more or less, as the worst thing to happen to Christendom since Charles Darwin.

I enjoyed the technical aspects of making the programme, I enjoyed being back in the LWT building, even if I did get stuck in a lift on the way to the studio one day with a rabbi, a bishop and a hermit, a situation which cries out for a punchline. The programme itself, however, was not a success. I looked uncomfortable, it lacked the edge of other less constrained quizzes, and I began to discover how difficult it is in religion to achieve accessibility without lapsing into whimsy. I invited a party from King's once to watch an episode being taped and could tell from their faces, a mixture of boredom and *schadenfreude*, that it was not going to be listed among my triumphs. So when the lady from LWT called one day to say the ratings were in and we had three times the numbers of the previous programme in that slot I called Dazzle, one of the programme's most trenchant critics, and crowed. I put the phone down and it rang again and it was the same lady from LWT who said she'd made a mistake and the ratings she had given me were really for *The Little House on the Prairie*. Needless to say, *Divine Inspiration* lasted only for a season but my picture was up on the LWT wall of heroes for years to come, alongside Hale and Pace, before being tossed on the bonfire of the vanities following franchise reorganisation.

What a strange sort of student I must have seemed to my peers and my teachers, picked up by BBC drivers to go and speak to the nation, even the tiny fraction of it listening to Radio Five, paying for stationery at the Student Union shop with a Gold Card and getting a look of withering scorn from the Socialist Worker on the till, lunching in the staff dining room, which had a carpet and choice of potatoes, because the student canteen was so ghastly. I already had a life in London, unlike those who had arrived after school or a gap year, and I remember slightly disconcerting my fellow students by taking them for supper at the Groucho Club or to the opera at Covent Garden, hospitality they would struggle to return on a student grant. We went once on a Chaplaincy trip to Vienna to see the relics of the Habsburg Empire and then on to Budapest to see Brother Roger, leader of the Taizé community, lead an ecumenical congress. I was keen to go, too, but made my own arrangements, travelling separately and staying not in the youth hostels the others stayed in but at the Hotel Sacher in Vienna, where I entertained some of my scruffy fellows to tea and *Sachertorte* as the maître d' looked on with undisguised loathing. The next morning a limousine arrived to take me to the station where I was booked on the train to Budapest, but the driver mistook my instructions, or I gave him the wrong instructions, and he drove me to a different station. When I realised the mistake, I snapped at him and he apologised so abjectly I was ashamed of myself and gave him a huge tip. In Budapest I stayed at another grand hotel where I spent the day in the steam bath before going to hear Brother Roger preach in a featureless stadium to a crowd of thousands, young people from all over the world, whom he invited to say together the Lord's Prayer in our different languages. 'Give us this day our daily bread,' I murmured, but dined later on goulash and *nokedli* and the nicest cherry strudel I have ever eaten.

It was hardly a life of evangelical poverty and humility and anyone seeking to discern in it the makings of a monk may have struggled. My academic performance was more encouraging. I was diligent, far more motivated than I would have been at eighteen, and I worked hard. The harder I worked the more I enjoyed it and I discovered that I was quite good at Church history, quite good, too, at New Testament Greek, not so good at philosophy, but I persevered and began to get good marks. Adam Mars-Jones had introduced me to the London Library, the wonderful private members' library in St James's Square, where ticket holders can access the vast labyrinth of the stacks and fall asleep in leather armchairs in the Reading Room to be woken by a gong, respectfully struck at closing time. One morning I was working there, the Reading Room as silent as a crypt in those pre-laptop days, and just before eleven o'clock a voice came over the tannoy to remind us that it was 11 November and asking us to kindly observe two minutes' silence. The hour struck, and we shifted a little in our chairs, maintaining a rather more solemn sort of silence than the silence we had maintained so far, and then returned to our noiseless study. I wrote most of my essays there thanks to an excellent theology section, less frequently visited than the theology library at King's, so I could have almost unlimited access to our texts.

 I may have been absent from the college library and the student canteen but I was very much present in the choir. I was an indifferent bass but got better, and enjoyed myself more and more as we worked our way through the Anglican choral repertoire, which I half remembered but still felt stirred by, and Renaissance polyphony, contemporary music and early music. One Christmas, for the carol service the Director of Music, Ernie, decided we would do a piece by the fourteenth-century French composer Guillaume de Machaut, 'Ma Fin Est Mon Commencement', a trio for male voices, one of them mine. Ernie was not a great organiser and we never got round to rehearsing it until the day of the carol service itself, when an assistant breezed through it, confident of the competence of his three singers. That confidence was, alas, misplaced, for that evening, as candlelight flickered round a full chapel, Ernie marked the first beat of the bar and we came in in three different places and at three different speeds. That attempt was aborted and he tried again, to no better effect, and I remember his face of woe and a dismissive gesture indicating our commencement was in fact our fin. Good for me, the chart-topping artist, to fail so lamentably and look a fool, and I heard later my disgrace mimicked by the other members of the choir.

I may have seemed wildly exotic at King's but my friends and family were simply relieved that I was functioning again. It was difficult for some of them to understand my religious allegiance, when there had been so much media coverage of fundamentalists insisting that AIDS was divine punishment for our wicked ways. Some of us, involved in the London Lighthouse or other places where people with AIDS and HIV were looked after, encountered Christians in a very different light, as carers and as volunteers and as organisers of simple goodness, but these exemplars of charity were sometimes obscured by the preachers of judgement. Goodness, however, abounds and may surprise us. One young man I particularly remember was admitted to the Lighthouse in a desperate state. He was from a small town, the first person there to be diagnosed HIV positive, then the equivalent of a death sentence. His life fell apart. Too frightened to tell his family and friends he one night got drunk and went out on his motorbike, missed a corner and ended up lying in the middle of the road, covered in blood. I don't suppose anyone ever felt more wretched.

And then, out of the darkness, a tall figure walked towards him, brilliant with light. It was a police officer, in a high-visibility jacket. The man lying in the road did not expect to be sympathetically treated by anyone, let alone a policeman dealing with a crashed drunk, but nevertheless, mindful that he was bleeding and incapable and infectious, he said to the policeman, 'You need to know I'm HIV positive.' The policeman knelt beside him, put his arm around him, and said, 'And you need to know that someone loves you.'

As I recovered from the disaster of the previous year, I began to function again socially, not in gay clubs, their enchantments rather dulled since my humiliation, but in a new circle which opened when I met, through Emma Freud, Helen Fielding, then earning her living as a journalist and living in a little flat in Primrose Hill. Helen had been at Oxford with Richard Curtis and Rowan Atkinson and that circle of comics and writers and musicians who became famous in the eighties and nineties. As Helen and I got closer so I got closer to them, a part-timer in their glamorous world. This was attractive not only because I was star-struck and quite liked the idea of spending a week in a villa with Mr Bean but because it was a world untouched by AIDS. I couldn't face another sick room, those dreadful acronyms, another horribly shortened life; but I did re-establish contact with old friends, like Hugo and Kevin, survivors of our original gang. Kevin was steady as a rock, still living in the same flat in south London he'd lived in when we first met, still working for the same council, and he was one of the few people who had seen me at my lowest who I could still bear to be around. Hugo was now living with Jimmy, an unlikely friendship between a working-class Glaswegian and a public school-educated posh boy, and perhaps that is why I felt a little awkward about it. Hugo, however, matched Jimmy – almost – in his appetite for sex and clubs and having a good time and domestically they matched, too, Hugo patient with the pitch and toss of Jimmy's passions, Jimmy at last at ease with a flatmate who knew how to take care of Le Creuset cookware. They, too, had moved to Islington, to a lovely Georgian house in the conservation area, but I used to arrange to meet up with Hugo in town because I did not feel entirely at ease around Jimmy, although nothing was ever said. One day Hugo and I met for breakfast and he was in a foul mood, a hangover I thought, and he got into a row with the waitress about the state of his fried egg. It was not just the egg that was in a state. A few weeks later Jimmy called to say that Hugo had been admitted to St Mary's Hospital.

He was in the HIV unit, which was agog to see Jimmy as a visitor, only one step down from Lady Di or Elton John in celebrity value. My awkwardness with him did not seem very important now in our shared devotion to Hugo and the demands of dealing with someone dying; for Hugo was dying, the immune system good for nothing, his body collapsing in the undiagnosable let alone irresistible assault of the disease. The medical staff made him as comfortable as possible, understanding that while smoking around an oxygen supply is inadvisable not allowing him to smoke or drink – Campari was his poison – would not be either. He was very frail and thin and I remember miserably asking a nurse if they could give him some vitamins, and she looked at me and said nothing and I realised he was going to die. Dying takes some doing, and those who are undergoing it have enough to be getting on with. So it is those around them who flap, wanting to make this event especially meaningful or solemn or tender.

We decided that we wanted Hugo to come home and demanded the hospital staff obliged, full of the righteousness of the soon-to-be-bereaved. A charge nurse talked us down and said Hugo would probably not survive the trip in the ambulance and that even if he did they would not be able to provide as good a level of care for him at home as they would here in hospital. Jimmy disappeared, and came back an hour or so later with rolls of wallpaper that Hugo had chosen for a makeover, and his bedside lamp, and some of his things, and we tried to make the hospital room as much like home as possible.

I don't know how much of this Hugo was aware of. He had moments of lucidity. After a period of intense hallucinating, when he was convinced the Abbot of Downside had come to say hello, he quietened down. 'Am I dying?' he asked. I said, 'I think so.' He said, 'Thank fuck for that.' His friends sat with him in shifts as he went in and out of consciousness, topped up with morphine administered through a motorised device. The Abbot of Downside appeared again – Hugo had been at the boarding school run by its monks – so I got in touch with the community, and his former housemaster, and they prayed for his soul. His mother appeared, too, but in real life, and his younger brother came up from Devon and burst into tears when he saw Hugo wasted on the bed. I was trying to make myself useful, preparing people who were arriving to see him for the shock they were about to receive, telling them how to interpret his hallucinatory monologues, trespassing, actually, where others belonged, caught up in the drama of what was happening and a bit off my face on cocaine, with which we fuelled the long night watches.

One day I was sitting with him alone during a period of lucidity and he suddenly doubled up with pain and shat himself spectacularly. We were both covered in it, and, trying to contain my retching, I did my best to clean us both up. I thought he had passed out but as I knelt at his side, he leaned forward and kissed me on the cheek. He died the next day while I was in Garfunkel's having a break and a burger. In the press of weeping friends around his bedside I awkwardly held his toe for a moment and then we prepared his body for the crossing of the Styx, a bottle of Campari in the crook of his arm and a packet of Marlboro in his hand.

We bade Hugo farewell in two goes. He had a friends' funeral at the London Lighthouse, where his nephews and nieces left drawings of Uncle Rat, as they called him, on his coffin, not really understanding that he was in it, and there were readings, which we surreptitiously squabbled over until his friend James said, 'It's not a competition.' And we shared memories, the politer ones, and some of his favourite country music, which was execrable. And a few days later I arranged a Requiem Mass in the crypt chapel at Westminster Cathedral, where four of us sang a Mass setting among the tombs of Cardinal Archbishops, and his brother read from Job and his mother led the mourners; the rival funeral, Jimmy called it. Hugo's old housemaster was celebrant and I put him up at the Groucho Club, the first time, he said, he'd slept in a double bed since entering the monastery.

In the middle of one of those long nights, when Hugo was dying, I went down to the chapel in St Mary's and lit a candle and read some of the prayers left on the board and sat alone at the back. I wondered if I might there be overwhelmed with anger at his underserved suffering, and rail at God's cruel indifference, but I did not. I remembered an expression of Hugo's – 'safe in the arms of catastrophe' – and thought then of Julian of Norwich's utterly insupportable conviction that 'All shall be well, and all manner of things shall be well'.

24. *Tu Es Citrus*

After Hugo died there was something I had to do, something I had been putting off, but could put off no longer.

I spent the next fortnight taking deep breaths on friends' doorsteps, before telling them – the good news – that I was not HIV positive, and – the trickier news – that I had made it up. I had no idea how people would react, especially considering the grief they were suffering as a result of all our friends who had died not from a fiction but a reality. Jimmy was first. He said, 'That took something to admit, doll' and that, more than anything, confirmed that the terms of friendship that had been lost in the pressures of pop stardom were restored. I told Kevin, who was angered, but swallowed it and said, 'Oh, Elsie.' I told Emma in a letter rather than face-to-face – there's only so much humiliation one can endure – and that afternoon a biker arrived at the door with a box of muffins and a note saying 'Best news I've had in a while'. And I told Matthew, who did not take it so well. In fact he was angry, which caught me by surprise after a run of generously uncritical reactions. In guilt, and a bit frightened, I went to a posh gents' barbers in Holborn and bought a large basket of manly grooming products, and sent it to him in the hope that this would be acceptable. It was not. I called and got no reply. I wrote and got no reply. I wrote again, with what I hoped was passionate eloquence, but again received no reply, and I realised that I had been called on my behaviour and had not got away with it. It was a while before it occurred to me why this might be, that maybe Matthew actually cared about me enough to find the prospect of my illness and death upsetting.

After a while I stopped knocking on the door. I just had to get used to it, as I had had to get used to Billy's unwillingness to say it was all all right really. It was a bitter lesson for me to reflect on – that as AIDS took friend after friend by *force majeure* I had managed to lose these through my own efforts.

If adoption of Christian faith did not bring about an immediate and obvious improvement in self-awareness, let alone elementary ethical competence, I don't think this was because my conversion had not been genuine or profound. I had been in a deep, deep hole and I was climbing out of it, like Adam in the orthodox icon of the resurrection, yanked by Jesus into unimaginable light, and I was blinded by it and too used to the darkness to leave it entirely behind. A dramatic conversion, like mine, takes time to work its way through your thinking and doing, and even after years of discipline and practice the old Adam may reappear for time to time, looking over his shoulder at that dark hole and missing the familiarity of its shadows and grip.

It was a whole year before Matthew and I sat down and talked; a painful conversation, in a pub in Hampstead, and I had to hear an unadorned account of my shortcomings as a friend, a man and a human being. He was completely right about that and all I could do was hear, mark, learn and inwardly digest and pray that would be enough to eventually make things right.

My thirtieth birthday arrived and I marked it with a big party at the Groucho Club. I hired the upstairs, gave a big dinner, stocked a generous bar, hired a magician who did rather dazzling things with cards and coins, and commissioned a *croque en bouche* which towered trendily and stickily over very mixed company. The photographs show Dazzle in a dog collar and silk rabat taking to a leather queen, Peter and Keith from St Alban's Holborn with Harry Enfield, a gay porn star of my acquaintance and my parents. I had a whale of a time, blew out my candles with gusto, made a speech, had a snog with someone I shouldn't have snogged in a place I shouldn't have been, but it was a remark of Andy Lipman's that still resonates. As we talked about *Framed Youth* days in Brixton and how it all began, he looked at me and said, 'This is your goodbye, isn't it?'

I sat for my finals at King's in the summer of 1993. I worked hard revising, so hard my shoulder locked and Chris, the handsome ex-Commando, came back to my house and gave me a massage, the high point of physical excitement in all my undergraduate years, and I will remember it with happiness for the rest of my days. For the exams Sara's husband, Donald, lent me a tertiary relic of St Joseph of Cupertino, patron of examinees, and it sat on my desk, a speck of stuff that the citation claimed had come from a blanket he once used, as I worked my way through papers on the first epistle of Peter, and Jansenism, and the ontological argument of St Anselm.

St Joseph's intercession evidently paid off, for I got a First. I also won three prizes, for Doctrine, New Testament Greek and distinction in the exams for the Associateship and for the first time I began to feel that there was something to back up the rumour of my cleverness.

I celebrated, rather unusually for a new graduate, by renting a house in the south of France for the summer, a house on a hill outside La Garde-Freinet, with a wonderful view across Grimaud towards the Gulf of St Tropez. Guests were staggered, family first with Lorna, as near to family as not. It was just idyllic; the weather was perfect, the house was perfect, big but not grand, and we played boules and swam and went to Port Grimaud so Dad could have his favourite lunch of fish soup with garlicky bread and rouille. After family came friends, in batches – famous, glittery ones and notorious ones from the London club scene – there was nude bathing, and dancing all night, and an unscheduled visit from the son of the owner alerted, I supposed, to our enormities. That dropped off a bit in the last week, when we were joined by Adam and Sara, whose bathing manners were more seemly. On our last night Sara, a stargazer, made us lie out on the lawn, fragrant with thyme, to watch the Perseid shower pass overhead. Something else was passing, that kind of life, at least as lived by me. I thought of Andy Lipman's words at my birthday party, drank a bottle of marc, and thought this is not au revoir but adieu.

I passed also from Radio Five to Radio Three. As *The Mix* came to its end I was asked if I would like to review an Oscar Wilde play for *Night Waves*, Radio Three's arts and culture magazine programme. Then they asked me back, to sit in when the regular presenters were on holiday, and, in that typical BBC fashion, never asked me to go away again. It was just as well my degree had given me some intellectual confidence, for *Night Waves* was terrifying, distinguished people in their fields talking to the no less distinguished in theirs.

For the first six months or so I felt like a complete fraud, on the brink of being exposed. Of course I was a fraud, and was exposed regularly, once when I found myself having to pronounce on air the artist Gaudier-Brzeska, which I tried to obscure by pretending to cough at the same time. There were German architects, and Romanian sculptors (it is BrrnKOOSH, not BranCUsi), quotes I misattributed, and lofty pronouncements on things I knew nothing about, which I hope provided some entertainment value for those listening at home. After six months or so I realised, first, that most of the contributors thought they were frauds, too, and, second, that it did not really matter.

My vocation, perceived perhaps more steadily by Andy Lipman than by me, required some attention, and at Dazzle's suggestion – more like insistence – I signed up for a series of talks at Archbishop's House, next to Westminster Cathedral, arranged by Cardinal Hume to encourage men exploring vocations to the priesthood. The first was hosted by the Cardinal himself, a Benedictine monk before the cloister gave him up for greater things. We sat in a drawing room and his chaplain played a video that had been made about the life of a young priest, designed to show how vibrant and engaged such a life could be. It wasn't bad, but, like most of the efforts of the unworldly to be worldly, it was woefully out of date, and showed him wearing white socks, trendy in the eighties, not in the nineties, and definitely not with a black clerical suit. And he kept on going to the gym and working out and running round Hyde Park in a singlet. When it finished the Cardinal asked if there were any questions, I said, 'Is jogging compulsory?' which made him laugh.

I was invited to another evening at Archbishop's House but I was a little late in arriving and stood in the dark outside the door and rang the bell. It was not answered, I suppose because the session had begun and there was no one to answer the door. I thought about ringing it again, but decided not to. Knock and it shall be opened unto you, says Jesus in the Sermon on the Mount. But it did not open unto me, providentially, because I think I knew by then that the Catholic priesthood was not for me.

So what door should I knock on? I went on a vocations weekend with the Jesuits at Osterley Park, where I laboured through a stalled conversation with one of the priests as I tried to explain myself and he struggled to imagine my Jesuit future. Dazzle took me up to Ampleforth, the Benedictine monastery in Yorkshire where Cardinal Hume had been Abbot, but it was too soon after Hugo died and I was all over the place, and people were kind but not perhaps fully prepared for a grieving gay man in the midst of the AIDS crisis. Also my notoriety preceded me and one of the younger members of staff at its college said he'd heard that I was in a pop band and when I said I was, he replied, a little too quickly, 'Well, I've never heard of you.' A put-down, rather typical of the tweedy, beagling culture of the place, but I loved the liturgy and the scale of things and the activity that you find only in big communities, a sense of confidence and purpose, even attracting vocations from young people, who leavened its well-ripened lump.

I was much more at home in the parish in Islington where a different sort of Catholic culture pertained, more mixed, more grounded in common experience, or so I thought. There was a priest who had been connected with the parish, who was quite well known as the only openly gay priest, or fairly openly gay priest, in the diocese. I went to see him and asked him if he thought it was possible to be a reasonably well-adjusted gay man and a Catholic priest and he said yes, undoubtedly, but he looked away as he did and I thought, 'I don't believe you.' Why *would* a gay man want to be a Catholic priest? One answer is that it offers much to someone who is called or obliged to live the celibate life. Catholic priests can get alongside others, especially the poor and the marginalised, better than most because they do not have to be home for dinner, or to read a bedtime story, and have room in their emotional lives for those who would tax others too much. The abuse scandals of recent years have obscured a much greater truth: that priests can live lives of extraordinary dedication and service of a kind that can only be realised when priesthood is your first and primary commitment to others. For some being a priest simply made loving possible. I often thought that of Dazzle, for whom intimacy was so difficult, and who could be so waspish and sometimes snarly, and whose childhood was a desert of affection, but who was finally able to love people through his priesthood.

I learned a bit more about his loving priesthood when he was dying. I met him one day at the V&A where the Pugin exhibition had just opened, to which the High Church clergy of England flocked. Dazzle, unusually, was trying to avoid them, and told me over coffee that he had been diagnosed with something horrible and possibly incurable. I thought he would be quite resilient, but he declined very quickly, and – a terrible invalid – he took to his bed and began willing himself to death. Dying drew an extraordinary mixture of people – Princess Margaret, Alec Guinness, a French monk who made the journey from Mont Ventoux to his vicarage in Ealing with oils to anoint him, and a succession of county ladies who called in with jars of game broth from their estates – even the nurse who came to take care of him turned out to be an Italian contessa.

The game broths, the holy oils, the famous names – nothing made any difference and it became obvious he was about to die. I called the Cardinal's chaplain, and at teatime on a dark, cold January day, as his friends sat at his bedside reading passages from the sermons of John Henry Newman, the Cardinal arrived. He went upstairs and we went downstairs and were sitting at the kitchen table when the Cardinal appeared in the doorway and said, 'He's gone.' After he'd prayed for Dazzle, he'd started saying the Gloria in English, but couldn't remember it and reverted to Latin, which the patient would have much preferred, and on the word Amen Dazzle had given up the ghost and expired. The *bona mors,* the good death, he would have wanted. I discovered that through the weeks of his illness he had spent hours hearing confessions at Westminster Cathedral, the agent of God's mercy relieving people from the burden of their sins so that they could live renewed.

I left Dazzle's deathbed and went back home, where I found on the answerphone, with unthinkably bad timing, a message saying that Andy Lipman had been admitted to hospital and was dying. I went straight there but Andy did not know who I was and I thought, I am ashamed to admit it, 'Thank Christ, I don't have to come again' and I left. As he declined, a friend called me to say that I should come if I wanted to say goodbye, but I could not bring myself to do that, I could only pray for him, and then felt so guilty I hadn't been I didn't go to the funeral.

One afternoon I took Foggy for a walk and a run in the church-yard round the corner. I sat on a bench reading Evening Prayer, the two-birds-with-one-stone approach to my obligations, but was distracted by a commotion. A drunk guy who had fallen asleep on the grass awoke to find Foggy eating his sandwich. In a rage he belted the dog, so I ran over and said, 'Please don't hit the dog' and was about to say, 'Let me buy you another sandwich' but he hit me, so hard he knocked me out, and the next thing I knew I was lying on the ground, unsure how I got there, with the taste of blood in my mouth, which I spat out along with a chip from a tooth. Some-one came to help me as the drunk wandered away and, rattled, I put Foggy on his lead and went home. It was not being knocked down that rattled me so much; it was the clear and irrecoverable realisation, as consciousness returned, that I did not want to be a Benedictine monk.

Something had shifted. I began to look forward and saw not a cloister but a different kind of retreat, a different kind of goodbye, not the drama and romance of the Abbey door closing behind me, but something better matched to the reality of who I was and where I was and what I was and what God might do with that. At first I settled on redecorating the house, covering up the painterly extrav-agance of the post-pop band makeover with soberer, solid colours, putting down coir and putting up curtains, but I was no less restless than before. I went up to Northamptonshire one weekend with Rosie and a friend in his 2CV and I took them to see some of the places I loved when I was growing up, the tiny limestone and thatch villages along the Nene and around the great houses of the great estates. I felt the pull of the landscape as strongly as I ever had, I felt the pull of my own past and my parents and the place I came from; and I felt something fall into place.

I decided to move from London to Northamptonshire. I broke the news to Rosie, who had put up with my self-centredness for years, and she cried. I learned to drive. I found a home for Foggy with a woman who lived in Berkhamsted and had a dozen dachshunds already. I resolved to test my vocation not against a backdrop of the monkish paintings of Caspar David Friedrich and the novels of Evelyn Waugh, but in the place I grew up, and in an attempt, I think, to rediscover the child and the youth abandoned when I escaped to reinvent myself in London, so full of opportunity and possibilities for transformation, and fame and fortune and the big glitter.

25. The Comfort of Strangers

In an estate agent's window in Kettering I saw a house for sale. It was in Grafton Underwood, one of those villages built to work a grand estate, an idyllic place, with a street of thatched cottages along a duck-filled brook, a tiny post office, a pretty fourteenth-century church and a dairy herd which ambled up and down the street twice a day, knocking off wing mirrors as they passed. It was four miles from Kettering, with its mainline station and Catholic church for my travel and sacramental needs, but distant enough not to intrude on its rural charm. The house, Bird's Farm, in limestone and thatch, with a 'bide-a-wee inglenooke' according to the particulars, was one half of a double cottage built around 1620 at right angles to the brook. An extension with a new kitchen and utility and shower room had gone on in the eighties, but it needed some work so the builders arrived and there was a comedy when the wrong sort of door appeared in the wrong place and was reported by neighbours to the Planning Authorities whom I had to placate and persuade that my intentions were honourable and in line with its Grade II listing.

I had thought that I would live alone at Bird's Farm, for the three or four days a week I was there, but I had been seeing more of my brother Will, then living in London and working for a housing charity, and we had begun to talk a lot about childhood, checking my memory of an event against his, thinking how we fitted into the family narrative, how the past connected to the present. Will, who had always preferred Northamptonshire to London, liked the look of Grafton Underwood, too, so when the offer of a job came up for a social worker to help Vietnamese refugees settle in the county, he took it and moved with me to Bird's Farm. Unpacked, our townie clothes hung on a rack by the back door – Moschino jackets and Nike trainers where you would expect to see waxed jackets and wellingtons.

Moving to the country is more than a change of scenery and costume. It is a change of life, especially social life. London's tightly packed tribes create particular social patterns, but in the country things are different – there are fewer people you have dinner with, you dine in rather than out, and you have to drive miles to see them. Staying over is the price you pay as a single man who wants to drink with dinner and there was a lot of waking up in beds other than my own, but alone now and sometimes awkwardly in a bottom bunk under a Harry Potter duvet. And then people kept coming for the weekend. I got a bit carried away with this, inviting people up until the bin bags of bed linen, taken for service washes in Kettering every Monday, became too much. Visitors were spaced more evenly, and more carefully mixed, especially London friends with local friends, whose manners might not quite match. One friend from London, flamboyant, noisy and drunk, tried to steal a car to get back home after a spectacularly disastrous dinner when his brilliant conversational sallies, or so he thought, were met with appalled silence.

I started going to the Catholic church in Kettering, to the Vigil Mass on Saturday evening, where you could sit at the back and no one bothered you, and I helped out playing the organ at the little church in the village at Evensong, that most durable and distinctive Church of England liturgy, which first got my attention when I was a boy chorister, which called me back that afternoon in Edinburgh, that called me still: *Almighty and most merciful Father, we have erred, and strayed from thy ways like lost sheep. We have followed too much the devices and desires of our own hearts . . .*

I am not sure it was erring or straying exactly but I was diverted, certainly, by *Night Waves*. The programme's brief was to cover everything in the arts apart from the concert hall, already covered elsewhere on the network. I knew a bit about music and theatre but nothing about contemporary painting, dance or sculpture, so *Night*

Waves was like a finishing school or, rather, a very congenial cram-mer. I would spend the week looking at lovely things and going to the theatre and the opera, trying to work up sufficient familiarity to survive a fifteen-minute conversation with an expert on the follow-ing Tuesday. Promiscuity is in the nature of a weekly programme and I found my own taste in things shifted simply because I was obliged to try things I would not normally have touched. There's a lot to be said for being made to try things.

I was also working again for Radio Five, now rechristened Radio Five Live, presenting its complaints programme, *Clear the Air* (it went out just before the football phone-in, *606*, but my suggestion we call ours *YOY* was not taken up). Listeners phoned in from Pinner and Motherwell and Truro, and we roped in colleagues to voice their letters in the days when hardly anyone used email. Most of the complaints were to do with areas in the BBC I knew little about, sports coverage and the news, a rather more macho and journalistic world than that of arts and culture. Some complaints were more wide-ranging, and my favourite came from a lady who called in one day: 'Marjorie is in Hemel Hempstead.' I said, 'What's your point?' She replied, 'I'm absolutely DISGUSTED with EVERYTHING' and put the phone down.

I came to feel at home on both networks, soft-voiced and slow-paced on Radio Three, brisk on Five Live. I felt at home, too, in the different worlds of London, where I worked and stayed for a part of the week, and the country, where I tried to spend most of my time. I bought a new bike and became addicted to cycling, on-road and off-road, rediscovering the landscape of my childhood and youth, or what was left of it. In the years since I had moved away much had changed; roads that were once there had gone and new roads had appeared, so I kept cycling in and out of the familiar, with a jerky, in-terrupted nostalgia. One day I cycled to Burton Latimer and decided to visit my grandfather's and great-grandfather's grave in the ceme-tery, not far from the field where my father watched the Hurricane shoot down the Dornier, and where today huge wind turbines slowly turn. I could not remember where the grave was, but as I looked I saw my brother Will, who by a mysterious coincidence had decided to do the same. We found it, marked with a Masonic symbol, and stood there, trying to locate ourselves in the narrative it told.

We were lucky my grandmother Kathleen was still alive – Grandy we called her – my father's mother, a contemporary of both Queen Victoria and Verdi, living now in a flat in Kettering and doing everything she could to stay out of the nursing home. Grandy and I became close in her last years. I had been a bit scared of her when she was the unchallenged materfamilias of us all, but we had both relaxed in our attitude to one another and she would talk to me with a frankness and humour, mostly about her husband, my extravagant and hilarious and philandering grandfather, as vivid in my memory now as he was in my childhood.

I was getting to know my parents on different terms, too, with the subtle shifts in power and gravity that occur in parent–child relationships. We would not only go to theirs for Sunday lunch, but they would come to ours, too, and the provided-for became providers. Moving five miles away meant that I could see them much more often, but regularly, and for an hour or two, rather than as infrequent overnight visitor, a scenario in which it was too easy to lapse into the habits of teenagehood. I was also, in this shifting balance of power, becoming the treat giver my father had been to us when we were boys. As a surprise I took my parents away for their wedding anniversary. I told them to pack for smart evenings and bring a passport. A car picked us up and drove us to Heathrow from where we flew to Venice in as much luxury as British Airways could afford. At the Gritti Palace, an old palazzo on the Grand Canal that had been turned into a small and very luxurious hotel, I heaved a bounty into the concierge's hand, and he ensured we ate in the fashionable bit of Harry's Bar, got tickets for La Fenice and had a launch to take us to Torcello, and the Lido, and the palazzo where Peggy Guggenheim stashed her bibelots. The hotel was lovely, a little jewel, with Murano chandeliers, dowager-dignified with age and, my favourite, proper linen bedlinen, changed every day, the chambermaids tossing the all but unsoiled sheets and pillowcases into a laundry barge which drew up alongside. We went to Murano to see glass being made by an impatient man who mustered a little enthusiasm when he tried to sell shimmering shelves of 'crystal ware' for tens of thousands of pounds until I told him firmly that we were not interested. My father, embarrassed, offered him a tip for his trouble, but he refused it with disdain. We visited a Franciscan friary on one of the islands and met a delightful old friar who had lived in High Wycombe and we talked about John Betjeman and British Rail while the waters of the Venetian lagoon lapped at his sandalled feet. He did not decline my father's offering, discreetly sealed in a Gritti Palace envelope.

There was more embarrassment than I had expected on this trip, not only my father's but mine, because in my excitement at the largesse I was about to endow them with I had not really thought what it might be like for them. Perhaps they were not entirely comfortable in the Gritti Palace, surrounded by unsmiling Americans in blazers and Rolexes, lunching at the Cipriani and paying for cappuccinos at Florian's with their Platinum Cards. Perhaps this kind of glamour and luxury was best left to legend. On our last day we came down to find the lobby in six inches of water, the concierge in wellington boots handing out umbrellas, and pelting rain outside. This little drama, far from spoiling things, rather made them, and as the stiff regime relaxed we all relaxed, too.

The glory of former days. My father's nostalgia for the Cap d'Antibes in the years after the war, his stories of Atlantic crossings on the *Queen Mary*, the theatres and restaurants and dances, were part of our family history, but they were history, tales of things gone by, preserved in a present that was very different. I, too, was beginning to look back at my glories, a little more distant every day, and this distance was noticed not only by me. Looking at a car one day the salesman recognised me and asked me what I was doing now. I said I was working for BBC radio and he said, with a faint note of triumph, 'Well, I've never heard you.' If I winced at these comments on my return to the ranks it was not for long, because it was also a release into a form of life that felt so much more livable than the dream-life of the past few years. It was not only my circumstances that were changing. I was changing, too. My conversion to Christianity – when the chains that bound me fell away – was just the beginning, a moment of vision, which dazzled and confounded, like the burning bush stopping the traffic, but people have to be on their way, and these moments of vision fade. The real work of conversion is gradual, the turning away from our fascination with ourselves, in so far as we can ever find a subject more fascinating, to give the completely unexpected reality of God a look in.

There are ways of doing this, primarily by following the discipline of prayer. And in spite of my eternal self-absorption and hard-heartedness and disinclination to give up any of my pleasures or privileges to follow Jesus Christ more faithfully, I did say my prayers. I was using the breviary, the Roman Catholic prayer book used by its clergy, which sets out, morning and evening, a round of psalms, Bible readings, prayers and hymns in tune with the seasons of the Church's year. For the slightly obsessive person it is a deep joy, immensely complicated, requiring more ribbons than a maypole, bits of card you stick in here and there, a constant turning forwards and backwards, until, like a run-in engine, it all comes together to permit what to many sounds like the most perfunctory prayer imaginable, as rushed as supper in a boys' boarding school, without relish or even savour, the words as undifferentiated as numbers in a telephone directory. But saying your prayers is not reading Shakespeare, and in a sense the more mechanically they're done the more effectively they achieve a detachment from the present moment, and in their drone the antennae unfurl that pick up the so often drowned-out or ignored frequencies by which God broadcasts his strange grace. Many religious traditions, I find, have something similar at the contemplative end of their practice. I am not saying it is the only way to be in communion with God – there are many ways to skin that cat – but it is the one in which I am most at home.

Even though I struggled to maintain this discipline amid all the distractions of work and play, I think it still opened up some cracks in my self-regard through which grace could leak. I had no idea how surprising and how powerful this grace could be, and how unexpected. And the biggest surprise for me was this: I began to have a great deal of sex.

I thought it was behind me. Christian faith gives you a respectable reason to retire from that fray, elected celibacy looking more like a sacrifice than a failure. But the truth was that I could not think of myself as someone desirable, I could not approach another man without the conviction, displayed in every word and gesture, that I would be as attractive to them as Quasimodo, Charles Laughton in a rubber face, leaping from sounding bell to bell in a peal of frustrated desire. Becoming a Roman Catholic, going to live in the country, was in some sense a repudiation of the desperate search for sexual satisfaction; the irony was that it was there I finally got some.

I had, without quite meaning to, got fit. I was cycling everywhere and going to the gym three times a week and I suppose it must have showed because even though I still thought of myself as Quasimodo, others did not. Like an expat calling in at the High Commission, I went to the gay club in Northampton once in a while to refresh my credentials. Gay life in the provinces, like social life, lies thinly on the ground, and the club was very inclusive of all kinds of gays, from bearish men with moustaches, to hysterical teenage screamers, to ordinary blokes who looked like anyone else, to veterans of the gay politics of the 1980s. I hung around at the back but my exotic past was revealed and I enjoyed a moment's vogue, even as an object of desire, for I supposed my anecdotal value was high if not my allure.

There, I met a semi-professional footballer with the unusual handicap of haemophilia, a story I did not press too hard, and he and I had the odd fling which invariably ended with him passing out drunk in the bedroom of the house he shared with straight footballing friends in the rougher end of town. The television was on permanently and as he snored I would get up to the sound of exotic football games from Malaysia or the Faroe Islands broadcast through the night, and drive home alone through the dawn, trying not to run over baby rabbits. Once he told me, with unusual vulnerability, that he would prefer it if I stayed, so he could wake up beside the person he went to sleep with. I knew I was very far from being that sort of a date, but thought it only polite to oblige, so that night I lay there awake while he snored beside me, the television on faintly in the background. Something was not right, and I realised it was what was coming out of the television – no cheers, no boos, but terse speech. I went downstairs and saw a grave-faced presenter say the Princess of Wales had been seriously injured in a car crash in Paris and that her lover, Dodi Al Fayed, had been killed. Curiosity triumphed over politesse, and I left him snoring and drove home as anxiety ratcheted up on the radio. I fell asleep on the sofa and woke up to discover that Diana was dead.

My abandonment of the semi-professional footballer for the death of a princess put an end to that faltering relationship, but I started to long for the comfort of strangers, and turned, in these pre-internet days, to ads in the local press for 'men seeking men' and went on a couple of dates. It was through one of these I discovered that more men were seeking men and in more surprising places than I had hitherto been aware. There followed some months of sexual adventure, and occasionally misadventure, conduct unbecoming a clergyman, but I was not a clergyman and to those who would think it unbecoming a Christian I would say yes, but also that this period of adventure allowed me finally put to rest the persistent and deeply damaging myth of my own undesirability. The glory of God, said St Irenaeus in the first century, is a person fully alive, and while he could not have had in mind late-night lay-by debaucheries at the turn of the twenty-first century, through them I got closer to being fully human than I ever had before.

I shared intimacies of the most profound and tender kind with people I would have only passed by in any other place or at any other time. A man who worked in a factory making tractors, disabled and all but unspeaking, spoke for hours about his life with such originality and wit I have never forgotten it. I lay under trees, the sun filtering through the leaves, with another man, a pork pie maker, whose soul was as unshadowed as any I have ever encountered. There were angrier, darker encounters, too: a man who walked through a park in Northampton where people went to meet anonymously and late at night, carrying a metal bar which he slapped threaten-ingly into the palm of his hand, and yet no one moved, perhaps, like wildebeest at waterholes ignoring the lion because the danger did not compute, or because we knew that his behaviour was ambigu-ous. There was comedy, too, bushes parting on a scene of complex debauchery to reveal a Buddhist monk in saffron robes doing a Walk for Peace across Britain. We all stopped what we were doing and said hello and he carried on his way, smiling evenly from beginning to end.

My great discoveries in the commonwealth of these encounters was, first, that men sometimes wither for lack of intimacy with other men; and, second, that rejection was not an ontological negation but merely the expression of a preference by a particular person at a particular moment, and that I was neither so loathsome, nor so significant, as I thought I was. There were occasional visitors back to Bird's Farm, a car not seen before parked in the drive, never un-noticed by Nancy Brains, my neighbour, who saw everything, but never gave a look, nor judged, nor spoke of it. But hardly any of them stayed. Like a true romantic, I chose to sleep alone – one way of putting it – though in truth I had no idea how to be close to people in that sort of way.

In what sort of way could I be close to people? When August came I took the High Road to Scotland, to the annual media junket of the Edinburgh Festival, and there I found a sort of answer to the question.

26. Recrossing the Tiber

I went to Edinburgh for *Loose Ends*, Ned Sherrin's Saturday morning programme on Radio Four on which I played a bit part, decamped with half the network to the Fringe, trying to get to the rising comedy acts before agents signed them up and Perrier, awards sponsor, anointed them kings. For the duration media people moved into flats vacated by locals, who took the rent and left for their holidays, leaving the New Town and the hotels and restaurants to the invaders. I was billeted in a flat that had been converted inexpertly from a Georgian house, so inexpertly the loo was wedged into an angle by the front door, a space so narrow you had to sit on it sideways to get your knees in. I realised I was too old for this and phoned Martin, Russell's friend whom I had last seen at his funeral, who at once invited me to come and stay with him.

Martin lived in a flat not far away in the New Town, too, on the top floor of a building at the edge of what is known as the gay village. It was bright and full of pictures and colour and shrines, almost, to Martin's abiding passions, the Kennedys, Glasgow Celtic Football Club, the saints of the Catholic Church and Native American heroes. The bed in the spare room was covered with a wolf blanket and in the guest bathroom a life-size plaster statue of Santa Maria Goretti, a young woman martyred protecting her virginity from an assailant, looked down on me mournfully as I sat in the bath while a procession of tiny figures in pointed hoods stood to attention around her. They can't be Klansmen, I thought, and they weren't – they were models of the figures who process round Seville in Holy Week, but the effect was unnerving.

Martin quite liked to unnerve. He wasted no time pretending to share the conventions of those around him and if he felt like raining on your parade he would. Sitting beside a river eating ice cream, watching a family of swans glide by on an idyllic summer's day, out of nowhere he said: 'I hate swans. Nasty, hissy things.' He was funny, he was honest, he was committed to his faith, to his work – his vocation – with abused children and those who victimised them, and he carried the burden of his own tough childhood without sentimentality or self-pity. We sat drinking and talking and went out to dinner and came back and drank and talked into the small hours.

We had so much in common – both gay, both Catholics, both on our own, both on the left – both had gone through the terrible darkness of the AIDS years, and both had lost, in Russell, someone we loved, a loss we did not speak about but it bonded us nonetheless. There was, however, much we did not have in common. Martin had been abandoned as a child and had grown up pretty much unwanted in a tough working-class Glaswegian background, the only mixed-race kid on the street, the only half-Scottish half-native American kid in the city, if not the country. He was as at odds with his childhood, I realised, as Jimmy Somerville with his, and like Jimmy he kept the harshness and dourness of those years at bay by turning himself into a walking talking protest, sharp, smart, with comeback. At Midnight Mass one year Martin was passing the cup of wine to people when they came up for communion. Midnight Mass brings out the infrequent attender, and one of them, a well-spoken woman, was unused to being invited to drink from the cup as well as share the bread. As she came up to Martin she said, 'Oh, is it the wine?' Martin replied, 'Well, it's not the Pepsi challenge', and thrust it in her hand.

And he was dogged in the faith. He cared little for theology, he hated churchiness, he had no time for conservative Catholics, ordained or lay, but he went to Mass faithfully, and said his prayers, and fought his corner if challenged by his friends, gay or straight, who thought his adherence to the Catholic faith was an inexplicable lapse of sense and judgement. But faith in Martin was not a self-inflicted and unhealing wound, and definitely not the enervating, pallid thing it can so often look like, but something he carried like a charge. I loved that. And I loved Martin, not as a lover, but as a friend beyond the normal call of duty, and wondered for a while if we would find in each other a companionship in life we both lacked. We talked about it once and I proposed buying a house to share in Edinburgh but when we made a list of the things that would be essential to our wellbeing it included two kitchens, two sitting rooms, separate front doors and no direct access from one to the other.

Martin and I may not have fallen in love, but I think I fell in love with Scotland in the same way you might fall in love with a person – headlong, and not always wisely, but there is nowhere I would rather be (faint echo of the Proclaimers) when the midges aren't too thick, and the sun shines a bit, and it's neither too punchy nor too dour. I got to know his friends and through them a new social life opened up and I was so often in Scotland that I began to be recognised by the train crews.

My life had settled into a pattern in which I was as happy as I had ever been. Will's life settled happily, too, when he met Julia, and they got married and went to live in a village down the road, but my older brother Andy's marriage was getting into trouble and when it broke up he moved up to Kettering, too, so the three of us were now back where we came from. I don't know why, but that provoked a strange period of tension with my parents when I began to resent their non-acknowledgement of me being gay. My brothers' relationships, wives and girlfriends, were fully woven into the family tapestry, but mine weren't and I began to feel not just overlooked in embarrassment, but deliberately slighted. I went round and had it out with them, and complained that they didn't seem to think that my relationships were real in the way my brothers' were real, and if that was so awkward for them perhaps it would be better if . . . ? Eventually, as I stopped for breath, my mother pointed out that it was difficult to accept my gay relationships into the family narrative when I didn't actually seem to have any.

I had not, since Russell, ten years earlier, and I suppose I wanted to blame them, in an obscure way, for my failure to make lasting intimate relationships. To make intimate relationships that involved lying down would have been an improvement on my then form, but day-to-day I found single life suited me well enough. I liked the freedom to take off and do what I wanted when I wanted, accountable only to myself. I liked the unchallenged command of the TV remote. There were moments when frustration broke through – coming back to my empty cottage after a fight at work and just wanting to talk to someone about it – and, worst of all, I once tried to put up a self-assembly double bed on my own.

I suppose I had got used to being alone. The habits of the single person took root – getting up early, becoming slightly obsessional about *EastEnders*, ritualising everything – and I began to find interruptions to the schedule difficult to take. I loved having people to stay, but that was on the schedule and on my terms, and if guests were dilatory in rising I would make so much noise downstairs they would soon appear, bleary-eyed. At the BBC, too, as I approached my forties, I was slipping into habits, expecting things to be done my way, and getting worked up if there were changes to the running order or guests. I was becoming, I discovered, 'difficult to produce', which means not doing what the producer wants, but I was by now longer-serving on *Night Waves* than most of the producers, and tended to think it was them not getting it rather than me. I did fail to get it, spectacularly, when I was asked to interview Edward Said. We went to see him in Cambridge, where he was a visiting fellow at King's, and we talked in his flat there about his childhood in Jerusalem, in the same Anglican school as Omar Sharif. All went well, but I had been primed by my editor not to give him too easy a time about the Palestine/Israeli conflict and I asked – not unreasonably I thought – how he squared throwing stones at Israeli border guards with the commitment to reconciliation evidenced by his work with Daniel Barenboim and young musicians from across the divide. He resented the question and grew heated and then accused me of hectoring him and in a tantrum got up and walked out. Unfortunately he walked out of his own flat and a minute later there was a tap on the door and I let him in as we let ourselves out. There was a complaint, and those who needed to be placated were placated, but I had no say in that and it left a bitter taste and I began to feel no longer quite as at home on the programme as I once had.

In my single state, however, I did enjoy bachelor privileges. If there was a party I was good to go, and there were a lot more of them when Helen Fielding's book *Bridget Jones's Diary* became a bestseller. Helen never really needed an excuse to go on holiday but her success, and the need to write a screenplay once the film rights were sold, meant we were away a lot, on yet another of those sunny fortnights that seemed to blur into the long holiday of my thirties, meeting at Nice airport or Pisa or Rome and heading off to lovely villas with great views, clear-blue swimming pools and famous people. My fascination with the celebrity circuit had yet to pall, though the penalty I paid for my bachelor privileges was kipping down on the camp bed in a corridor rather than in a grand suite, a short straw that fell to the single gay man and made me feel a bit like one of the characters in an Evelyn Waugh novel making up the numbers. My photo albums from this period look like test shots from *Vanity Fair* covers, with unlikely celebrities arranged around different swimming pools or playing the hat game after dinner in linen trousers and pink from the sun.

My own celebrity had dwindled to almost nothing, though, if being fictionally famous counts, as part of Helen's group I had rather got used to recognising myself in her prose. Bridget Jones had begun life as a column in the *Independent* and one of Bridget's friends was Tom, a gay man who used be in a pop band in the eighties and had honorary status in Bridget's inner circle of girlfriends. I immediately assumed Tom was me, but details from a common friend's life began to turn up in Tom's. A tiny tug of love would break out between us from time to time, culminating when we both outed ourselves as the model for Tom to journalists, and then rather retreated when a little further on in the narrative he secretly had a nose job.

There were moments when I was still recognised as me, but more often I was mistaken for someone else. In Harvey Nicks in the week before Christmas I got into the big lift laden with presents. It was crowded with people, all the buttons were pressed, and, as we began our slow, slow descent to the ground floor, a young man standing right next to me said, 'I recognise you.' I smiled and said nothing in that gracious minor royal sort of way, but this did not deter him and he said, 'You were in that band weren't you?' I just smiled and looked at my feet, embarrassed, but this seemed to provoke him and he said, 'I know who you are, you're Neil Tennant from the Pet Shop Boys.' I continued to smile and said nothing and hoped he would back off. Then someone else said, 'No, he isn't. That's not Neil Tennant' and looked at me accusingly. I said, 'Actually, I was in a band', but by now the mood had turned and other people started looking at me as if I had been trying to pass myself off as Neil Tennant. I said 'I was in the Communards', but I sounded a bit desperate, and I thought of that scene in *Julius Caesar* when the poor man about to be lynched says, 'I am Cinna the poet, Cinna the poet!' Eventually the lift reached the ground floor and I slunk away like a fraud.

Shortly after Tony Blair was elected to power in May 1997, Helen invited me to accompany her to Number Ten, where the Prime Minister was holding a reception for people from the world of arts and entertainment. Number Ten. It had seemed as remote as Berchtesgaden to the likes of us for the past eighteen years, and suddenly its doors were thrown open. We were let through the huge iron gates – a symbol of Thatcherism to me – walked past the Mosimann's catering trucks – a symbol of New Labour – and arrived at the glossy black front door, the portal to power, and joined a long queue of very famous people going slowly up a staircase to a landing and a reception room where, like an enthusiastic prep school headmaster greeting parents on Speech Day, Tony Blair took your hand in his, pumped it twice, looked you in your eye and said 'Hi! Hi!' We passed on into the room and set about the canapés and drank the wine and saw some friends and then Cherie Blair was upon us, thrilled to meet Helen. She loved the book and said she was trying to read it in bed when she had a minute in a way which suggested that the aphrodisiac effects of power were indeed as one hoped. After a minute or two of Cherie bonding with Helen I tried, a bit desperately, to introduce myself by saying, 'I'm Tom', meaning the character in the book. Cherie looked at me, said nothing, then turned back to talk to Helen, and I thought, sulkily, that not so long ago I was the one who would have been invited to parties at Number Ten had Labour actually won an election and that there should have been a veteran's badge and a place of honour for the likes of us. But, no, New Labour was interested in the celebrities, just like everyone else, and in the end Harry Enfield, who had just had a little spat with Peter Mandelson, and I found our way to the staff room by the front door where I was allowed to smoke a fag with some of the ladies who worked there. 'Who's the nicest person you've had to deal with round here?' I asked, and they replied, with one voice, John Major. 'And who's the nastiest?' asked Harry. They looked at each other and said nothing.

At first it looked as if I – or Jon – was going to be immortalised by Robbie Williams in the film version of Bridget Jones and I wasn't slow to tell people about it. But if Robbie was ever in the frame he soon fell out and in the end the part was played by a brilliant actor, James Callis. I met him at the premiere and if it was a little odd to meet the person you had just watched playing you in a film I was much more distracted by something else, for my date that evening was Billy.

I ran into him one day in Barking where he was living with a girlfriend and instead of the cold shoulder he came to me and said hello, the first time I had seen him in nearly ten years. He was bare-chested and now mightily tattooed and pierced, and in a nervous gesture of friendship I remember casually waggling his nipple ring. He gave me his number and I called and we met at the Groucho Club and I told him how sorry I was that I had behaved so badly and he just gave me a peck on the cheek and that was that.

I don't think men get broody, as women get broody, but I did in my late thirties wonder what it would be like to have a child. Some gay friends of mine had done this – Adam Mars-Jones and his co-parent Lisa had a daughter, Holly – and I even discussed the possibility of doing the same with a friend. But it came to nothing and I began to believe that I was much better suited to unclehood and godparent-hood than fatherhood. My brothers had both become fathers, Andy, who had been married to Claire, had two daughters, Rose and Lillie, and Will and Julia produced three children, Alice, Ellie and Oliver. I delight in them all. That broodiness faded before long and I don't feel it now, but when it was high it evoked for me that feeling I had in adolescence of being at odds with the core business of existence, childless, single, a noncombatant in the battle with entropy.

Emma, an old flatmate from Stratford-upon-Avon, called one day. 'How do you fancy working with Franco Zeffirelli?' she asked. I said I fancied it very much and she, now a casting agent, arranged for me fly out to Rome a month or two later, where I spent a bizarre fortnight living in Zeffirelli's house between the city and the Alban Hills to write a version of a song from his new film that could be released as a single. Although my feverish passion for Roman Catholicism had burned away, and my observance of its discipline had lapsed a little, Franco's Catholic piety, which endured in spite of his unbridled love of life in all its glory and disaster, inspired me to go to confession, which I had not done in a while. I went to St Peter's, where I found an American Franciscan priest and knelt down: 'Forgive me, Father, for I have sinned . . .'

It had an unintended consequence. I wanted to talk about some of the consequences of my homosexuality – not being kind to some-one – he wanted to talk about the fact of my homosexuality as if that were in itself the sin. I found this – and find this – very frustrating. When I seek the Church's forgiveness and counsel in matters of sexu-ality it is not because I think it is in itself wrong. I think it is the morally neutral context in which my less than loving, less than gen-erous, actions occur – that's where the trouble lies – and no matter how much the Church may want me to, I cannot repent of a sin that I do not think a sin. It's as nonsensical as those so-called therapies that claim to cure homosexuality; for how can you cure something that isn't a disease?

However, I needed the Church to help me to be more attentive, more forbearing, more clear-sighted, more just, more loving, in my relationships with other people, the person with whom I would be intimately involved, those with whom I was only glancingly involved, and especially those with whom I would much rather not be involved at all. I had to interrupt the confessor to explain that was not what I meant, and to try to get him to see past the fact of homosexuality into the fact of my messed-up humanity. He was kind, and he gave me a light penance, and absolution, but as I walked away I looked back and saw him leaning out of the box looking after me as if I had walked by accident into the wrong place.

Back at home in Grafton Underwood I continued to help out playing the organ at services, often a comedy of errors, when everything went wrong, and the prayers wandered slightly from the theme, and in the absence of the vicar someone said the Magnificat three times, and there were screaming rows at the south porch when someone forgot the key. But even on the wheezy, squeaky two-manual organ rescued from a northern chapel, the hymn tunes with names as familiar to me as my own family – Rockingham, Down Ampney, Hereford, Laudate Dominum, Gonfalon Royal – expressed an integrity that still held and that I still believed in, not to a Roman Catholic standard of belief, but a Church of England standard of belief, nearer to a mood than a dogma, some would say, but persuasive precisely in its gentleness and hesitancy rather than its rigour and its clarity.

One evening I went to see the vicar and explained my problem. He said he feared he would not be able to help me much, but he knew a man who might, and gave me the number of a former Rector of Lowick, just over the hill, who, after some adventures in Roman Catholicism, had returned to the Church of England and was now Rector of St Mary and St Martin in Stamford. His name was Michael Thompson.

A few days later, one evening in late spring, I found the rectory in Pinfold Lane, a rather disappointing house typical of the Parsonages Board in the seventies, built on the cheap to accommodate a household of the kind Robert Robinson would interrogate on *Ask the Family*. The priest who came to the door, however, belonged to another era entirely. He was shaven-headed, not much older than me, in an old slightly off-black cassock with a broad watered-silk cincture with falls – tattiness girded with splendour – and he looked at me searchingly through rimless glasses before inviting me in. I noticed a biretta hanging on a peg by the door, and, incongruously, a racing bike with drop handlebars parked beneath it. We sat in the garden, amid a splendid show of dandelions, on chairs that looked like they had been stolen from a classroom and a rusty old table with a Formica top, and he produced a bottle of Crémant de Bourgogne and some olives and we talked until it grew too cold to sit outside and retired inside, to a room not quite up to the furniture it contained.

As it grew dark he asked if I was sure I could no longer continue as a Roman Catholic and I said, without having to think about it, yes, I was sure. He waved his fingers at me. 'Welcome home,' he said.

27. Remember Ye Not the Former Things

What impressed me most about Michael that first night we met was not how well he fitted the part – the good furniture in the drawing room, the good wine in the fridge, the invitation to a Garden Party at Buckingham Palace framed and hung up in the downstairs loo – but quite the opposite; it was his honesty, his utter indifference to the things he should have said, and his unadorned account of the state of the Church of England and the state of its clergy. He spared me nothing, and more than once his eyes filled with tears as he spoke of his own disappointments, from Westminster Abbey, where he made the Ecumenical Patriarch gasp by decorating the shrine of Edward the Confessor with a thousand twinkling lights and lost his job, to being a parish priest in the inner city, crunching discarded syringes underfoot as he went from vicarage to church, just trying to keep things going.

I had met enough Anglican clergy who seemed oblivious to the inconsistencies of the life, behaving like Victorian gentlemen when they were really inexpert social workers, or imagining they were indispensable to their communities when in reality their communities looked on them in puzzlement if they looked on them at all, or – worse – talking the kind of corporate talk which can never admit to anything being bad or failing. Michael had no time for those half-truths or evasions, and his honesty, not only in matters of Church order but also in matters of faith, was bracing. I guess I must have looked startled, for years later he said to me, 'You remember that night you came to see me? I assumed you were mad.'

I did not think he was mad, though he did at first seem impossibly remote from me in temperament, style and conviction. He loved order and hierarchy and rank – stability in a chaotic world – in a deeply romantic way, and used to buy a French magazine chronicling the daily affairs of the royal dynasties of the world. I once found him in tears in his study looking at an internet site dedicated to the doomed Cambodian royal family. Like many romantics in an unromantic age he was often frustrated and angry and could be extremely irascible. He was most readily provoked by the new forms of worship and patterns of organisation, which the Church urges upon its members from time to time. I remember going with him once to the installation of a new vicar at the Evangelical church round the corner, as far from Michael in the Anglican spectrum as could be, all jeans and trainers and drum kits and mateyness. Michael arrived in traditional choir dress – cassock, surplice, gown, hood, scarf, tabs and a mortarboard – looking like a character from Trollope who had accidentally strayed into Woodstock. He joined in half-heartedly, tapping out a ratatatat on his mortarboard during the chorus of 'Shine Jesus Shine'. But he did turn up, dutifully, for he was dutiful, only he saw his duty as preaching the word of God and administering the sacraments, which he did with great diligence and indeed brio, as I discovered when I started going to his church and found a chancel crammed with retired clergy, who turned out for Michael for he did it properly, everyone vested as they should be vested, everything in order, never an ugly sentence or an ill-tuned hymn. It was not only the clergy who turned out for him; the congregation did, too, and would have done anything for him even if he was occasionally bad-tempered and unpredictable.

I started coming regularly and Michael soon had me serving, which I did with a clumsiness that irritated him and the other clergy, some of them more forgiving than others. When one asked Michael who I was, he told him that I'd been 'a gay icon'. 'Well, that's one icon we won't be kissing,' the clergyman replied. There was sometimes a froideur to what Michael once called 'God's frozen people'. Most were perfectly amiable and supportive and one or two became friends, but a couple of the ladies there never spoke to me once, although one shouted out 'rubbish!' at the end of, I think, my first sermon.

Radio Three, as the year 2000 approached, decided to look ahead at the dawn of the twenty-first century and, with an ambitious use of alliteration, invited me to work on a series called *Fifty Futures*, which proposed to visit fifty cities around the world to see how they were going into the new millennium. Budgets thwarted ambition and we never got to fifty – I'm not sure we got much past five – but I went to Bangladesh, Sweden, Atlanta and Sydney before we adjusted our trim, and had a wonderful time in what was to be my swansong on *Night Waves*. Bangladesh I remember most vividly, visiting a tribal village that we could only reach by walking through jungle, and being woken up in the morning with a just picked mango brought by a Bangladeshi who shyly asked me if I could answer a question. I said I would try. As the sun rose on the bustling jungle and the fresh mango fizzed on my tongue he said, 'How do you account for the pessimism in the novels of Thomas Hardy?'

I had been lucky with the BBC, and would be again, but after the debacle with Said things soured a bit. The culture in the radio arts unit had changed, too, imperial behaviours tolerated where once collegial values had prevailed, and although there were some fantastic people there it was less fun than it used to be. Perhaps I had simply been there long enough.

I love the BBC. I love the Church of England. But it is not wise to love organisations because they do not love you back. They do what organisations do, sometimes close ranks, lie, betray, disappoint, take you out at dawn and shoot you. All institutions are demonic, a cleric once observed, but the ones that have the clearest sense of their own high calling are most vulnerable to demonic activity. I suppose it is because where aspirations are high and reach is limited there's plenty of room for disappointment and frustration to play out and that can curdle one's feelings for a place.

It is not unusual for broadcasters to fall out of love with the BBC after twenty years or so of service, but there was more to my growing

sense of disenchantment than that. I was not able to smother entirely
the insistent call of God, a call that I found harder and harder to
ignore. My dilatoriness in deciding what to do about it began to bore
my friends but it was Mo Mowlam who final challenged me about it.

Our paths had crossed back in the eighties when I was with Red
Wedge and Mo was a young and rising Labour politician. By the end
of the nineties she was a government minister, Secretary of State for
Northern Ireland, and the right person at the right time when reconciliation and peace there became suddenly, tantalisingly, possible.
It was then I met her again through Charlie Parsons and Waheed
Alli, media tycoons who were partners in life as well as in the television company they founded, Planet 24. They had been neighbours
of mine when I lived in Islington, but we became friends when they
started inviting me to their country house in Kent for weekends.
These weekends, of royal hospitality, brought together an eclectic
mix of people, from the worlds of politics, journalism, media, as
well as friends and neighbours, and Mo and I hit it off immediately.
Within a weekend we were trading confidences, although hers, at
this hugely significant moment in UK politics, were rather more
thrilling than mine. I remember one New Year's Eve as we sat at
dinner going round the table saying what had been most memorable
about the year just passed. Waheed had been made a peer, Mo had
brokered the Good Friday Agreement, I'd given up smoking, but,
crestfallen, started again that very night.

Mo had also been treated for a brain tumour and, like many who
experience life-threatening conditions, she had no time for nonsense. She was utterly unconcerned with the Ps and Qs, unusual in
the risky politics of Northern Ireland, and I remember one weekend
at Hillsborough Castle, the sovereign's official residence in Northern Ireland and Mo's home when she was there, getting drunk and
streaking round the Throne Room for a bet while Mo, whisky in
hand, looked on unfazed. She was, we found out later, suffering the
effects of her illness, which returned, but while her powers of concentration and memory for detail may have faded, she engaged with
people with quite extraordinary intensity. She had that politician's

way of making you think you were the only person she was interested in, but more than that she looked straight into you and saw
the issues and the tensions and the evasions that obscure desires and
potential. As we sat one evening in the garden on deckchairs, she
said without preamble, 'What are you going to do with the rest of
your life?' I said, 'I don't know.'

The millennium had come and gone, something I had looked
forward to since the seventies, for then the *Blue Peter* time capsule
would be dug up and I supposed that when it was I would be like
my dad, a managing director of something, driving a Rover, with
children at Wellingborough, and going to functions in a frilly shirt
and bow tie. But I was disappointed by that, just as I was by the time
capsule which was opened to reveal only sludge within. My life was
not sludge, but I felt nonetheless without form and disappointing as
I came to where the road diverged.

'Have you thought any more about what you are going to do with
your life, Richard?' said Mo. I said, 'I think all the time that I should
maybe get ordained.' She looked at me. 'I don't get religion at all,'
she said. 'But if you do, you need to do something about it. The next
time we meet I want you to have made the call. OK?'

I made the call. I went to see the Diocesan Director of Ordinands
at Lincoln, the diocese that covers Stamford. She spoke to Michael,
who put me in a cassock, a horrible thing that blew up in a wind and
exposed my knees, and made me follow him around town to learn
the rudiments of parish ministry and I was sent on a Diocesan Ordinations Day, when I rather misinterpreted the instruction to bring
a packed lunch by choosing a lovely jar of chicken liver parfait with
brioche and dessert of a *tarte aux fraises des bois* and a half-bottle of
Sauternes. Everyone else had Dairylea sandwiches and a packet of
Quavers.

I talked to one of the Diocesan Selectors. She said, 'Do you want
to give up your comfortable life and enjoyable job for half of what
you earn now [a quarter, I said to myself] doing something you
have never done before? Do you really?' I said, as I seemed always to

say, 'I don't know.' I talked to my father and he said, with unusual feeling, 'For God's sake, don't get ordained.' I wondered why he said that. Perhaps it was a memory of being made to stand to attention on a pew during the sermon as a boy, his father making up for his own lack of piety but imposing this as penance on his son? Perhaps it was an expression of frustration as his son leaped yet again into an unknown world? Perhaps he thought it simply wouldn't suit me, like Ned Sherrin, who said to a mutual friend, 'He'll jump over the wall in a week.'

One day I was in Stamford, wearing my cassock, running an errand for Michael. In the alleys behind the high street I came across a group of boys, ten or eleven years old, dressed in Boden, like middle-class kids in towns like Stamford. One of them looked at me in my cassock and said quite fearlessly, 'Oi, you fucking paedo-philiac. Don't fucking touch me!' Two instincts warred within me, one to slap his insolent head, another to correct his vocabulary, but I was so taken aback I didn't know what to do. So I ignored them. Another said, 'Paedophiliac', and another, and I thought discretion the better part of valour so walked away. But they followed me, out of the alleyway and into the high street, busy with people. I walked its length, in my cassock, with them in a crocodile behind me going, 'OI! PAEDO!' which drew the attention of the crowd. I made a sort of 'Kids! What can you do?' face but I could sense the adults were not all comfortably on my side. In the end I went into WH Smith to try to shake them off and fortunately they went on their way. But I was shocked. I called on a retired priest on the way back to the rec-tory and he told me to call in at the police station and report it, not to get back at the kids, but to protect myself against someone else reporting it first. And then he said: 'It's horrible, I know. But once you're ordained the Grace of Orders will protect you when things like this happen.' I thought, there's a piece of pious nonsense I could do without. Actually, he was right.

Angela, the Diocesan Director of Ordinands, recommended that I should go forward for a Bishops' Selection Conference, a notorious debacle called any number of names as the Church confuses itself over how it wants to train people to serve as ministers and priests. It is based on the army's method for selecting people to train as officers, although a test of physical fitness is wisely omitted, and takes place residentially over three days in a college or retreat house near a cathedral. It was important because it would decide which fork in the road to take, whether I should be recommended for training, not recommended for training or advised to go away and maybe come back. Mine was to take place at Ely in six months so I had time to prepare for this strange procedure of deciding whether God has called you to a particular ministry in a way that is practically realisable and without too much damage to the parties concerned. How do you measure that? I was to find out.

Much more difficult is working out what is going on in oneself. I had realised as soon as I admitted that the Church of England was my natural habitat that priesthood came into focus in a way that other roles did not. I could imagine myself as a monk, but only in the way I could imagine a character in a story. My sense of myself in priesthood was neither so clear nor so pat. At first I took encouragement from the support of other priests who also thought I might have a vocation. I could imagine myself doing the things that priests do, or some of them. I never had any difficulty imagining myself preaching, nor doing anything at the dressier ceremonial ends of things.

But did I have the forbearance, the patience necessary to endure with people and situations – doubtful on present showing – and, the undodgeable question, could I make holiness look real? Not on my own, in spite of my clamorous effort to acquire all the accomplishments of priesthood, confidence in the role, familiarity with the traditions, public and private, fluency in its public and private language. That's not enough to look a person in torment in the eye, that's not enough to stand untrembling beside a person falling apart, that's not enough to point beyond the horizon of their farthest imaginable despair towards the possibility of an unimaginable life transformed, renewed, made glorious, without looking like a scarecrow in a field of aimless wind. The only person who can do that is

Jesus Christ, and our job as priests – as Christians – is not to get in the way, not to make it impossible for Jesus to make his home in us, taking on our strange shapes and dissonances and tuning them to his purposes.

There were moments of grace. A lovely stranger I met and blurted it all out to said nothing but took me to a field where we lay beside a river and looked at the sun filter through a canopy of leaves until the sun went down and went away. A man on the tube, aggressive and full of edge, followed me when I got off and I turned round and faced him and asked what he wanted and he said his name and told me he was just out of prison for crimes of violence against his girlfriend and wept because he had ruined his life. I met a former chaplain who I'd tormented at school, and mocked relentlessly, taking a service as a locum one Christmas. I said after the service, 'I bet you never thought you'd come across me in a place like this.' He said, 'Of course I did.'

The day arrived for my selection conference and I drove off to Ely with Tom, the chalk to our cheese, from the Evangelical church round the corner and as nice a fellow as ever shook a tambourine. As soon as we arrived and checked into our narrow rooms, just vacated by bishops of the Anglican communion who must have found the spartan conditions even more challenging than I did, I developed a migraine, a migraine that throbbed for the duration of the three days and gave it, when I look back, a strangely trippy tinge. We began with a liturgy of Compline, the very beautiful night office from the Book of Common Prayer. Our preparatory material had contained much on the subjects of the breadth of our tradition, of the use of inclusive language for candidates both male and female, about new patterns for worship in the challenges of a rapidly shifting world; so it was an irony that the first word we heard, gathered as a praying community was 'Brethren'. After Compline it was easy-going, dinner, then getting to know you, meeting our selectors, and then we went into groups, inevitably, and did some work.

Our group sessions were interrupted by one-on-one interviews with the selectors, a group of clergy and lay people. With one I had to discuss my personal life, and this was tricky, because homosexuality, although very commonly found in clergy of all denominations, is still the love that dare not speak its name, and the Anglican Communion is particularly divided over the fitness of those so made up to serve in ordained ministry. I resolved to tell the truth, but nothing more. 'Has your sexuality ever been a challenge?' I was asked. 'Sexuality is always a challenge,' I replied. 'Was this person who influenced you so deeply gay?' 'That was one of the things he was,' I replied. Nothing was pressed, but I think enough was understood. Finally, I was asked to see the head selector, a grey-haired Archdeacon who invited me to sit down. He had my file open in front of him on the desk and said, 'Why would someone like you want to get involved with a broken-down, failing institution that's lost any sense of its tradition, hasn't got a clue where it's going and can't pay its bills?' I replied, 'Actually I'm thinking of leaving the BBC.'

A week later, Michael called and said, 'You've got through, but I'm not meant to have told you, so sound surprised when Angela calls.' I put the phone down and had to get up and walk round the room, somewhere between elation and tears. I had got through, and the road less taken stood open before me.

I had to find somewhere to train and it wasn't easy to decide which college to pick. Most, from the bishop down, said Westcott House, the liberal catholic theological college in Cambridge. But there were other options to consider: St Stephen's House in Oxford, catholic as they come but more conservative then Cuddesdon, the liberal catholic college just outside Oxford. I knew I was a liberal and to Cuddesdon I went, set on its ridge, and had a yogurt in the refectory with the Principal while Soapy Sam Wilberforce, fierce in conventuals, stared down from the wall. Then I went to Westcott, with its divided college garden – half cultivated, half wild – a statement, like everything at Westcott, and had a civilised conversation with Angela Tilby, its Principal, and the author of the book Sara Maitland had given me when I went to see her in the first rush of conversion. I liked both of them, I could have gone to either but before I made up my mind Michael suggested I try yet another, up in Yorkshire.

The College of the Resurrection at Mirfield is attached to the Community of the Resurrection, an experiment in Anglican monasticism founded by Bishop Charles Gore and Walter Frere in the nineteenth century. These two men, Gore a bishop and an aristocrat, Frere a gent and a scholar, dressed bachelor Old Etonian dons in grey scapulars and put them in an old beer baron's mansion on a sooty hill between Dewsbury and Leeds. It seemed an amazingly eccentric thing to do, but since then the Mirfield Fathers have given much to the Church of England, through its college, which trained working-class northern men for the priesthood, and its presence in South Africa. Bishop Trevor Huddleston was a monk of Mirfield, and Mirfield monks trained and supported Archbishop Desmond Tutu, Hugh Masekela, Steve Biko and a host of other African and Europeans who fought and defeated the evil of apartheid.

It was not, by the turn of the millennium, in great shape, and it was not the powerhouse of learning it had once been, nor a dynamo of energy in promoting the social gospel. It was also stuck between a chemical plant and the M62 and I really, really didn't think I wanted to go there. But Michael thought I should try it, so I did. I booked in as a potential student and drove there on a filthy rainy night, conditions so appalling I could not make out the road signs, nor see anyone out and about to ask directions. I drove round and round, in growing frustration, and then saw a gap in a high wall with a gate and room to pull in, so I could get my bearings. The gate swung open of its own accord, and my headlights fell on a sign. The College of the Resurrection.

I parked, I rang a bell, someone came, a fey young man in a cassock and scapular, and took me up some stairs where I saw on the wall a framed print of a Native American depiction of the Trinity, not well known at all, but by coincidence I had just used it to illustrate an article I had written for a book. By coincidence? The magic gate; the destination that found me rather than I it; the Native American Trinity; if spooky music from *The Outer Limits* had floated along the cloister it would not have seemed out of place.

Spooky music floated beautifully round the aisles and nave and

choir of the community church, which looked like a Mexican basilica transported to Yorkshire and given a smart green copper roof.
The monks, in grey scapulars, the students in black, were gathered
for Evensong, in boxy stalls and chunky wooden chairs, arranged in
the simplest of spaces, singing plainchant settings of the psalms and
hymns in English rather than Latin. It was beautiful and done with
such supple strength and assurance that I was completely taken up
by it. We ate afterwards, in a booming refectory, on school food,
which was whisked away almost as soon as it appeared, by ordinands in white scapulars instead of black, who got up and sat down
and turned this way then that in unpredictable ways, as High Table
departed.

I had an interview with the Superior of the Community, Fr
George, who seemed simultaneously utterly relaxed and agonised
with shyness. There were long silences, for a radio broadcaster all but
intolerable, but I endured them and the few words that he uttered I
still remember: 'Dig where the shit is.'

There was Compline, in semi-darkness, and then a late-night
sherry party with dreadful sherry in one of the ordinands' rooms,
with slightly too hysterical laughter, and that febrile atmosphere that
closed communities create so readily, and I went off to bed knowing
that in spite of this I was, God and Principal and Bishop willing,
going to train for ordained ministry at the College of the Resurrection at Mirfield.

28. Cloistered

There is something about handing in your notice that gives joy to the heart, a moment's shift in power from employer to employee, and the happy knowledge that you jumped rather than waited to be pushed. *Night Waves* very generously did me a leaving do, arranged, at my request, at the south Indian restaurant near Broadcasting House and where I had been eating masala dosa since 1987. I had worked out a speech, a clarion call for sustaining serious arts broadcasting as civilisation collapsed around us, but all I could think of in the end was to say how much I had enjoyed the company and friendship of my colleagues, and to apologise to the dearest among them, Horatio Clare, for having drunkenly suggested same-sex fiddlededee in the back of a cab near Clapham, an offer he didn't even remember. A couple of days later there was a programme jolly, a rounders match and a picnic at Primrose Hill, the last farewell, where I finally said goodbye and walked away to waves and shouted good wishes. A little further on, like Aeneas, I unwisely turned round to acknowledge yet more of their good wishes but saw that they had all gone back to the game of rounders.

I did a circuit of friends, home and abroad, to say goodbye, as if I was going to Australia on a ten-pound emigrant ticket never to be seen again, and arranged a holiday for my family, two weeks in Cornwall in two houses, side by side, just off a beach near Bude, my parents, my brothers and their families, proper bucket and spade, and on me. It was an idyll, the weather was glorious, and the only shadow that fell across us was the first symptoms of my father's Parkinson's disease. We had to cross a rocky strip strewn with boulders to get to the beach and halfway across one day he said, 'It's no good, I can't do it' and went back to sit in the garden reading the *Daily Telegraph* in a deckchair. The houses looked out over a stream with a rope swing where the kids could play, and my bedroom had once been the study of Parson Hawker, vicar of nearby Morwenstow, the most eccentric clergyman of his day and inventor of Harvest Festival. The window was formed in the shape of a cross and cast a cross-shaped light across my prayer book diligently set up with ribbons and bookmarks as I prepared myself for entry to the clerical life. There was another family staying on the other side of the brook, one of them a Scottish advocate. I told him what I was doing. 'Are you sure you really want to do that?' he asked and I said, 'I don't know.'

I worked out what to do with Grafton Underwood. I had just had it re-thatched at ruinous expense (one of the taxes middle-class people pay to live in their dreams), but did not want to sell it or let it, so asked Will and Julia if they and the children would like to live in it, look after and re-thatch it when the time came (Northamptonshire longstraw being not only expensive but about as durable as butterfly wings as a roofing material), and, subject to review, change of circumstances, return it to me to live in when I got to retirement and their kids were grown up. Michael said, 'You will never live in that house again.'

I set off for Mirfield from Stamford on Sunday after church, where my parents came to see me – vested in a gorgeous tunicle – preach a sermon. I had exchanged my bright blue VW Beetle with a gerbera in the dashboard vase, which made me think of both Big Ears and Rachel from *Friends*, for a sober, lowest-of-the-range Polo in dark red, more suitable I thought for a cleric, and it was loaded with what I considered essentials: a cocktail cabinet, a small Bridget Riley, a Bose home music system, cassocks and a cloak into which my mother had sewn name tapes she had found in her sewing box unused since 1970. Will, in a hired van, was driving up with the rest of my things, which Michael looked over and observed that he had arrived at his theological college, St Michael's Llandaff, with just one suitcase. As I said goodbye to the man who had taught me so much, he said, first, he wasn't going to make any speeches, and, second, that the cassock fund, a traditional way of a parish providing a cassock for an ordinand off to theological college, stood at twenty-five pounds, the sum I put into it myself.

I had thought that the journey would be itself an experiencing of letting go, of sloughing off one skin so that a new skin could grow, but it was nothing like that, as we stopped at a Burger King on the M62, and then turned off when we saw the Mexican basilica just visible at the top of a hill. Another fey young man opened the door to us and we found my room on a corridor over the old stables, and unloaded my essentials for living into this spartan space with, oh, great blessing, an en suite bathroom. I said goodbye to Will, put on my cassock, and made my way to a common room where our first evening began with a sherry party for the new boys, once we had browsed the pages and pages of notes explaining how things were done, and not done. As we waited for Fr Christopher, the Principal – tall and shy – and Fr Peter, the Vice-Principal – short and silky – to welcome us, I looked at the photographs of previous years, of men in cassocks and new scapulars, in black and white in the wire-rimmed specs of the thirties, in the ugly beards of the 1970s, in the hair-oiled fifties, and then, the eighties, with the appearance of wives and children, breaking the monotony of black on black, rank on rank preparing for the parishes of the biretta belts of Blackburn Diocese, the slum parishes of Sunderland, the vicar-and-six-curates parishes of Leeds and Manchester and Liverpool, the townships of Johannes-burg and Pretoria, the mission parishes of Zimbabwe.

And I looked at us. The youngest was in his thirties, the oldest twice his age. We had a food scientist, a football referee, a head teacher and a florist. We were six in number, but this thinnest of years would be padded out by two Romanians, a Zimbabwean and South African and an Armenian monk. And a woman from Hert-fordshire along for the ride, for Mirfield, at that time, did not take women students for training for the priesthood. These were my peers for the next two years and if that seemed a challenge, we then met the year above us, who had looked at us with spiritual tenderness when we came to sniff round, but now looked at us rather like Flashman looked at Tom Brown on his first day at Rugby.

I don't think I really believed in evil until I went to Mirfield; not as an objective force, certainly, with purpose and character, but my first year there made me change my mind. It was not so much that there were nasty people doing nasty things – though sometimes there were, as there are anywhere – it was that a group of people living together in an attempt to realise a common experience of the risen Jesus Christ could, by the very nature of that effort, destroy that life and themselves with it.

Things for me did not begin so badly. I made friends with one of my peers, Neil, the football referee, although I did not know that then, who had worked as a lawyer in a magistrates' court in Rotherham. He and I had a glass of wine together and I thought – I hope he thought – that two years in each other's company would not be so bad. There were two quite camp boys in the year above who I thought were an item, with whom I went out for a drink on our first night to a pub as characterless as a petrol station on the A1. There was our only woman, Ursula, with her teenaged son, Simon, who lived in a college house round the corner, whose ordinary life was already looking like an oasis in a desert. Not long after I arrived I was invited to tea, with two of the Romanian monks staying with us, at the house of a married student in the senior year. I thought he looked even more monastic than the monks, pale with practically a tonsure and deep-set eyes, but he had a slightly bumbly clerical way about him, which I think he had acquired rather than been born into, and an American wife, who seemed very proper, whom he called rather formally 'Elizabeth'. They lived in a bungalow outside the monastery grounds which smelled of mildew, a smell which clung to his cassock, so I could tell when he was in church even in the dark. The bungalow was full of photographs of their wedding, which was conducted by a bishop judging by the number of times a mitre appeared in shot, and we sat in the sitting room, which was dominated by a grand piano a little too big, even baby-sized, for the room. We had tea and cake and a slightly stilted conversation, and the afternoon concluded with Elizabeth and me playing duets of popular songs that segued into carol tunes. Grateful though I was for their hospitality, and we were in time to become friends, I felt a sudden pang for the fleshpots and the mires.

By the end of the first month I realised that I had eaten nothing delicious since arriving and that if I didn't soon I would surely die. We had school food, lots of it, and it wasn't bad, but it came in stainless steel dishes on rumbling trolleys, and was eaten on refectory tables that smelled faintly of bleach, and there was nothing to cheer the heart and my homesick heart needed cheering. So on Saturday, our day off, I looked in Egon Ronay and found a place not far away where I could go for lunch. I drove there in civvies and asked for a table for one and when the waitress came to take my order she said, 'Do you want rice with that or chips? Or rice and chips?'

Rice or chips? We were put on endless weekly rotas to take our turns in various duties and in the first week mine was clearing away dinner and lunch with our Zimbabwean ordinand, Luke, a lovely quiet and reserved man from a country far away that was falling apart under Mugabe's increasingly mental rule. After supper, scraping spuds into a black plastic bin, he seemed more than usually quiet and I asked if he was OK. 'You have just thrown away more than my family sees in a month,' he said, without any emotion.

In spite of this profligacy, spiritually our regime was austere and rigorous. We got up early to say our prayers, no excuses were acceptable, save mortal illness, we met again for Mass and for Evensong, no deviations from the set forms were permitted or even tolerated. House rules were no less exacting or inflexible, and we had our duties and we performed them, without thinking, as drilled a body of men as any army corps. The benefit this brought was that the liturgy, our worship, soon became second nature, and instead of having to feel things or put ourselves in the right mood, we simply fell in with what was already happening, the heartbeat of Jesus Christ in the prayer of his people. The cost was that it licensed the occasional authoritarian behaviour of those participating in it, and my first year at

Mirfield was so tainted by an outbreak of that I seriously thought of walking away from my troubled corridor and returning to a world of maturity and friendship and familiarity.

Sometimes it was just low-grade hectoring. If you missed a cue or were three seconds late in swinging your thurible or stood two feet shy of where you should, someone would shout at you, like a comedy sergeant-major in a fifties British comedy. Sometimes it was worse than that. One of my peers thought a fellow student not up to standard in personal hygiene, but said nothing about it, only opening the windows, even in dead of winter, when he was around and once surrounded his door with air fresheners.

Sometimes it could be worse. One of the more tiresome aspects of life at Mirfield was the culture that prevailed among those in the student body known as the Bags, a High Church coterie, conservative in politics and theology, but screamingly camp, some – though not all of them – gay. That culture had emerged in the days when homosexuality was not only intolerable in the Church, but illegal in the world, so its expression was coded and oblique and sometimes brilliantly funny. That was fine in the fifties, but by the twenty-first century, even with the Church's slowness to catch up with the normalisation of gay people, it had really had its day. Camp can quite often be a form of toughness, a refusal to subject oneself to hateful power, and its humour a way of refusing to acknowledge wounds; and there was a badinage that characterised it, sometimes shrill, sometimes cruel, which took no prisoners, expected no quarter and could hate with a perfect hatred. A sound I grew to dread at Mirfield was a high-pitched cackle that rose over a victim's humiliation, like smoke over a Balkan village. That cackle would stop when you walked into the room, so I was not only a joke but a joke you weren't in on. You probably would not have wanted to be in on it, but the culture, which was pervasive, began to affect the life of the entire college. Each year the tradition of the conclave was observed, when the Bags rechristened all the new ordinands *in absentia*, with a new Name in Religion, just as a monk or nun is given a new name when they join a community. Only this name was a drag name.

Sometimes these could be clever and funny. A Mark Davis who arrived at Mirfield became Dark Mavis; a former Principal at a different college, who had tried to crack down on such things, was immediately rechristened Ina the Cruel; and when some Anglican clergy went over to Rome in the Archdiocese of Birmingham, the then Archbishop, Maurice Couve de Murville, was rechristened Maureen Cocoa de Bournville. Perhaps that makes you laugh, perhaps not. The Conclave that met and pronounced on my intake rechristened me Britney, due to my pop past, which did make me laugh. Others were less kindly treated, which contributed to a tense atmosphere that accompanied us on our Advent Retreat, mercifully silent.

Advent is traditionally a time for repentance, so we went off to see our spiritual directors, monks of the community, one by one. I sat with mine, in a little room with a box of tissues and a clock in his sightline but not mine. 'How's it going?' he asked. 'Really bad,' I said. I told him about what had been going on, which I was sure he knew about, and let rip about the foolishness and unkindness of some of the people who I had to live with and work it out with. 'Go on,' he said. I paused and thought and said: 'I'm not as kind as I thought I was. I'm not as brave as I thought I was. I'm not as tolerant as I thought I was. I'm not as clever as I thought I was. I'm not as honest as I thought I was.' There was a pause and he said, 'Oh, that's good.'

And it was. The problem was not the awfulness of others, the problem was the awfulness of me, so stuck in my self-regard that I had not seen how marginal my angst was to what was happening all around me. And the only thing I could do about it was deal with my own awfulness, because the awfulness of others was for them to deal with and, besides, how could I even begin to see straight until I had cleared my own eyes of obstruction. I fantasised about escaping back into my old life, and when some friends came to stay for a weekend nearby I almost asked them to take me home with them. But I knew there was no escape, there never is, and I waved them off to return to that intense little world of slamming doors and endless drama and my own moral incompetence, and what had to be done.

This realisation was the beginning of wisdom, and the beginning of a new way of living the college life. I became much more disciplined in my prayer life and started getting up early and going to a little chapel in the basement of the church to pray in silence for half an hour before Mattins in the morning and then again for half an hour before Evensong in the evening. It sounds so simple, but it is so difficult, to find the time and the space to pray (although how easily we find the time and space to do other things); difficult to accustom ourselves to silence in a world of relentless noise; difficult simply to surrender, to let go of our own needs, as we disingenuously call them, to ignore our internal commentaries, with all their evasions and incompleteness, and to tune in to God's frequency, to find the signal among the static. One of the Romanian monks gave me a *metanoi*, a knotted string a bit like a rosary, and I got into the practice of saying the Jesus prayer on each knot – 'Lord Jesus Christ, Son of God, have mercy on me, a sinner'; that slowed down my breathing, altered the rhythm, and although I would often find that, in spite of my best efforts to focus on the mystery of the incarnation, I was really thinking about the snooker, by observing the external discipline of saying the prayer, knot by knot, I began to yield to something not entirely of my own making.

Prayer, like life in the Kierkegaardian sense, is lived forwards but experienced backwards. On my knees, or, rather, on the little prayer stool tucked under the bum to spare them, the trickle of thoughts, impressions, mood, distractions dominate; it's only when I look back I see an odd angle, a surprising shape, left by a pressure I wasn't aware of at the time. It's a bit like going to the gym and sweating for six months to no visible end until one day you discover you have an ab. And, like the gym, it doesn't get easier.

I found keeping this discipline of prayer got harder, but I kept it up, not refreshed by a deep well of piety rising within me, but because I needed it. Without it I was simply too susceptible to self-absorption and the temptation to close down when beset by a sea of irritations.

And there was absolutely nothing twee about it at all, and if I ever lapsed into whimsy or tried to get away with disguising self-seeking motives as altruism, from the silence and the space there came back an echo, a disquieting ping like sonar, which I had to attend to.

It seems obvious, but it is often overlooked, that there is nothing more important for a Christian to do than to pray. It is so easy to duck it, to move prayer to the margins of our lives and to the life of the Church; but what's the point of us if we don't? And if prayer seems to have moved to the margins of the life of the Church, how marginal has it become to everything else? It seems extraordinary to me that having prayed for millennia human beings in the last hundred years or so in places like Western Europe just stopped. Abandoning a practice so central to the lives of individuals and societies, for whatever reason, is inevitably going to have an effect, whether you think it fruitful or not. If we're made for prayer, and some have said there are neurological as well as theological grounds to think so, then how is the appetite for it satisfied in a prayerless world? Perhaps one of the causes of the unhappiness which so many seem to think of as a characteristic of our culture is this unsatisfied hunger, this spiritual starvation.

Round and round the *metanoi* I went in that dark winter at Mirfield and if things didn't get better I think I got better at dealing with them. Some of us certainly settled into more adult relationships, though there were lapses, for something in that form of life infantilises you. I can remember writing notes to a fellow ordinand and slipping them to him at the back of a class when the teacher wasn't looking. I was forty years old. There was also an opportunity to neutralise the more intense hatreds at the Christmas panto, a savage student-penned *Gesamtkunstwerk* we performed at the end of the Advent Term; not completely neutralised, perhaps, but at least laughed at.

And there was Scripture. It seems extraordinary now, but it was not until I arrived at Mirfield that I really started taking the Bible seriously. I had read it, of course, and studied it, too, but I thought of it as simply a complex and jumbled record of the human experience of God; but now I began to experience it as the power of God, active in the lives of the people he loves.

I had started a research degree at Leeds University, looking at the textual history of the New Testament, a minority interest, but I loved it when I was an undergraduate and I think I had a feel for it. A new edition of the Greek text of St Paul's Epistle to the Ephesians had been published, and I decided to look at that. Not by St Paul, not an epistle and nothing to do with Ephesus was a summary of what I thought I would argue, but it did not quite work out that way (for the record, it is not by St Paul, it is not an epistle and it is nothing to do with Ephesus, but that's not what's important). There's a passage in it, Ephesians 2.13–14, which I came across not studying the text but reading it liturgically in church: 'But now in Christ Jesus you who once were far off have been brought near by the blood of Christ. For he is our peace; in his flesh he has made both groups into one and has broken down the dividing wall, that is, the hostility between us.' This was read out loud into as divided a community of Christians as I have ever lived in and ever since I have known that the only way we can live alongside other people without deceiving them or ourselves about our competitive, incomplete and occasionally murderous natures is because Christ has made it possible by dying for us so we can live. If we want a share in his life, we must accept a share in his death, too. It says so when we are baptised, that in the waters of baptism we share in Christ's death so that we can rise to new life with him.

On our college retreat, at a convent on the cliff tops at Whitby, I went for a walk alone. It was a beautiful cold afternoon, the sky smudgy and opal, the sea dark and fierce. I climbed down a long flight of steps, which led down in a zigzag from the cliff top to the promenade and walked towards the harbour. Big waves were rolling in from far out to sea, turbulent, the colour of iron. But nearer in the waves calmed down and settled in a band of still water, almost glassy, where the seagulls were resting; there it seemed to gather itself and begin its push into the shore, picking up power and movement and forming a greeny-dark ridge which then – so beautifully – curled over into itself, releasing a crest of off-white foam which rolled over the now darker water like a mushroom cap curling over the dark gills beneath. And then it spent itself in a crash of white foam, breaking on to the rocks with amazing violence.

I walked on and saw a red sign ahead mounted on a pole saying 'STEPS'. It stood at the top of a flight of stone steps with metal rails leading down not on to the beach, revealed at low tide I supposed, but into the crashing, foaming sea. I stood and looked at this sign. Was it a warning or an invitation? Step this way, it seemed to say, not on to the pleasure beach you seek, but into this chaos that awaits you and promises you a new birth.

29. Triduum

In Holy Week the monks left Mirfield to lead retreats in parishes so it was left to the ordinands to take over the everyday running of the monastery for the most solemn week in the Church's year, beginning with Palm Sunday, commemorating Christ's entrance into Jerusalem, and culminating with his resurrection a week later on Easter Day. It is also the most theatrical week in the Church's year, the re-enactment of the climactic events in Jesus' life and what lies beyond; and to experience it in the concentration and exclusion of a monastery is extraordinary.

Guests arrived to spend the week with us: a barrister, the head of a primary school, a civil engineer from Sweden and a couple of young guys who the friendlier of the ordinands eyed up. I liked having guests to make the journey with us, but I also liked to retreat myself, so after Compline I went to Calvary, to the monks' graveyard, to do another row of departed brethren; I was praying for them, one by one, through Lent, a private devotion in a week of very public ones, and with the monks away the entire burden of the daily round fell to us.

Maundy Thursday arrived, the first day of the Triduum, and the beginning of the great drama of Easter. In the evening, marking the night before Jesus died, we celebrated the Eucharist as he shared the last supper with his disciples. As he washed the feet of his disciples ours, too, were washed by the priest; and then the blessed bread – his body – was taken in procession into the Lower Church where an altar symbolising the Garden of Gethsemane had been prepared, covered in flowers, so you could smell their perfume from the floor above – useful to have a former florist in your number – and there we left him as his disciples left him in the garden, praying alone in his agony. Upstairs the high altar was stripped and left bare and all departed in silence.

I was up at five to rejoin the watch at the altar and stayed there beyond my allotted hour because whoever was due at six thirty didn't show up. My knees were sore by then, so I sat on a bench waiting, but when I heard footsteps approaching I leaped back on to my knees in a dishonest show of piety.

It was Good Friday, the day of atheism, when God is dead, and his Church the abandoned junkyard most people I know think it really is. The blind leading the blind, we made a circuit of the Stations of the Cross in the monastery grounds, pausing at fourteen places to recall the agony of Jesus' trial, torture, his walk to Calvary and his execution; and by the time we arrived at Calvary I knew what had been causing me so much anguish since I'd been there.

It wasn't the uselessness, nor the infantilism, nor the awfulness of the Church of England, nor the hell of other people. It was my own chaos; hidden at first behind the prestige of my accomplishments, the glittering or at least shiny prizes of life, the motley I had learned to put on. As we stood before the Cross and the abandonment of Jesus to the chaos of death, I thought again of the steps at Whitby leading down into the crashing sea.

The Liturgy of Good Friday is also complicated, barefoot, and unnourished. Three cantors sing the Passion, three sacred ministers prostrate before the bare altar, and the veiled cross is brought into the church and carried in procession to the front, where we come up one by one to venerate it with a kiss. Everyone made mistakes, we didn't know what we were doing, we didn't pay attention. I remembered one of the monks saying, 'You know what sin is? It's not paying attention.' That night one of our members marked this most solemn of fasts, the Day of Chaos, by shagging one of the guests so noisily that someone had to come and tell him to keep it down.

It kept me up, and I had to rise at three in the morning for the Easter Vigil, so I was yawning when we met just before dawn outside the south door to the Upper Church to light the new fire of Easter. A big wax candle was produced and marked with a cross, the number of the year, the letters alpha and omega to signify the beginning and the end, and then pinned with five grains of incense symbolising the wounds of Christ, and finally lit from the new fire. The Paschal Candle was carried by the deacon into the unlit and empty church, Jesus' tomb, and as the light flickered in the fathomless darkness the deacon sang 'the Light of Christ' to which we responded 'thanks be to God' and we all kindled lights which spread through the church as the dawn broke and we celebrated the first Eucharist of Easter. Jesus Christ is risen from the dead and as we sang those words the possibility of new life for us began to rise too.

I thought again of the great Icon of the Anastasis, the Resurrection in Orthodox tradition, and Jesus reaching down into the pit of hell and yanking out of it the souls trapped there, their chains and padlocks falling away as they are hauled into the light. So it is with us at Easter, but until the end of all things, something of the shadows clings to us, something of the prison house endures, and we are never entirely free. The first year came to its end and the senior year met in church to celebrate its last Eucharist together and one of the most wounded of that year refused to exchange the peace with another. You might as well not have bothered, I thought.

After Easter I went to London and spent a fortnight staying at Lorna's and catching up with friends. It was wonderful to be away and to spend some time in rooms rather than in echoing spaces, but it was also more difficult than I thought it would be. I was bound up in our life at Mirfield, its dramas were so enveloping, its walls so enclosing, that I was not tuned into life outside. There are many similarities between life in a monastery and life in a prison, I have since discovered. It is not just pallor that endures after release, the locked-in patterns of relating that total institutions produce endure, too. I noticed this when I went on day release, so to speak, to see Helen Fielding's mother, Nelly, who lived nearby. A friend of hers came to supper and I realised not only that I had no conversation, for I could only talk about Mirfield, but that it meant very little to anyone else. The forming dynamic intended to produce in us solidarity and collegiality – although there was little of that in my first year – also distanced us from those outside; a mixed blessing to be sure. I would also observe that, in spite of prison mythology, living in seclusion with a group of other men is wonderful practice for celibacy. One or two of our number, young in years, had enthusiastic sex lives, but most of us, gay or straight, were wretchedly chaste; although one day when I was putting post in people's pigeon holes I noticed a number of large brown card envelopes from Amazon France. I found out later it was the Dieux du Stade calendar, in which the French rugby squad posed naked in strikingly homoerotic ways.

The summer lay ahead and I had chosen a placement, not in a local church or somewhere slightly beyond my ecclesiastical comfort zone, but in the belly of the beast itself. I was going to Uganda to be part of the Chaplaincy team at Makerere University in Kampala. One of the members of staff at Mirfield had arranged it for me, having worked there as a missionary. Before I left, he called me in to say goodbye. He had told the chaplain that I was a dynamic person, full of ideas . . . he paused . . . but you might have to . . . I chose an ending for his sentence: to observe discretion? He looked relieved.

The Ugandan Church had been – and still is – one of the most vocal in its condemnation of homosexuality. This was before the days when people there were calling for legislation to imprison and even execute gay men, but it was definitely not Soho, which was one of the reasons why I wanted to go. We are often told that the future of Anglican is African. Take me there, I thought.

I arrived at Entebbe at night after a hideous flight, where every penny I'd saved by flying on a less expensive carrier I spent on a hotel room at a stopover in some desert oven for an hour of sleep before the onward journey to what Churchill called the Pearl of Africa but what looked to me more like the Heart of Darkness. The man who was meant to meet me did not show up, so I made my way to the guest house I had booked, which had no record of a booking so I ended up at the guest house at the cathedral on Namirembe Hill, basic in its comforts, and a favourite with noisy pilgrims who were so full of the Lord Jesus that they burst into spontaneous choruses of Alleluia! throughout the night, most vigorously just before dawn as the Muslim call to prayer struck up. Also staying was a party of young Evangelicals from Britain, public school boys with a rather tiresome way about them, as if they were subalterns on an exercise with something to prove, who looked on me with suspicion.

Everyone – except me – was obsessed with homosexuality. It was denounced on television by evangelists, it was denounced by the local clergy from pulpits, it was denounced in the countless newspapers and magazines that proliferate in that country, it was denounced by countless mysterious American right-wing preachers doing what they could to stir up authentic African godly resistance to this satanic infection from the former colonial masters. Ben, however, the chaplain at Makerere, was not that bothered, or did not seem to be. He was a shrewd laid-back man, in his sixties, who had been involved in one of the quasi-revolutionary fundamentalist movements that arose from the Balokole revival in the 1930s which had come into conflict not only with the Anglican authorities but the colonial authorities, too. Ben had lived a full life. He was not fazed by things, he was not censorious, I liked him a lot, although he was hopelessly disorganised, and kept talking about 'my programme' but not putting it together so in the end I did my own thing.

The university followed a familiar model – central buildings with a chapel and halls of residence – but in my first week some students found a pedlar in one of their halls of residence and lynched him. Downtown Kampala, at least where the western hotels were, was prostitute central – I had never seen so many women offer themselves in so many ways to so many men in one place ever before. In spite – or perhaps because – of these eye-opening realities the churches were full to bursting, as I discovered when I preached a sermon one Sunday in the chapel, packed from seven in the morning until lunchtime, with Sunday school under a banyan tree all afternoon. People in church would be disarmingly friendly, offering you their hand to hold during prayers, but then pulling away, embarrassed if you held it too long. They were enthusiastic practitioners of glossolalia, speaking in tongues, which they fell into without any self-consciousness at all, leaving me in embarrassed silence, and tremendous singers of hymns, which I could at least join in with although the dancing left me again looking like a Puritan at a knees-up. The cathedral, near where I was staying, seemed weirdly old-fashioned and English, with a robed choir of men and boys, and clergy in cassocks and birettas, until the service got under way and was anything but old-fashioned and English. I suppose when the colonial era receded it left an uneven heritage behind. I began to spend more time out in the city, paying a couple of quid to be taken around on the back of a two-stroke moped, or in the lovely city of Jinja, on the back of a push-bike, where I took a trip out to the source of the Nile in a boat piloted by a Westerner who turned out to have been on a lifeboat my friend Horatio had skippered in Pembrokeshire. At Makerere I passed my time in the university library, immersing myself not in the literature of East Africa but the novels of Evelyn Waugh, for it had shelves and shelves of English literature, acquired before Amin took power in 1974, when acquisitions stopped.

I felt as at odds with Africa as Basil Seal in *Black Mischief*, for I had no idea what was going on. One day, back at the guest house, I met an old English couple who had served as teachers in Uganda in the sixties. He had been head of a mission school of the kind Ben had been taught at so I invited them to church at the university that Sunday. They came, and afterwards I introduced them to Ben and knew immediately that something was wrong. They did not hang around, and when I had a cup of tea with Ben later I asked if he had noticed. He told me the man had not only been his headmaster but had also expelled him for being involved with one of the revivalist movements. But Ben was an orphan, with no home to go to, and the school was all he had, so he was effectively turned out and made homeless and lived for some years on the street, where he had nearly died several times, of hunger, or of disease; so to see the man who had put him there produced complex feelings.

I got it wrong with Ben a couple of times. Once he hosted a big dinner, a fundraiser for a project he had under way at the university for a new chaplaincy centre. The guest of honour was the head of the National Bank, who pledged a sum of money to get the ball rolling. A couple of other big men – it was a big-man culture – pledged the same amount and I, too, pledged the same amount, about five hundred quid, I think, which I could easily afford. But it was too generous an offer from someone who was not a representative of the big-man class but a student on placement at the chaplaincy. I immediately wished I'd done it anonymously, but among the big men I wanted to show off, too.

Another time we were at an event and one of the other clergy asked me about homosexuality in the Church in Britain. I said it did not bother me, nor any of my friends, and we regarded it as something quite normal. They went quiet. One sucked his teeth. They all melted away except one who said, intending to be kind, 'You must understand there is no homosexuality in Africa.' And then a drama group came on stage to entertain us and I could see at once that there was homosexuality in Africa, just like everywhere else.

It was an uncomfortable experience for me to be somewhere where gay people are not only held in suspicion, but actively hated. I was disgusted to see how active those mysterious American evangelists had been in fomenting hatred of gay people, although there was also so much to admire about American and British Christians there, like those posh boys on a mission, working with orphanages and hospitals and schools, putting the gospel into action and trying to narrow the gap between our rich lives and their poor lives and maybe to heal the wounds left by white people's exploitation of black people. I remember talking to an American medical missionary who spoke of her frustration at preaching abstinence to girls who were nonchalantly sexually active but, being a realist and because she cared about them, as she preached she distributed free condoms.

Most Christians I know who have worked in Uganda fall in love with it. I wish I had, but the hatred of gay people was so intense I found it strange and frightening and it made me want to come home.

I found I liked Africa much better from Mirfield. Back from

my travels I was talking one day to Fr George, the Superior of the community, and he mentioned he'd just had Hugh Masekela to lunch. Masekela was writing a musical about Archbishop Trevor Huddleston, one of the leaders of the fight against apartheid, and a monk of Mirfield. An odd subject for a musical, I thought, but it turned out that when he was Superior at the Priory in Johannesburg, Huddleston had given Masekela his first trumpet. A teenager then, he had come to the Priory to ask for help to start a band. So Huddleston wrote to the most famous trumpeter he could think of, Louis Armstrong, in America and told him about these boys. Louis Armstrong not only sent him his own trumpet as a gift but got a rich businessman to pay for instruments for everyone else. One day Huddleston invited these kids round to tea and when they walked into the parlour there were the instruments set out for them and the young Masekela burst into tears.

Then Fr Aelred, one of the monks at Mirfield, died. He had been ill for a while and in a nursing home and, while many of us hadn't known him, we were mustered for his funeral, the first monk's funeral I had attended. Monks get two big dos in their lives – their profession, when they enter the life of the community for good, and their death, when they leave it for good. Aelred's body came into the church before Evensong and lay in an open coffin in the porch all night. In the morning the church was packed with mourners, former students, black Africans, ancient clerics and the gathered community. I was a cantor that day, and the funeral began with the singing of the plainsong for a requiem as we all processed into church to where Aelred's coffin lay on a bier under the pall (which the Bags called the Wendy House). In the address Fr George introduced a middle-aged African lady and a young African man who were sitting in the stalls. It was Steve Biko's widow and son, who'd flown from South Africa just for the funeral. I found it incredibly moving and had to compose myself to sing the Kontakion of the Dead, the Russian hymn, which so powerfully gives voice to the paradox of the Christian funeral: *All we go down to the dust; and weeping o'er the grave we make our song: Alleluia, alleluia, alleluia.* Then the coffin was loaded on a little hearse and we processed down to the Calvary in pale autumn light. The leaves fell from the trees as four of the brethren lowered Aelred's coffin into his grave and an old monk, Aelred's contemporary, supported by two students, hobbled to the graveside to sprinkle the coffin with holy water. The Bikos followed and then the rest of us. And I thought of a community of Old Etonian Englishmen in cassocks living quietly in a monastery in Yorkshire in the fifties and sixties, so outraged by the iniquity of apartheid that they devoted their lives to fighting it, and loving its victims, and getting arrested and imprisoned and exiled for their troubles. And whenever I hear of the Church in Africa mistreating gay people, and think 'screw the Anglican Communion', I think of Aelred and Steve Biko and Trevor and a fifteen-year-old boy crying because someone he had never met gave him a trumpet.

The year that followed at Mirfield was mercifully different. The year above had departed, taking with it its aggro, and while the arriving year brought its own aggro it brought also its blessings, a new mixture of people, and there was an outbreak of peace. Perhaps because the year before had been so awful we all resolved to make it work, and although there were the usual rows, which are inescapable where people locked up with strangers discover the limits of their tolerance and patience, we handled them better. There were the usual partisan issues which divided us, those in favour of women's ordination, those against, those in favour of eighteenth-century French fiddle-back chasubles with spade-ended stoles so heavy with bullion they clanked as you put them on, those against. But there was a willingness to be open to each other, to understand each other, to get on with each other, and to live like we were trying to work out the life of Christ in the muddle of our own.

For my year, it was a time of looking ahead. We were on the market as potential curates and our dioceses were looking for churches to send us to once we were ordained. I was sent to look at Boston Stump, the parish church of St Botolph in Boston in Lincolnshire, one of the great medieval churches of England. There I was to be inspected by its vicar, Fr Robin Whitehead, whose approval was needed before

I could be assigned. He met me at the station after a journey on a little train through fields of cows and kale and cauliflowers, and we walked up to the enormous church through the little town of thirty thousand people, not big but the civic centre for the whole district. There were supermarkets, an arts centre, a general hospital, a working docks (Boston: Gateway to Europe), and a large population of Portuguese – 'Pork and Cheese' – migrant workers who were there to pick the mile on mile of brassicas that were soon to draw the first flows of workers from Poland and Eastern Europe.

Wherever you went in town, whoever you met in town, you saw the Stump, this misnamed three-hundred-foot-high triumph of civic pride and the Perpendicular. Triumph, too, of the Decorated, its horizontal part belonging to that period of English ecclesiastical architecture, and known, too, as a calendar church, with fifty-two windows and twelve pillars and seven doors and three hundred and sixty-five steps to the top of the tower. Count them and it doesn't quite work out, but the point is one of comprehensiveness. It is a building designed for all of life and beyond.

Robin gave me a quick tour, or as quick as you can in a church which takes twenty-five minutes to lock up, then we went to the vicarage, where I met the dogs – important – then Robin's colleague Nicky, vicar of the church down on the estate, where lives could be as rough as any lives anywhere. She told me that the bishop had been recently to confirm some of her kids and asked them before the service if they had any questions. There was silence, apart from one girl who said, 'I've nicked this top from me nan, but do you think it shows too much tit for church?'

I barely slept that night – the excitement of a new place and new people – and I heard the Stump chime one, two, three, four and five; and then I was up at seven thirty for breakfast, Morning Prayer, and a tour of the rest of the town, including St Thomas's, also 'ours', out among the bungalows, and like a bungalow itself but with lovely furniture and fittings. And then to see my house, the 'best Curate's House in the diocese of Lincoln', according to the present occupant, an American called Charles, who spent twenty-two years translating dictionaries into Turkish in Istanbul before getting ordained. He met me at the gate and threw it open to reveal a garden so overgrown with nettles and weeds you could barely see the front door. 'Let a thousand flowers bloom!' he exclaimed. The house was very seventies, built by a boat builder and full of tongue and groove, and Artexed ceilings, and a huge bathroom, and the largest downstairs lavatory I'd ever seen, with a loo incongruously at one end looking like something by Duchamp. And light, with big double-glazed windows on the south-facing side. And location, location, location, right on the river with access to the water from the back garden. And the swirliest carpet I had ever seen on the stairs and landing, which would have to go, but nevertheless I could see myself living here, I thought.

Robin walked me back to the station. The train was delayed and we talked about this and that and Robin said, shyly, 'Well. Are you interested?' I said yes, of course I was. 'Well,' he said, 'we'd love to have you.'

30. Into the Harvest

Mirfield finished half demob happy, half high anxiety, for our end of year coincided with the college festival, to which a star preacher was coming, the Archbishop of Canterbury, Rowan Williams, who had taught there in the seventies. The atmosphere grew febrile, with rows over who got to do what, and during a seminar on marriage, tempers erupted and there were tears and a walkout while a nice woman from Relate explained to us the importance of communication.

For those of us leaving there was a winding down and one evening we sat in a common room and talked, for the first time, about our childhoods and our first memories of public events. Mine was the moon landing in 1969, another's was the resignation of Eden, another's was her first day at school. Luke, from Zimbabwe, without any alteration of tone, said he remembered helicopters landing in his town and soldiers getting out and everyone running away but they caught his mum and him and took them to a prison camp. He didn't know what happened to his dad.

In the last weeks of term visitors from what are called the Tat Shops – the clerical outfitters, ranging from Wippell's, high-end traditional, to J&M budget lines made by two ladies from Newcastle – arrived to set out their wares in a common room. I was one of the first to visit and tried on a clerical shirt with a tunnel collar, for everyday wear, but the only one they had in my size was bottle-green. I went into the gents to change and came out to see my peers, now gathered, staring at me in horror. Green, you see, is not a colour for a clerical shirt in the Mirfield tradition, where the only colour is black. Not grey, not dark blue, but black, clerical back. No one tells you these things but they are true nonetheless, and I, too, knew that it was so. Fortunately I was able to pre-order in black – and even more fortunately I did not have to pay for them, for Helen Fielding picked up the tab for my entire clerical trousseau, which was substantial, and I thought of a time years ago when she had been broke and I'd bought her a dress from Joseph, and how very, very much in my favour that had worked out.

We were rather rushed through our last lectures. The marriage seminars obliged me to stand in as a groom at a dummy run when I married the gayest of our number who chose to be bride. Everyone clapped and cheered and when I looked out of the window a small congregation had gathered on the path to watch.

The day of the Archbishop's visit came, and the first item on the schedule was to have the college photograph taken with our star guest, but he was delayed and in the end we went ahead but left a gap in the middle for the Most Reverend and Right Honourable Primate of All England to be Photoshopped in. I went up to church to say my prayers and sat for half an hour with my *metanoi*, praying, knot-by-knot, 'Lord Jesus Christ, Son of God, have mercy on me a sinner . . .' When the organ began playing five minutes before the Mass I stood a little awkwardly and genuflected and stepped back, just missing a figure kneeling behind me. The Archbishop of Canterbury. He was then in the thick of battle trying to reconcile the irreconcilable, African bishops who hated gays and American bishops who were gays, and he preached without notes that day on the theme of patience, on the necessity of waiting for God, but noting that the word patience is derived from the Latin 'patientia' which means 'suffering'.

One of my last duties at Mirfield was to go through my final report with the Principal. I was quite looking forward to it. Last year's report had been warm and generous, but while this final version was also complimentary, two things stood out. *Richard is convivial and highly sociable . . .* and *Richard does not bear fools gladly . . .* Both statements were followed by praise for my efforts, but later that day, having found myself brooding on it, I thought anyone reading that will think 'boorish drunk'.

I also went to see my spiritual director for the last time, Fr Eric, who was in his usual circumspect mood. He told me he'd once done a mission at Crowland Abbey, not far from Boston, and thought it, and Lincolnshire, a strange place. 'Did you know that at the dissolution all the monks from the Abbey were thrown out except one – must have been awful for him – who stayed on as parish priest. But by some oversight no one arranged a stipend for him so the poor man had nothing to live on. Apparently the whole community . . . just watched him die.'

It was my last of Mirfield, a strange happy–sad tailing off, with a leavers' party where everyone got plastered, and the handing over of college responsibilities to those in the year below us. I handed over my duties as Precentor, co-Master of the Musick, to Ringo, so called after he let slip that he was named after John Lennon, and to fortify him for this role I gave him a relic of the Curé d'Ars, patron of priests, some stuffing from his kneeler which I bought on eBay.

The corridors were full of boxes and people squabbling over the trolley and the lift and showing our faces at slightly desperate parties thrown by those who really did not want to go; and then it was our last Evensong. I was fine until the hymn, 'Quem Pastores', and those with ears to hear had teary eyes and those without looked their usual blank selves. As we left the organist improvised a voluntary on the same tune, sending us out as uncertain shepherds to uncertain flocks.

After dinner that night a few of us went out to see an extraordinarily vivid one-man show based on the life of the Singing Nun. Not, unfortunately for the handful of people who showed up, a tribute; more a searing indictment of the breakdown of ecclesial identities in the wake of Vatican II. This was memorably conveyed when the performer, a middle-aged man dressed in a wimple and skirts, reeled round the stage retching on the combination of brandy and barbiturates which he'd poured down his throat for the finale.

In the morning I said goodbye to those who were still there and packed my car with the fraction of stuff that had spilled forth from my room and I set off for Boston. It took longer than it should as I got stuck in traffic in roadworks, but I got to the new house, still

being painted, by teatime. As soon as I was there I felt completely
in the present-becoming-future rather than the present-out-of-past.
The same thing happened when I left the BBC; I expected to feel its
claim upon me, but I didn't.

I went round to the vicarage where I met Robin. We had supper
in the pub, a thick greasy beefburger for a fiver, and then we ran into
Nicky outside the church, who'd just officiated at the wedding of a
bride supported by a chunky Lincolnshire lass in a deep red shiny
dress, 'she looked like a fookin' plum'. By the end of supper I had
been made Chaplain to the Air Cadets, the Burma Star Association,
ASDA and Deputy to the Chaplain to the Admiral of the Wash for
the Annual Inspection of the Beacons and Buoys.

I had some time off before my ordination so I went down to
London and stayed with Lorna in Clapham, savouring these last
days of liberty like a volunteer awaiting his ship. Mo's husband, Jon,
called to invite me down to lunch at their farmhouse in Kent, where
they'd semi-retired, he from the City, she from politics, so I put my
new folding bike on a train and cycled there from Sittingbourne,
through acres of unprepossessing industrial estates, through fields of
grubbed-up orchards where ponies rolled around in the dust, on a
day of wonderful weather. The trees, in thickening leaf, were sprout-
ing that fizzy green colour and I saw a kestrel hovering over a hedge
suddenly swoop and make a kill.

I arrived at the farm to find Mo and Jon outside by the pool.
Mo was in bad shape and couldn't walk without help and Jon said
her brain tumour had returned and she'd been having radiotherapy
which had badly affected her balance. So she sat in a chair in the sun,
eyes shut, occasionally dropping off, wrapped in a blanket, joining
in from time to time. She said she would not be able to make it to
my ordination and I said I would save her a piece of cake. My last
memory of her is turning round as I left and seeing her in her chair,
trying to shrug a shawl from her shoulder to catch the last of the sun,
her eyes closed, smiling.

The ordination was to take place at the Stump, but it was preceded
by a three-day retreat at Lincoln in Bishop King's Old Palace, from

which we would emerge on Sunday morning to drive to Boston where the Bishop of Grantham awaited with his ordaining hands outstretched in a church full of parishioners, colleagues, my family and my friends.

I went back up to Mirfield to supervise the removal of the rest of my stuff, which was lugged by two Poles into a van and lugged out of it again into my new house, painted now, and with the worst of the jungle cut back with Diocesan strimmers. I had been sleeping on an airbed on the floor and had also managed to come down with the worst cold of my life but Horatio volunteered to come and help me unpack, an act of supererogation for which I will be always thankful. The removal van with the container loads of stuff from Grafton Underwood that had been in storage arrived, too, and I was reunited with things that had been put away two years earlier, pictures, my bed, a kitchen table; my piano.

I was moved in. Horatio left me to it and said he'd see me at my ordination and I was, for the first time in what felt like years, alone. I went from room to room, summoned by no bells, wearing normal clothes, watching the telly, having a bath, unused to the everyday luxury of doing what you want in your own place.

People came round to say hello, some Jewish neighbours heard I had a cold and made me chicken soup. Robin called in to tell me that one of the children at the school had been knocked down and killed by a driver who did not stop. He wept as he told me this and said he was sorry that my first job after ordination would be assisting at the funeral of a child.

I spent these last days just walking round the town looking at things, listening to things, enjoying being anonymous and unnoticed. One evening I stood on a footbridge over the River Witham and looked up at the Stump's tower as six struck. The river was so high that boys in trunks were jumping off the bridge into the water, and off walls and the river bank all the way from where I was to the Stump. It looked like something from English pastoral until you heard them speak and I realised they were Polish, not English, and I suddenly remembered standing on a footbridge over the River Seine twenty years earlier after the Communards' first gig and knowing then, as I knew now, that life would never be the same again.

I thought, too, about one of my friends from Mirfield, like me a gay man in his forties who had endured the AIDS years of the eighties and nineties, and, although we were very different, we shared this formative experience. We were both on placement at St Peter's Huddersfield, a typical Yorkshire town centre church, large and galleried, and with an organ twice as loud as it needed to be. But on this day, Remembrance Sunday, it couldn't be loud enough. It was the biggest service of the year, with six hundred in church, in uniforms, mayoral robes, sober suits. There were serving military, cadets, old soldiers in baggy blazers and wheelchairs, and to mark the occasion we put together a choir to sing, of all things, Gorecki's *Totus Tuus*, an eleven-minute-long motet composed for Pope John Paul II. It had nothing to do with Remembrance Sunday but it shifted the mood from the bang crash of the calls to arms to something much sweeter and more tender. And then a bugler played 'The Last Post' beautifully and it was all bangs and crashes again as we watched the parade go off.

A couple of days later my friend and I drove up to Harrogate and he asked me what I had made of the service. I said I had been deeply moved by it. 'Why?' he asked. Because poppies and bugles and uncomprehending boys and girls in uncomfortable uniforms mourning a generation they did not know but whose loss was inescapable, chiselled on memorials the length and breadth of the land, touched our grief for another lost generation – and I thought, in a great rush, of the people I had lost, and of those my friend had lost, too, less well remembered, but who had brought us to this place, driving through North Yorkshire silently with tears in our eyes, into a life so shaped by that loss it was never the same again.

Never the same again. I walked back along the river bank to my new house and there packed into a bag my new black suit, my new black shoes and my new black shirt with its new white dog collar still wrapped in cellophane and waiting to be worn.

At the Old Palace in Lincoln in my tiny room, with its narrow bed and uneven curtains, I unpacked them along with my new cassock and my stole, a long coloured scarf, worn crossways for a deacon and straight for a priest. The colour for ordination is usually white and a certain latitude is permitted to personalise your ordination stole, in so far as you can personalise something that is really not about you at all. Mine was quite showbiz, its broad ends embroidered to symbolise the dark waters of creation yielding to the light of the fiat lux and the alpha and omega of the beginning and end of all things. At Mirfield we clubbed together and bought one for Luke, whose Zimbabwean money was worth less than the ink it was printed with, a white stole with the lamb and flag of the College of the Resurrection embroidered on it. At our last college Mass these stoles, entwined, were blessed by the celebrant as a reminder of our common life as priests of the Church, even if they did resemble, in a certain light, snakes in a pit in the darkness of that Church.

On the first evening of the retreat we left the Old Palace in our cassocks and walked where Lincoln's bishops had walked for centuries into the cathedral, and were invited to sit in the choir for Evensong. In the prayers priests who have served in the cathedral are remembered by name on the anniversary of their deaths, and there is something very moving to hear them read out, equal in dignity, whether still alive in people's memories or dead for eight hundred years; and it was even more moving to hear our own names when we, too, were prayed for. It was the first time I had ever heard 'The Reverend Richard Coles' and I have tried to keep it that way ever since.

The retreat was led by a retired bishop, grey-haired and wise and venerable, so it was slightly surprising to discover that he had been at school with John Lennon. We had to do some old-fashioned things, swear our oaths to the Bishop's Commissary in a chapel at the cathedral famous for its mural by Duncan Grant, a sumptuous piece of exuberantly homoerotic art which seemed rather at odds with the occasion. And on the night before we were ordained the Bishop of Lincoln came to see us and to give us his Charge, rather a touching, fatherly business followed by a fork buffet.

On retreat I tried to spend as much time in prayer as I could, discovering very early in my clerical career that the times when it is most necessary to pray are very often filled with necessary trivialities. But at Evensong, on the eve of ordination, I prayed as earnestly as I have ever prayed that I may 'hereafter live a godly, sober and right-eous life'. I got up early on the morning of the ordinations and in Bishop King's private chapel made promises to God that I would to the best of my untested and uneven ability be his faithful servant.

I peeled open the cellophane packet and took out my shirt and put it on and tried to smooth its creases before fixing for the first time my dog collar, a fiddly business with metal poppers and a tongue of fabric that seemed to do nothing, and when it was all in place I looked at myself in a mirror and saw, for the first time, what everyone else would now see. I saw Dazzle looking back at me, and John Gaskell, and Peter and Michael, and intimated for the first time from within the tension between the person and the calling. Would my friends, would Sara and Billy and my sceptical father see looking back at them someone who could make it look possible?

I sat, a layman for just a few hours longer, in Edward King's chapel saying the Jesus prayer until eight o'clock and thought of Housman's unlucky hero on the scaffold hearing the quarters as the first chime of eight gathered force to strike him from the land of the living. In-stead of eternity I went to breakfast and entertained myself in silence by looking at everyone else in their new dog collars, and then left with my friend Paddy, who was being ordained with me, and drove the back way through the wolds to Boston. It was a beautiful morn-ing when we arrived at my house and made final adjustments before presenting ourselves to the world as clergymen. We walked to church and crossed the footbridge over the river and there at the bottom saw the first person from my life before to see me, dog-collared, in my life to be. It was my brother Will.

The beginning of the service was a blur of faces and a wash of sound, as we were welcomed by the bishop and the community we were to serve. I knelt and watched a spider walking slowly across the fourteenth-century flagstone at my feet, indifferent to this day of solemn purpose. I got up to read the second reading, from the Letter to the Romans: 'I appeal to you therefore, brothers and sisters, by the mercies of God, to present your bodies as a living sacrifice, holy and acceptable to God, which is your spiritual worship. Do not be conformed to this world, but be transformed by the renewing of your minds, so that you may discern what is the will of God – what is good and acceptable and perfect', and looked up from the lectern to see an indefatigably atheist friend looking back at me with tears in his eyes.

The Bishop made us stand and face the congregation and asked them if it was their will that we should be ordained: *IT IS,* they shouted back. Will you support them? *WE WILL.* As we turned back and took our places kneeling before the bishop a shaft of light struck the altar and a pigeon, lost in the vast space of the nave, fluttered along the clerestory towards us.

Afterwards, sweating in four layers of cloth, I greeted people at the door. I greeted, it seemed, almost everyone I had ever known, and I thought of the Epistle to the Hebrews and the 'great cloud of witnesses' that surrounded those first communities of Christians, those who had gone before, living and dead, who have pointed us to heaven and the things of heaven and walked beside us over the hills and through the valleys and stood with us at the edge of crashing waters.

I looked into people's faces, faces that had seen me at my best and my worst, at my most vulnerable and my most triumphant, at my sleaziest and my finest, and we went to the church hall for tea and cake and speeches and presents and I ducked out for a moment and went into church, the new curate on his new patch, for the first time.

I noticed a man having a coffee at the base of the tower where ladies were serving teas. He was looking at me and when I went over to talk to the ladies he came up and said, 'Aren't you Richard Coles?' I said yes, and he told me that he was a huge fan of the Communards and that our music had been a big influence on him in the eighties. He was very nice, effusive even, and we talked for a couple of minutes longer. As I went back into the party I realised he had made no reference at all to my dog collar or asked why I was there.